FIRST CROSSING

THE 1919 TRANS-ATLANTIC
FLIGHT OF ALCOCK AND BROWN

D1535130

ROBERT O. HARDER

SUNBURY
PRESS

Mechanicsburg, PA USA

Published by Sunbury Press, Inc.
Mechanicsburg, Pennsylvania

www.sunburypress.com

For information about special discounts for bulk purchases, please contact Sunbury Press Orders Dept. at (855) 338-8359 or orders@sunburypress.com.

To request one of our authors for speaking engagements or book signings, please contact Sunbury Press Publicity Dept. at publicity@sunburypress.com.

FIRST SUNBURY PRESS EDITION: April 2022

Set in Adobe Garamond | Interior design by Crystal Devine | Cover design by Tobi Afran | Edited by Sarah Peachey.

Publisher's Cataloging-in-Publication Data
Names: Harder, Robert O., author.
Title: First crossing : the 1919 trans-Atlantic flight of Alcock and Brown / Robert O. Harder.
Description: First trade paperback edition. | Mechanicsburg, PA : Sunbury Press, 2022.
Summary: The first to cross the Atlantic non-stop wasn't Charles Lindbergh, but two long-forgotten British officers. Captain John Alcock and Lieutenant Arthur Whitten Brown flew their flimsy wood and fabric Vickers *Vimy* from St. Johns, Newfoundland to Cliveden, Ireland on June 14–15, 1919—eight years before the "Lone Eagle." This is their story.
Identifiers: ISBN : 978-1-62006-876-2 (softcover).
Subjects: BIOGRAPHY & AUTOBIOGRAPHY / Adventurers & Explorers | BIOGRAPHY & AUTOBIOGRAPHY / Aviation & Nautical | TRANSPORTATION / Aviation / History.

Product of the United States of America
0 1 1 2 3 5 8 13 21 34 55

Continue the Enlightenment!

Cover photos – Top: The Vimy *just seconds after its incredibly hazardous takeoff. (Science Museum Group)*
Bottom: Alcock & Brown kitted out in their flight suits minutes before mounting the Vimy, *June 14, 1919. (Science Museum Group)*

To all the Early Birdmen whose total landings
were one less than their takeoffs.

Author's Note

During the centuries-long history of marine and air navigation, more technical advances have been made by Great Britain than any other nation. Arguably, this preeminence reached its zenith a century ago when the first *non-stop* aerial crossing of the Atlantic was flown by two former Royal Air Force officers, Captain Sir John "Jack" William Alcock, KBE, DSC, and Lieutenant Sir Arthur "Ted" Whitten Brown, KBE, on June 14-15, 1919. It is a story that has been told before but not often and not always accurately. Probably 100 out of 100 laypersons and 98 out of 100 *aviators* believe that particular claim belongs to Charles Lindbergh in May 1927. But the truth is Alcock and Brown made the first aerial voyage from North America (Newfoundland) to the British Isles (Ireland) eight years before Lindy made his extraordinary *solo 3,000-mile flight from New York to Paris*. And that historical confusion is something of a shame, because what Alcock and Brown and the other three British *Daily Mail* Atlantic teams competing for Lord Northcliffe's £10,000 prize did during that half-year following the end of World War One marked a major turning point in aviation history. It was during the Great War, and just after, that truly capable airplanes, modern cockpit instrumentation, and precision air navigation aids were first born, marking the beginning of transoceanic air travel. Today, in our world of Global Positioning Systems (GPS), automated "glass" and fly-by-wire cockpits, and remotely controlled, pilotless airplanes, few know when, where, or how the experimental years ended and the modern air age began.

Our story is told largely through the eyes of navigator Whitten Brown, an American turned Englishman. Cerebral, well-rounded, and a capable (often colorful) recorder of events, he more than Alcock has left us with the flight's most memorable impressions. The format used is called "creative nonfiction," a genre where the narrative and dialogue convey significant and accurate information in a near novelistic manner. Writer Allan W. Eckert used this approach in his 1992 book *The Life of Tecumseh*. "Such dialogue," he wrote, "is not invented conversation but, rather, a form of painstakingly *reconstituted* [emphasis in the original] dialogue that lies hidden in abundance in historical material." Herman Wouk offered a similar perspective in the Foreward to his epic novel *The Winds of War*: "[The] words and acts of the great personages [are] either historical or derived from accounts of their words and deeds in similar situations."

It is also high time to correct what has become the greatest myth about this flight, perhaps most solidly set in concrete by a very popular 1955 nonfiction volume titled *The Flight of Alcock and Brown: 14 – 15 June 1919* by Graham Wallace (see bibliography). In the book's most spectacular passages, Wallace allowed himself to uncritically believe an account written by Captain John Alcock's younger brother, E.S.J. "John" Alcock, who must have misunderstood what he had been told, an especially unaccountable lapse when one considers this younger brother himself became a highly accomplished RAF and airline pilot. According to the younger Alcock's story, as repeated by Wallace, a crippled Ted Brown crawled out on the lower right wing some half dozen times to chip ice off either an engine "fuel gauge" or some kind of engine air intake—it's never quite clear. In fact, no fuel gauges were on or near either of the engines, and the idea of a crippled man venturing out on an icy wing traveling at 100 mph in continually rough air to do either of those two things—especially chipping ice off an engine air intake obstructed by a whirling propeller—is preposterous. What Brown actually did is stand up in the cockpit into a terrifying slipstream and chip ice off and read the critically important Fuel Overflow Gauge—more later on that—located on a strut three feet above the crew's heads, an extremely difficult feat in itself, especially for a man with Brown's physical limitations. This gross misrepresentation alone sufficed to taint what was otherwise a well-told tale (though Wallace made a few other factual errors and the professional screenwriter in him resulted in too many Hollywood-style embellishments), with the unfortunate fictitious incident just mentioned continually repeated in many subsequent works. It was not fully rebutted until the 2012 publication of Brendan Lynch's exquisitely researched book *Yesterday We Were in America* (bibliography).

The skill, courage, and resourcefulness of pilot Alcock and navigator Brown need no such imagined heroics from me. Their magnificent achievement, as it actually happened, stands on its own as the highest of dramas. My purpose here is to faithfully tell their story as they would have wanted it—truthfully, technically accurate, and in the vernacular aviator language of a century ago.

One may ask why use a "creative nonfiction" approach at all, when sufficient documentation is available for the usual straightforward nonfiction book? Frankly, because I did not wish to put the reader to sleep with yet another heavily footnoted, carefully documented, too-often-dry scholarly work such an effort would demand. I also wanted to explore what made these flesh and blood men tick—both personally and professionally; to dig into the very human side of the fellows who operated those rickety early flying machines. Further, I wanted to bring readers closer to what it would have actually *felt like* to live through the incredible experience of flying the stormy North Atlantic in an *open cockpit* airplane! To twenty-first-century aviators, the extraordinary determination, deep reserves of strength, and just plain guts of early birds like Alcock and Brown are nearly incomprehensible. Whatever in the world, I wondered, possessed them to gamble their lives seemingly so recklessly?

As a former US Air Force navigator, commercial pilot (piston/propeller), and US Federal Aviation Administration (FAA) Certificated Flight Instructor (CFI), I had confidence I could render the complexities of the subject matter into text understandable to the layman. I also wanted to strip away the bravado that often attends these kinds of exploits in uninformed writers' hands. To further enrich the readers' experience, I wished to bring to light the many long-forgotten pioneers of modern flight, weaving their procedures, discoveries, and inventions into the narrative, connecting the dots between the experimental and modern eras of flight. Most of these lines of inquiry would have had to remain unexplored, risk becoming incomprehensible to the uninitiated, or most deadly of all—*boring* using a standard, nonfiction format.

Aviation purists may quibble over the title's veracity. Technically, America made the Atlantic's first crossing by air a month earlier than Alcock and Brown's flight. Out of three US Navy flying boats at the start, only the NC-4 (Navy/Curtiss) completed the journey. Its six-man crew, led by Lieutenant Commander Albert Read, made four en route stops from Newfoundland to the United Kingdom via the Azores and Iberian Peninsula, landing at Plymouth, England, on May 31, 1919. The NC-4's journey took a harrowing fifteen days; the Vickers *Vimy* flew non-stop in sixteen-plus hours. I will leave the matter of "firsts" for the reader to adjudicate.

All the named individuals in this work were real people; I have done my best to portray them accurately as I thought they would act and according to written records. And, due to the story crossing so many time zones and the confusion that brings, I have converted all takeoff to landing times to Greenwich Mean Time (GMT), the international aviation and marine standard. It is also important to note that the specific technical data available about this flight is meager. Because Brown left little written evidence in his in-flight notes and later recreated log, it was necessary for me to reconstruct much of what actually went on during the flight.

Further, Brown's charts and most of his calculations, particularly with regards to celestial work, required the use of nautical miles for measurements and knots for speed (the two terms are unrelated phonetic coincidences). However, pilots of the time worked only in mph, with their dashboard instruments reflecting same. It was therefore necessary for Brown to make the conversions when communicating with Alcock. This naturally necessitated great care; a nautical mile (6,076 feet) is equal to one minute of arc around the sphere of the earth and is equivalent to 1.151 statute miles. A speed of 100 knots (nautical miles per hour) equals 115 mph. I have therefore taken the liberty of smoothing all this out by uniformly stating all distances and airspeeds in statute miles and miles per hour. It was also essential to reconcile several knots/mph discrepancies between Brown's hastily scribbled in-flight notes and his later written narrative and formal log. Interestingly, this navigator/pilot terminology confusion continued through World War Two when finally high jet airspeeds made it all much too dangerous, and military and airline aviation, in particular, converted their instrumentation, charts, and manuals solely to nautical miles and knots.

Important events, times, dates, and locations have been as faithfully rendered as I can make them. In a very few scenes, time has been compressed for the sake of continuity and a smoother narrative. In regard to matters pertaining to the flight itself, the descriptions of the Vickers *Vimy*, and the airplane's instrumentation and navigation aids, I have made my very best effort to be scrupulously factual, though at times that proved exceptionally challenging. All the same, any errors remaining of that type must be laid at my doorstep. For further reading, I have included a selected bibliography of reference works used in the telling of this story.

"[Although] I cannot pretend to follow technical progress as closely as I could wish, I am told that the men and machines are, at the moment, ahead of the organisation on the earth which should facilitate flying in mists and fog, and also at night."

—LORD NORTHCLIFFE
May 17, 1920

"Before a transatlantic airway is possible, very much must be provided—organisation, capitalisation, Government support, the charting of air currents, [and] the establishment of directional wireless stations . . . But sooner or later, a London-New York service of aircraft is certain to be established."

—SIR ARTHUR WHITTEN BROWN
Summer, 1920

Over Nord-Pas-de-Calais, France
November 10, 1915

Second Lieutenant Arthur "Ted" Whitten Brown, a twenty-nine-year-old Royal Flying Corps observer, had been unable to see a thing through his soaked, fogged-over goggles for nearly ten minutes, and he finally ripped them off. A moment later, a wall of 65-mph rain pellets nearly blinded him. He instinctively jerked his head to one side, rapidly blinkering his eyelids while trying to peer over the side of the fuselage at the ground 4,000 feet below. Brown's job was to photograph German artillery positions over Valenciennes near the Belgian border and well behind enemy lines, a circumstance no British airman ever found comfortable. Even more confounding, in all the murk, it was highly doubtful the vertically mounted Watson Air Camera strapped to the fuselage side was going to capture anything useful.

Brown was sitting in the forward bay of the already ancient B.E. 2c single-engine, reconnaissance biplane, with his pilot, RFC Second Lieutenant Harold Medlicott, flying their machine from the rear bay. The Bleriot Experimental, sneeringly known as the "Quirk," was so slow it was widely considered a deathtrap whenever Imperial Army Air Service fighters were prowling, but of course, Brown and Medlicott had been given no choice in the matter of taking it up. The RFC made doubly sure of their airman's dedication to duty by forbidding aircrew to wear the new so-called "parachutes," believing their use might encourage men to abandon a fight if it got too hot. To make matters even worse to Ted Brown's more practical way of thinking, the puffed-up RFC pilots themselves considered it unmanly to use the lifesaving silk canopies, which played right into the Crown's hands.

RAF Lieutenant Arthur "Ted" Whitten Brown. (Alamy Stock Photo)

B.E. observers like Ted usually had at least one swiveling, forward-firing .30 caliber Lewis machine gun in their planes, but this particular machine never had one fitted. With only their service revolvers for weapons, the two men were virtually defenseless, especially against ground fire and the fearsome new German Eindecker monoplane pursuit ship, a sleek, fast, single-wing machine that could literally fly rings around the Quirk. Ted quietly cursed senior British leadership—while it was one thing to deny parachutes on fighting machines, what was the reason to forbid them on unarmed reconnaissance flights? After all, even balloonist spotters were given "chutes" when they went up.

The threat this day was very real; B.E. 2c machines were dropping out of the skies like swatted flies. The RFC chaps considered the Quirk "Fokker Fodder," and no wonder—the Huns themselves had labeled it *kaltes Fleisch*, or "cold meat." British ace Albert Ball simply said it was "a bloody awful aeroplane." Only a month earlier, not long after joining his new unit, Brown had been shot down. He and another pilot were operating a B.E. at 8,000 feet near Lens when a burst of "Archie" sent metal fragments slicing through the fragile wood and fabric. A few seconds later, the plane abruptly heeled over and dove for the ground at a dangerous angle, flames spurting from the 90-hp Renault V-8 engine. The fire quickly spread into Brown's forward bay, forcing him to jump/scramble into the pilot's rear compartment, though not without getting himself and his flying coveralls singed in the process. The Quirk screamed downward, approaching speeds of 120 mph. Ted held his breath, expecting the wings to rip off at any moment. Only seconds before they would've smashed up, the pilot somehow managed to level the plane out, though still in a permanent descent. Fortunately, treeless level ground appeared directly in front of them, and, for a moment, it appeared all would be well. Unfortunately, at fifty feet, they flew through a pair of unseen telephone wires. The B.E. pitched down, and an instant later, its nose struck the ground, causing the machine to turn a somersault. The two men were thrown out by centrifugal force—while the use of lap belts in reconnaissance machines was slowly being phased in, none had been installed in their fleet of B.E.s. Incredibly, the men had been pitched onto a freshly plowed field, and the soft ground prevented serious injury—they suffered only a few minor burns and bruises. Both were further relieved to learn they'd crashed within their own lines, though just barely.

Ted had been thinking about that earlier close call when something made him look up and through an opening in the clouds. He gestured wildly at Medlicott; three fast-moving Eindeckers were diving straight for them. Only moments earlier every ounce of Brown's being had been concentrated on Watson camera operation, but now, in an instant, photography became the last thing on his mind. The Huns opened up, pummeling the B.E. with 7.92mm tracered machine-gun bullets. Both men clearly heard the angry *kak-kak-kak* of the German Spandaus. Brown banged his fists on the rim of his open bay, cursing the criminal derelicts who had ordered them aloft in a defenseless kite. Earlier, their two escort fighters had abandoned them because of the bad weather, but he and Medlicott had decided to continue on without cover, "doing our bit" for the Empire. A disgusted Ted Brown could only look back at what utter fools they'd been.

The enemy's first pass hit the plane hard, but the two men were not injured, and the Bleriot was still flying. Harold Medlicott winged it over and dove for the deck in an attempt to flee, searching vainly for a cloud to duck inside. With bracing wires singing at the top of their voices, Ted could only hang on as the pilot frantically rolled, skidded, and dived. It was not to be. The Huns caught up with them on the next go-round, and the B.E.'s Renault engine crumpled under the intense fire, trailing heavy, black smoke. One of the enemy bullets struck Ted in his left leg and he screamed—loud enough to carry over the slipstream and engine noise to startle Medlicott. As much as Harold wanted to come to Ted's aid, he was too desperately occupied keeping the machine from whipsawing into a fatal spin. No thought was left about getting home—they were going down behind enemy lines.

Providentially, Medlicott retained some control, though the B.E. was descending much too rapidly. Fortunately, the Eindeckers had disengaged—they considering the lone Bleriot fatally wounded. Harold had no thought any longer of the enemy machines; his mind completely fixated on getting himself and Ted down in as close to one piece as possible. Brown, seated in the forward bay, spotted the open field first, pointing excitedly at it. Harold nodded vigorously; while the terrain looked uneven, it was the only spot the B.E. could even hope to safely alight. Brown would later muse their "luck" held right to the end; twenty feet above the ground, part of the right lower wing gave way, and the pilot lost control. Had it happened at fifty feet, the Quirk would have fatally corkscrewed into the ground. As it was, the machine still struck hard. After skidding thirty or forty yards, they hit a ditch and nosed over on their back—exactly what had happened to Ted a month earlier, but thanks to a bit of earlier lap belt improvisation, this time the crew wasn't thrown out. Somehow, Medlicott came out of it relatively unscathed, but Brown had been seriously injured again in the crash. Harold wrestled the semiconscious Ted out of the upside-down cockpit and dragged him away from the wreckage. Brown would not realize until later that his left leg had been shattered by the earlier bullet, and in the crash, he'd suffered major dislocations in his hips and knee, along with a solid blow on the head that knocked several teeth out.

Lieutenant Whitten Brown had been pushing his luck for some time. When war broke out in August 1914, he enlisted in the newly formed University and Public Schools Battalion. At the time Ted was an American citizen and he understood that with this move he'd be required to declare for exclusive British citizenship. He was proud of his American heritage, and it had not been easy to give up his official connection, but loyalty to his adopted country had trumped all. By January 1915 he'd been recognized for both his engineering education and military leadership potential and was gazetted a second lieutenant in the Manchester Regiment, his hometown unit. Brown served in the trenches with the British First Army, enduring the terrible slaughter at Ypres before finally gaining acceptance as an observer cadet in the RFC. At the time, he was overjoyed at the chance to exchange the horrors of the trenches for the air, where he'd thought the odds would be much better. However, after completing the course and after a few weeks posting with No. 2 Squadron flying extremely dangerous reconnaissance sorties, he realized it had all along been six of one and half dozen of the other.

"Harold," Brown gasped through the pain. "The machine!" Medlicott understood at once—the standing order was to destroy your aeroplane if brought down in Hunland. The pilot raced back to the Bleriot and fished out a Very flare pistol, along with as many shells as he could gather. There was no chance to get at the fuel tank and discharge a flare into it, so he fired nearly everything he had at the fabric and wood wings. Nothing. The machine was so water-soaked from the rain, it wouldn't light. Out of the corner of his eye, the harried pilot noticed the classified charts and papers lying about in Brown's forward bay. He quickly gathered them in a pile and shot his final flare into the lot.

The frustrated pilot ran back to see what could be done about Brown. "It's quite clear I'm going nowhere," Ted muttered through his smashed mouth, his head lolling from side to side while rivulets of blood ran down his chin. "Make a run for it, Harold, quickly now while you still can." He tried to smile reassuringly. "I'll be all right."

Harold would have none of it. He knew Brown would never leave him behind. "Teddie, I can't do that. Come on, up with you. We went out together and we'll go back together." They were still arguing, rather oblivious to all that was going on around them, when several angry Hun soldiers abruptly appeared, their Mausers trained on the two British officers' breasts.

Lieutenant Arthur "Ted" Whitten Brown looked up at the lowered muzzles, near tears from the dreadful pain. "Well, old man," he squeaked out to Harold. "Looks like these fellows have decided for us."

And then he mercifully fainted.

Dardanelles Strait
0130 Local Time
September 30, 1917

Twenty-four-year-old Royal Naval Air Service Flight Sub-Lieutenant John "Jack" Alcock wrenched his two-engine Handley Page O/100 bi-plane bomber violently to starboard in an effort to dodge yet another "flaming onion," a German-made 37mm antiaircraft projectile that left a fiery trail. A heartbeat later, Alcock was forced to suddenly swing hard a-port when he found himself bracketed by a separate volley of standard "Archie"—explosive bursts that lit up the night and flung lethal metal shards in every direction, signaling their presence with an angry crump! crump! crump! It was almost as if the Turkish antiaircraft artillery batteries over the Gallipoli peninsula were toying with him and that at any moment they chose, they could finish off his machine, as does a cat finally tiring of playing with its prey. Never in over a dozen bombing missions to the north coast off the Sea of Marmara had he seen such a terrifying hail of fire. It was that much more horrific for Sub-Lieutenants Aird and Wise, his second pilot and observer/engineer, respectively, because all they could do was watch helplessly. All three believed their time had come.

Since June, Alcock and his fellow RNAS mates in No. 2 Wing had been flying night bombing missions from their Mudros aerodrome on the island of Lemnos in the Aegean Sea. Morale had never been higher—their state-of-the-art O/100s were proving devastatingly effective against Enver Pasha's Ottoman forces. John Alcock, a noted pre-war air racer and one of Britain's most accomplished pilots, had become the "ace" of the unit—a new French term coming into vogue, denoting pilots who not

RAF Captain John "Jack" William Alcock. (Alamy Stock Photo)

only flew bombing missions but had also brought down five or more of the enemy's aeroplanes. No. 2 Wing mechanics and ground support personnel were especially proud of Jack's exploits flying anti-U-Boat patrols and bombing flights over such enemy hot spots as Panderma, Adrianople, and Constantinople. On those evenings when an attack was scheduled, the mechanics vied with one another to be the first to proclaim, "I hear Alcock is raiding again tonight!" The gregarious flyer was widely known as the first man to bomb "Stamboul," otherwise called Constantinople.

Jack would later marvel at how fickle his luck had been on that September 30. In the early morning, he'd experienced what would become his greatest exploit of the World War, eventually earning him the Distinguished Service Cross. Alcock was merrily strolling to the bathhouse in his pajamas when the quiet skies over the Mudros field were unexpectedly violated by the distinct sound of enemy aeroplane engines. All eyes went heavenward; moments later, a shout was heard.

"Turk snooper machine!" Another voice chimed in. "And he's got two chums!"

Jack Alcock's sharp eyes zeroed in on the two single-seat escorts, both Rumpler R6B pontooned machines doubtlessly from the German Naval Seaplane Group.

Outraged by the impertinence, Jack and two other officer pilots, Mellings and Fowler, raced for their Sopwith Camel F.1's. Alcock, who was still in *dishabille*, signaled for two mechanics to join him. The enlisted men quickly removed the chocks and prepared to prop the 150-hp Bentley rotary engine. When Alcock yelled *Contact!* one of the fellows pulled the propeller through with all the force he could muster. The motor caught at once; unlike most other aeroplane engines, the Bentley had the propeller and engine whirling around a fixed crankshaft instead of the other way round. The rotary configuration enabled smoother running due to fewer moving parts and big weight reductions in that a radiator and water for cooling were not needed; the whirling engine cooled itself. Also, the standard crankshaft flywheel was unnecessary because the heavy engine itself provided the extra kinetic energy.

Alas, the Gods of Flight not only Gaveth, they Tooketh Away. The bigger and more powerful the rotary engine, the greater torque becomes in the direction of propeller travel, resulting in pilots having to constantly apply more and more opposite rudder to hold a heading. Engine controls were harder to manage as well and there was always a great deal of petrol wasted. Most irritating to Jack Alcock as he climbed up to meet the Rumplers, the Bentley constantly leaked large quantities of its lubricating castor oil. Alcock had already twice used his pajama sleeves to rub his goggles clean.

Prior to 1914, few flying machines had more than a half dozen cockpit instruments—an airspeed indicator, altimeter, compass, bubble level or inclinometer, fuel pressure gauge, and perhaps a pulsometer, a sight glass that monitored engine "health" via lubricating oil pulses. Alcock's rotary-engined Camel was also equipped with ignition switches, a "fuel fine" adjustment—a procedure that mitigated inadvertent engine stoppage—a throttle, and a "blip" switch. The blip allowed the pilot to cut the engine momentarily without having to use the throttle and "fine" levers, a valuable time-saving technique, for example, should a harried pilot be coming in too high and fast on landing.

The three German machines were complacent; Alcock was still undetected when he closed to firing range. The first Rumpler pilot likely never knew what hit him, going straight to ground after a short two-second burst from Alcock's twin synchronized Vickers machine guns. The other seaplane pilot, angered over the demise of his companion, swung around to engage. By then Mellings was also in the fight, and he and Alcock engaged the Hun in a "dogfight," as the action was being called, the aeroplanes twisting and turning into and out of alarming attitudes. Jack finally made a tight turn inside the enemy machine, and its midsection swung into the center of his pipper. Alcock rattled off a three-second burst. The Rumpler disintegrated, with wings, tail empennage, motor, and propeller flying hither and yon. Adding to the five other machines Alcock had already claimed, that apparently made him a solid "ace" with seven kills.

It should be noted, however, that postwar official tallies showed differences between RNAS records and Alcock's Rumpler claims, something that happened with a number of Great War British aces, particularly the Canadian Billy Bishop. No attempt at the time was made to reconcile the discrepancies, perhaps because of Alcock's then very public and heroic image. Also, in this action, it might have been that either Mellings or Fowler also claimed one of the kills—Mellings did state he'd damaged the second Rumpler. As with all dogfights, the action happens seemingly at light speed, and not even the pilots on that morning could have been certain of what actually occurred.

In any event, with all the aerial confusion and to Jack's colossal annoyance, the vulnerable camera carrier that had started it all managed to slip away unscathed. Alcock landed a few minutes later, shut down the Camel, and after recovering his usual good humor, slapped his mechanics on the back and resumed his bath. He capped the morning off with a sumptuous breakfast served with hearty congratulations all-round. Later that evening, determined not to be denied the big bombing stunt already on the docket, Alcock and his crew took off for the target—the railway station and marshaling yards at Hayda Pasha near Constantinople aside the Bosporus. All had gone well until they entered the narrow Darda-nelles Strait.

Just when John Alcock thought he might sneak his Handley Page through the fiery Turkish gauntlet after all, a shell blasted off his machine's port, or left, propeller and gouged a hole in a petrol tank. Bitterly cursing such wretched luck, he wrestled the machine back out of the Strait and headed for home. He nursed the heavily laboring starboard, or right, engine for another sixty miles before a combination of an overheated power plant and intermittent fuel flow became too much. The engine seized and the dark Gulf of Xeros near the Gallipoli shoreline rose rapidly to meet the Handley Page, the moon's light just enough to enable Jack to flare out a few feet above the relatively calm water—high breakers would have been cur-tains for certain. The ship sloughed roughly into the sea, with the tail tilting to nearly seventy degrees, before settling back into the water. The three men sat stunned, amazed they had somehow survived both the Archie and the ditching. That brief reverie ended abruptly when shots rang out from shore.

Lieutenant Wise was the first to understand what was happening. "Johnnie Turk is shooting at us!" Another volley echoed across the water and several bullets ripped through the wings and fuselage fabric.

"In the water, quick!" Alcock ordered. All three jumped over the sea-ward side of the aeroplane, shielding themselves from view.

"What now, Jack?" Lieutenant Aird croaked. He was breathing heav-ily and spitting out seawater.

Alcock stuck a hand through a rip in the doped fuselage fabric and grabbed hold, catching his own breath. "Sit tight and see what happens."

After a time, the shooting stopped, but Alcock could still hear activity along the shore. The enemy wasn't leaving. He worked his way along the fuselage to the tail and peeked around it. He was relieved to see no boats were coming out after them, at least for the moment. Jack looked up at the dark sky. A huge cloud bank was about to cover the three-quarter moon. He motioned for the others to join him at the tail, pointing at the approaching cloud bank.

"Now's our chance," Jack said. "It's less than a hundred feet to shore. We'll swim for it." Minutes later the flyers scrambled behind rocks and went into hiding.

By dawn, Alcock and his two wet-soaked, shivering companions had concluded their situation was completely hopeless. Not only could the exhausted flyers not get off the beach without being spotted, but there was also no place for them to go even if they did. Hundreds of enemy soldiers were camped nearby; the three cornered Englishmen were desperately thirsty and out of ideas. Still, no one could bring himself to be the first to suggest surrender until sometime past noon, when it all became too much, and they simultaneously agreed on capitulation. "Discretion finally became the better part of valor," Jack would later say.

Alcock fired two Very pistol flares to get the Turks' attention, a precaution against triggering a startled reflex volley of fire should the three suddenly stand up. Within minutes, the British flyers had their hands high in the air and were being forced at bayonet point up the slippery-rock hill. Three menacing-looking Turk soldiers then stripped the fellows stark naked and marched them barefoot five miles to a command post. Jack, who'd thought it was a cold he'd been fighting for a week or more, nearly collapsed from what would later be diagnosed as sand-fly fever. He and the others were at the end of their ropes by the time they arrived at the Turkish army base at Chanak, where they were formally processed as prisoners of war. It would be nearly a year and a half before John Alcock would again sit in the cockpit of a flying machine.

British Internment Camp
Grand Chalet, Rossinierre, Switzerland
October 15, 1917

There was a courtesy knock on the door before it opened. "Left-tenant?"

Royal Flying Corps First Lieutenant Arthur Whitten Brown—he'd been promoted during his nearly two-year imprisonment—was lying on a cot in his tiny bedroom, book in hand. "Yes?" During Ted's confinement his normally light complexion had become even paler, almost sickly looking. An already slender build had become wiry, just short of emaciated, more from lack of appetite than deprivation. Nevertheless, an observer could not have missed the fire still burning in his inquisitive blue eyes, the sole manifestation of an inextinguishable determination to live through the war and make his mark.

Speaking excellent English, the Swiss camp adjutant walked in waving a sheaf of official-looking documents. "Your repatriation has been approved. You are to be exchanged for an invalided German officer. Please prepare to leave for *Genève* on the morning train, continuing on to England via arrangements through the British Embassy."

Ted could not believe his ears. Although he had been made to understand such a thing was in the works, he had carefully avoided getting his hopes up. Now he was having trouble processing it. Could the miracle have finally happened? Was he actually going home to Blighty?

Ted Brown set the book aside and struggled to his feet, fervently shaking the official's hand. For a long moment, he was too overwhelmed to speak. Finally: "Thank you so very much, sir!"

"You are most welcome, Left-tenant," the Swiss official said, going along with the enthusiastic shake. "I'm quite pleased for you." It was rare to bring good news to the internees, and the fellow's demeanor clearly showed his own pleasure in at least making one man happy.

The adjutant took his leave, and Ted lowered himself back on his cot. He'd found it considerably more comfortable than sitting on his sole straight-back chair. Still in something of a daze, Brown could not help reflecting on all that had happened to him since he'd been shot down, particularly the deep uncertainty and heartsickness during those first weeks following capture. The experience had left a bitter taste in his mouth that would stay with him for the rest of his life. Then came those painful, half-delirious months in three French hospitals in and around the border town of Aix-la-Chapelle, or Aachen as the Germans called it. Over the centuries, the border region had changed hands so many times much of the area had acquired dual names. Brown had been astonished to discover his Hun doctors gave him the same consideration they did their own men. When he was well enough, he wrote his parents via the Red Cross that "I have had a series of eight operations and received the kindest treatment and consideration." He did not mention that he was in constant pain and had been told he would always walk with a pronounced limp.

After Ted had gained sufficient strength, he was trundled off to a prisoner-of-war camp. Fortunately, the commandant was neither a Prussian martinet nor sadist. Brown's requests to his family for extra clothing, food parcels, and especially air and sea navigation textbooks usually arrived fairly regularly. He continually marveled at not what he didn't receive but how so much *actually got through*. Brown had also been quite fortunate in one other matter—soon after he and Medlicott were captured, they began making escape plans. It quickly became apparent, however, that Ted's immobility would not only put Harold in that much more jeopardy but any attempt on his own would almost certainly be suicidal. Ted would assist his pilot in whatever way he could but not personally take part. Over the next year, Medlicott would make thirteen escape attempts. Each time he was recaptured and returned to the prison camp. On his fourteenth try, the enraged Germans murdered him on the spot.

Early in 1917, Ted and other severely disabled British POWs were handed over to the Red Cross "as ones not likely to recover" and relocated to a neutral Swiss camp near the small village of Rossinierre—de facto making him an internee rather than a German prisoner. Because of his injuries, he was unable to take part in the physical activities many of the others used to distract themselves from the unpleasantness of their confinement. Instead, Brown occupied himself via two useful pursuits—cooking for the men, which he became quite proficient at by brilliantly improvising excellent dishes from sometimes meager rations, and studying the problems related to over-ocean air navigation.

Ted was most intrigued to learn that not only had few men addressed the difficulties of long-range, over-water navigation but that, based on all he had read on the subject, even fewer had devised practical solutions. Since his confinement began, Brown had spent his every waking moment developing navigation techniques and procedures, customizing them to circumstances unique to over-ocean air travel.

Brown had been born on July 23, 1886, in Glasgow, Scotland, to American parents, Arthur George Brown and Emma Whitten Brown, both bearing a rich English heritage. His father was an engineer for British Westinghouse based in Manchester, England, where Ted grew up. Encouraged from a young age to follow in his father's footsteps, the young man took to the trade as if he'd been born with a slide rule in his hand. He enjoyed the complex mathematics and creative thinking required of engineers. After completing his formal schooling at Manchester's Municipal College of Technology, and thanks to his father's connections, he then served as a Westinghouse apprentice engineer in Manchester. It was quite an experience working his way through the several weeks of on-job training, which naturally included the hazing all young engineering apprentices received at the forge. Ted got a bit more than usual because of his father's prominence in the company. "I say, Whitten Brown, run along to the parts shop and fetch up a left-handed spanner." Another time: "Brown, point out on this diagram the alternate short circuit." Brown took the razzing splendidly. His coworkers described him as both intelligent and a "Jolly good fellow," though it was his rock-like character and deep inner strength that really stood out. A friend once remarked, "Ted would have made a very nice Roman Catholic priest." Those early years saw him spending his free time reading both novels and nonfiction, attending poetry reads and live theater, and perusing art museums.

After completing his apprenticeship, Westinghouse packed him off to Johannesburg, South Africa, for more seasoning, returning after a couple of years to become a full-fledged general manager in Manchester. Altogether those formative years from 1903 to 1914, as Ted came to think of them, had turned him into an educated, well-rounded, and somewhat worldly young man. Now, three years of brutal war had steeled him against the worst kind of adversity, and coupled with the rather astounding realization he was going to survive the slaughter, Brown found himself filled with a ferocious resolve.

Ted rolled out of his bunk, grimacing from the pain that effort always brought, to brew some tea. He shuffled over to a small, glazed pot that contained his treasured tea bags. Brown's parents had long-standing arrangements with an American tea merchant, one Thomas Sullivan, who a decade earlier had invented a clever silk bag that prevented the tea leaves from floating annoyingly in the cup. The wonder to Ted was its simplicity—why hadn't anyone thought of it before! Brown rarely threw a used bag away—the highly prized shipments did not always reach him—sometimes dunking together a dozen or more to squeeze the last out of every leaf.

After heating the water on his small electric plate and while waiting for the tea to steep, Ted exchanged White's *Astronomy* for his most prized volume, Nathaniel Bowditch's century-old *American Practical Navigator*, the seafarer's bible. He lovingly traced his fingers across the crowded, small-print book, filled to the brim with priceless and, at long last, *accurate* height observed celestial tables, nautical mathematical formulas, weather trends, and key ports' location coordinates—along with hundreds and hundreds of other hard-won nuggets absolutely critical to a successful ocean crossing. It had been largely the Bowditch and numerous other navigation textbooks and reference works received from his family—via the Red Cross—that had gotten him through his long and bitter imprisonment. And it was a thorough study of those materials, wedded to his extensive mathematical and engineering training plus wartime Royal Flying Corps navigation schooling and the Royal Navy marine navigation manuals sent by his father, that had enabled Brown to acquire the basic skills necessary to becoming a transoceanic aero navigator.

Brown had given much thought to Lord Northcliffe's £10,000 *Daily Mail* award for the first non-stop flight across the Atlantic. Aside from the challenge itself, that was an enormous incentive; his American side quickly calculated it at nearly $37,000! According to the newspaper clippings his family had passed along, Northcliffe was giving every indication the offer would be renewed following the end of hostilities. Ted's studies had further convinced him that such a flight could not succeed without the contributions of a skilled aero navigator. If ever came the chance, Arthur Whitten Brown wanted to be that man.

He sipped his tea, musing. The Atlantic, the second largest ocean in the world, was originally known to the Greeks as the "Sea of Atlas," first mentioned in the "Histories of Herodotus" in 450 BC. Long a great moat isolating the Americas from Europe, it was clear the new aero technologies were shrinking the planet to a degree that would have been unimaginable two decades earlier. For just that reason, the *Daily Mail* publisher had announced his prewar 1913 offer *"to the first person who crosses the Atlantic from any point in the United States, Canada, or Newfoundland to any point in Great Britain or Ireland in 72 continuous hours. The flight may be made . . . either way across the Atlantic. This prize is open to pilots of any nationality and machines of foreign as well as British construction."*

As tempting as this offer was to nearly every flyer, such an attempt was not something for the timid. Since the Vikings first crossed it a millennium earlier, the angry, remorseless North Atlantic had struck terror in the hearts of mariners. Bitterly cold and fraught with gale force winds, it continually demanded the utmost attention and respect from even the most experienced sailors. For aeronauts like Brown, the perils of transiting it were even more daunting. Freezing rain could form deadly wing ice, and the vicious winds were capable of suddenly blowing a pilot off course. In the event of an emergency, matters could get even worse; the shortest, most favorable route for an aerial crossing route was also well to the north of established shipping lanes. Ted Brown had no illusions—for anyone forced down into the sea, death from either hypothermic exposure or drowning was virtually a sure thing.

Before the war, there were no flying machines capable of making it across even the shortest route, though even that may not have stopped the most reckless of the pilot breed. Indeed, some English newspapers sneeringly derided Northcliffe for proposing something no less difficult than a journey to Mars, needlessly putting lives at risk. But the publisher, who fervently hoped British aero companies would be in the competition forefront, had made the seemingly impossible offer for precisely that reason—to spur the leaps necessary to catch up to the technological leads then held by France and an increasingly bellicose Germany. And while the Wright Brothers of the USA were the first conquerors of the air, the Americans had managed to squander their lead through a combination of the brothers' years-long patent intransigence, the public's perception of the flying machine as an impractical plaything, and parsimonious government funding. There was, in Northcliffe's view, a real opportunity for Great Britain to become as dominant in the air as the Royal Navy was on the high seas. All the country needed, he believed, was a good push. The following year, however, the Great War began, and commercial flying operations ceased. And as always happens during a high-stakes war, great advances in technology—including flying machines—were made, though certainly at a price no one would voluntarily have paid. But by 1919, the deed was done, those deadly wages settled in full. The world could only hope those new advances would mean a brighter future for all humankind, with aviation one of the most obvious places to make a first great leap. Everyone close to the flying game understood there were now several types of aeroplanes capable of making an Atlantic crossing.

Even before the war, it was generally agreed that, due to the Northern Hemisphere's prevailing westerly winds, the flight should be made west to east. Guglielmo Marconi had determined the shortest route in 1901, when the brilliant Italian inventor was ready to test the over-ocean capability of his remarkable new wireless telegraphy. After studying all the geographical factors, he decided to place his transmitter/receiver stations at St. John's, Newfoundland—the easternmost point of North America, and Cliveden, Ireland—the western edge of Europe, a distance just short of 1,900 statute miles.

In the same spirit, Lieutenant Ted Brown had decided on what would be his primary navigation aids. There would be *dead reckoning*, a method sailors had used for centuries that advanced a previously known position using only heading, estimated drift, speed, and time elapsed; a *drift bearing plate*, for determining wind direction and ground speed based on observations of a fixed point on the earth's surface; and a *marine sextant* he would modify for air use to observe celestial bodies.

Ted smiled to himself over the term "dead reckoning." "What does it mean?" a fellow observer candidate had asked rhetorically during their training, "If we don't reckon right, we're dead?" After the chuckling subsided, the instructor explained it was a corrupted version of the term "deduced navigation," which seemed to satisfy everyone. But one of the books Brown's father had sent him was Richard Hakluyt's 1582 book, *Divers Voyages Touching the Discoverie of America*. At one point, Hakluyt, a perceptive British writer of exploration and geography, wrote. "When you come to Orfordnesse, if the winde doe serve you to go a seabord . . . note the time diligently . . . and in keeping with your *dead reckoning*"— Brown had underlined the phrase—"it is necessary that you doe note at the end of every foure sand glasses what way the shippe has made . . ." For Ted, after this discovery, the origin of the phrase was even more perplexing than it had been before!

Brown had pondered for months as to how to deal with the most problematic issue—in-flight celestial navigation. Unlike a slow-moving ship's navigator, who could, if necessary, wait for clear weather to measure the altitude or angle from the ocean's horizon to a heavenly body, in a flying machine traveling at 100 mph, any cloud, fog, or darkness encountered would make it impossible to see the earth's horizon line. Ted's solution, which he later learned had independently occurred to others, was to use a modified "spirit level," a bubble device similar to that used in a carpenter's level, which could be adapted to a marine sextant *thereby creating an artificial horizon.*

Ted also understood he would have to precompute sets of time/day transparent chart overlays for each celestial body observed. There simply would not be time nor would he physically be able to do the required complex mathematics in a cramped open cockpit during the actual flight. Which further meant he would have to restrict himself to a limited number of heavenly bodies, probably no more than a half dozen.

An extremely accurate pilot's pocket watch with a second-setting feature was essential. Celestial observations based on faulty time readings were worse than useless; even a few seconds off could cause significant position errors. He'd already decided that if in the unlikely eventuality celestial observations somehow became impossible, he would rely solely on readings from his drift bearing plate and dead reckoning calculations. He would further need a special roll-off/roll-up map case that accommodated his entire route but still fit in his lap. It was also a must that the map show very accurate lines of *magnetic compass variation*—the difference between the geographic and magnetic North Poles. During a journey across the North Atlantic, that value would fluctuate up to thirty degrees, enough if not properly accounted for to cause the machine to career off into the unforgiving and trackless sea.

That map, Ted had decided, would be a Mercator Projection. Developed in 1569 by the Flemish cartographer Geradus Mercator, his projection was an attempt to portray the earth's curved surface on a flat sheet of paper. He used a format that throws the world onto a cylinder in such a manner that all the parallels of latitude are the same distance apart (60 nautical miles per one degree of latitude) at the equator as at the poles. At the time, the Mercator was the one projection that most closely represented a three-dimensional sphere on a two-dimensional practical chart. (Later would come the Lambert Conformal projection, which offered much less longitudinal distortion.) The downside of the Mercator was the immense longitude distortions that occur at polar latitudes—the classic example is the island of Greenland appearing larger than the continent of South America. Fortunately, this flaw would have little to no effect on a flight from Newfoundland to Ireland. Incidentally, most scholars believe the concepts of "latitude" and "longitude" originated with second-century AD Greek/Roman geographer and mapmaker Claudius Ptolemy.

There were no *aeronautical* Mercator charts in existence; Ted would have to use Royal Navy marine charts, modifying them to his specific requirements. In conjunction with these maps, the most accurate and reliable compass available was also essential. Should that instrument fail or prove to be unreliable, it almost certainly would be fatal to not only the success of the flight but probably to the crew as well.

There was to be much more to it, of course, some of which Ted had already anticipated, more he would later discover. But on this glorious day of his deliverance, with the sun setting and the light in his room fading, Lieutenant Brown was no longer able to maintain his concentration, nor for that matter even hold his eyes open. The adrenaline rush from his deliverance had flushed through, and fatigue swept over him. Ted gently set aside the Bowditch, repositioned his pillow to a more comfortable position, and threw a blanket over his chest. Although the constant throbbing in his left leg remained—the doctors had told him that would never go away—he nevertheless fell asleep in minutes.

Prisoner of War Camp
Kedos, Turkey
Monday, November 18, 1918

John Alcock clasped the small, cloth valise on his few personal possessions and walked to the assembly area. The Armistice ending the World War had been signed a week earlier, and he and the other British prisoners—mostly Scottish infantry captured along with the Anzacs after the Gallipoli debacle—were being repatriated to the United Kingdom. He'd been incarcerated for nearly fourteen months. Much had happened during that time, some of it affecting him personally. While still a prisoner, Jack received notification that in December 1917 he had been awarded the Distinguished Service Cross *"For the great skill, judgement and dash displayed off Mudros on the 30th of September, 1917, in a successful attack on three enemy seaplanes, two of which were brought down in the sea."* Additionally, word came that effective December 31, 1917, the Royal Naval Air Service had promoted him to Flight Lieutenant. Three months later, on April 1, 1918, the RNAS and Royal Flying Corps merged into the new Royal Air Force, and Jack's rank was laterally converted to RAF Captain John Alcock.

Born in Manchester, England, on November 5, 1892, John Alcock was the oldest of five children. He grew up in modest circumstances—his father, John Alcock, was a coachman and horse dealer; his mother, Mary Alice Whitelegg Alcock, a domestic servant. While still a child, he was designing and building model flying machines, their construction informed solely by his own vivid imagination. Impatient to get on with life, young Jackie left high school at age sixteen to begin an apprenticeship with Empress Engineering in Manchester. Shortly thereafter,

Alcock left Empress to attend an aviation school at Brooklands near London. The owner of the soon-to-be-famous establishment, a Frenchman named Maurice Ducrocq, had built himself a hybrid Avro/Farman flying machine, and Alcock's mechanical precociousness soon earned him the privilege of working on it. While developing into a first-class mechanic and self-taught aero engineer, Alcock fully succumbed to his true mistress—flying!

When Jackie reached age eighteen in 1910, the ever-accommodating Ducrocq, extremely impressed by his young student's abilities, gave him two hours of flight training in the only manner possible with the tiny Farman pusher—Alcock hunched over the French flyer's back and superimposed his own hands on the experienced pilot's, allowing Jackie to follow the control movements and how they affected the machine's attitude. A natural flyer if there ever was one, young Alcock soloed the aeroplane later that same day and never looked back. Within a year, he was competing in aero races against Britain's best pilots, including winning the 1913 Easter Aeroplane Handicap at Brooklands in a Farman B—the 50-guinea prize was big money for the still twenty-one-year-old! When war came, and because of his special flying skills, Alcock was made a Warrant Officer, Second Grade on November 12, 1914, and assigned as a flight instructor at the Naval Flying School, Eastchurch, on the Isle of Sheppey, Kent. A year later, he was promoted to Flight Sub-Lieutenant and reassigned to Mudros Aerodrome on Lemnos in the Aegean flying O/100s.

Despite all that John Alcock had been through during the war and in captivity, he maintained his robust, stocky frame, a shock of ginger hair that continually fell over his eyes, and an always enthusiastic and boisterous manner. While not good-looking in the conventional sense, many women thought his adventurous bearing had considerable appeal. As a friend once said, he was well-liked because "Jackie has no side to him." No matter the prison hardships and deprivations, Alcock's natural *bonhomie* always came through, providing that rare leadership that can only come from example.

Naturally, he was very unhappy with his confinement. In an early, rare letter to his family informing them of his situation, he sarcastically wrote that, of course, "We want nothing here, except our freedom and lasses!" And the trans-Atlantic flight was never far from mind. In a much later letter, in the summer of 1918, Alcock closed with, "Tell Coatalen I shall be ready for any big stunt after the war." Louis Coatalen, then Managing Director of the Sunbeam Motor Works, was an old mechanic friend from the Ducrocq Flying School with whom he'd often discussed the *Daily Mail* prize. The "big stunt" remark was Alcock's offhand way of stating his continued determination to make the Atlantic attempt.

The first four weeks following Jack's capture, when the three Handley Page airmen had been held in Constantinople's notorious Seraskerat Prison, were brutal. After he, Aird, and Wise received ragged bits and pieces of their own and other discarded Turkish uniforms, they were thrown into a stiflingly hot and verminous prison cell. Next came a hostile interrogation, the Turkish officers very angry about the British bombing their cities. Like every other country involved in the war, the Turks were having a hard time processing the idea of targeting civilians.

"Left-tenant Alcock, where did you take off from? What was your target? How many bombs in your machine? What is its weight?"

Jack was thoroughly in the grip of sand-fly fever and not in good humor. "I can't remember, what with your bloody Archie having knocked everything out of my head."

The Turkish intelligence officer already knew most of the answers to his questions, but he was becoming increasingly irritated with the Britisher's insolence. Alcock might have faced serious consequences if not for a squadron of German pilots detached from the Imperial Air Service stationed at nearby Chanak Field. Hearing of their flying brethren's plight, the Germans somehow pried loose the three English flyers and took them under their wing. Jack and his mates were astonished when the Huns went out of their way to make them as comfortable as themselves. At one point, the Germans even tried to get the prisoners transferred to one of their own POW camps, but the Turks drew the line at that, refusing to give up their special prizes.

There was one favor the German pilots were able to do that the airmen never forgot. "Left-tenant Alcock," an English-speaking Imperial officer said shortly after the Brit's arrival at Chanak. "Our commander has authorized a volunteer from our unit to fly over Mudros and drop a *laissez-passer* giving permission for a British airplane to fly to Chanak bearing fresh clothing, supplies, and mail for you and your friends."

"That's splendid, Herr Hauptmann" Jack said, grinning widely for the first time since his Handley Page splashed into the sea. "Thank you so much!"

The German captain smiled tightly in return. "I am further authorized to offer you the opportunity to write a short note to your friends."

Alcock thought for a moment before writing out a few words. "We are prisoners of war. All in good health. J. Alcock. H. Aird. S. J. Wise."

The comment on health was a bit of a white lie—after seemingly on his way to recovery, Jack's sand-fly fever had returned with a vengeance. But there was little to be gained by provoking his captors with the literal truth. After the pass and Jack's note had been delivered to Mudros, RNAS Flight Lieutenant Smyth-Pigott volunteered to fly to Chanak Airfield with the requested goods. To the surprise of many on the British side, he returned safely to Mudros after dropping the supply package to the waving Germans. While the spirit of old-time chivalry had utterly disappeared in the other services by that stage of the war, there remained a few Knights of the Air.

It was too good to expect their stay at Chanak Airfield would last for any length of time. Many months of captivity lay ahead after they were transferred to a more remote POW camp at Kedos, Turkey. While the guards there were relatively permissive and not inclined toward abuse—simple people, some even friendly toward their European prisoners—the local Turkish were more than a little puzzled about what the fuss was all about.

While Jack Alcock privately chafed at his stifling incarceration, he was careful not to show this bitterness to his fellow Anzac and other Commonwealth inmates, aware that his prominence as an RNAS officer and aeroplane "ace" meant assuming special burdens. Although he would have scoffed at the suggestion, Alcock's inborn leadership manner, even under great stress, was an important element in the camp's conduct and morale. His natural optimism was infectious; whenever the faces got too long, the pilot was the first to gin up a singsong and break the black spell. The other inmates called him "Honest John" because he never broke faith with them or the Allied cause.

This did not mean he was a saint—far from it. Alcock could some-times be thoughtless in what he said, needlessly offending with an off-hand comment. He was occasionally crude; a raunchy joke or sometimes thoughtless prank was to Jack Alcock an amusing, welcome diversion. He enjoyed and paid attention to women, but he was not a charming man in the classic sense. Jack often took his family and friends for granted, rarely observing the usual amenities. His failure to take full advantage of writ-ing letters via the Red Cross to his worried family back in Manchester bordered on the callous. Perhaps most irritatingly, Alcock could be short with people, easily bored and showing it with any conversational topic that didn't interest him.

In the prison camp, however, whatever personality negatives he bore were invariably canceled out by his never-failing and cheerfully applied good works. He volunteered to help with anything that needed doing—constructing a sanitary open-air latrine and bathroom, build-ing stages for the prisoners' amateur shows, preparing a bandstand for musical revues, even looking after the odd sick man. Alcock was also the Officer's Mess Superintendent, receiving high marks from the men for serving high-quality food and ensuring their health and well-being. Like Ted Brown, he became well-known for his cooking skills; especially remembered were the spectacular meringues. Those culinary skills had first manifested themselves at the tender age of thirteen; his younger brother Edward once proclaimed that "Jack's parkin and treacle toffee was the finest in the world." Best of all for Jack's personal well-being, the inland Turks had treated him reasonably well, and by the summer of 1918, Alcock had finally beaten the sand-fly fever and was restored to full health.

When he wasn't working on camp projects or performing his numerous other duties, Jack's principal means of passing the time was to mull over ideas for the non-stop Atlantic hop. While aware that Lord Northcliffe's prize offer had been suspended at the start of hostilities, he was certain it would be reinstated at the end of the war. The flight was no pipe dream for John Alcock, who was no pipe-dream pilot. He'd been awarded Royal Aero Club Aviator's Certificate No. 368 on his twentieth birthday, and by the time he was shot down some seven years later, he had accumulated an astounding 4,500 hours of flying time. His peers would have considered him one of a handful of men that had the necessary skill, experience, courage, and determination to make an ocean crossing. Because of his mechanical and engineering expertise, Jack understood perhaps better than anyone that, as opposed to 1913, there were now machines technically capable of actually making the journey. In early 1914, when he had first determined to try, it would have been suicidal. It was a great irony, Alcock had mused to himself, that the war almost certainly saved his life!

Night after Kedos night following lights out, Jack Alcock would go over the effort in his head, making mental notes in regards to selecting the right machine, making modifications on the aeroplane, planning the route, on and on *ad infinitum*. The more he thought about it, the more he realized it was essential he find a fully capable over-ocean aerial navigator—if there was such a thing. Alcock was secure enough as a pilot to privately concede that the navigator would be a more important crew selection than himself. While there were perhaps thirty or forty pilots in the British Empire with the necessary wherewithal, Jack doubted there were a half-dozen aero navigators willing and able to find their way across a great ocean without a speck of land to locate their position. His over-water flights from Mudros to Turkish targets, which had been difficult enough navigation-wise, had involved hundreds of miles; crossing the North Atlantic meant thousands.

Jack was to have one last great adventure in Turkey prior to his release. On September 27, 1918, in the middle of the British prisoner's production of the London musical *Theodore and Co.,* someone yelled "Fire!" But it wasn't a fire in the theatre—the entire city of Kedos was ablaze. The ill-trained Turkish prison guards panicked, racing about in circles, yelling and screaming conflicting orders. The English prisoners took charge, organizing the town's citizens into bucket brigades and doing everything possible to save property and lives. Unfortunately, and despite their best efforts, most of Kedos town burned to the ground. For the Brits however, because of their conduct during the emergency, their standing in the community soared. During the remaining weeks in captivity, they had virtual carte blanche in their comings and goings.

Jack and his crew were among the first to be released, probably because of their unusual standing as Royal Air Force pilot prisoners. Orders were issued to march to the nearby Port of Smyrna on the Aegean Coast. There, unfortunately, their brief spurt of good fortune ended. After a long period of unexplainable confusion accompanied by frustrating delays, Captain John Alcock finally sailed, arriving in Dover, England, on December 16, 1918, with only one thing on his mind. Unfortunately for his mental well-being, Alcock found himself dumped into a swirling maelstrom of RAF red tape, and he was not finally demobilized until March 10, 1919. What had made that agonizingly long winter so unbearable was the fine print in the renewed *Daily Mail* prize rules: No active Service pilots were eligible to enter. Jack Alcock, for so long as he was required to wear the uniform, had been forced to languish in a bureaucratic hell.

Vickers Ltd—Aviation Department
Brooklands Racing Circuit/Aerodrome
Weybridge, Surrey
Monday Morning, March 17, 1919

Former RAF Lieutenant Arthur "Ted" Whitten Brown and his companion entered the main entrance of the Vickers aeroplane manufacturing factory/hangar and were led upstairs to the executive offices. The Vickers plant, the sod aero field, and several other flying machine builders were located in and around the infield of the well-known Brooklands motorcar circuit. The aerodrome was Britain's largest, located about thirty miles southwest of London.

Ted Brown's presence this day was pure serendipity. While running personal errands, he'd run into an old chum, a former RAF officer who was now selling aeroplane engine parts. "Say, Teddie," the fellow had said after they'd gotten caught up. "I'm off to Vickers to make a sale. Why not tag along?" Brown eagerly took him up on the offer; tens of thousands of recently demobilized servicemen were swamping the employment agencies and there wasn't enough engineering work to go round. So far, he'd come up short himself, and there was always an off chance Vickers might have something for him.

Following his exchange from Switzerland and considering his severe leg wound, Brown had been seconded to the Ministry of Munitions in London. He'd stayed employed in the production of the larger aero engines used in bombing machines until the Armistice in November 1918. Soon after the first of the new year, Ted was demobbed, whereupon he began approaching various aero manufacturing firms with his thoughts about over-ocean, long-distance navigation, or more specifically, the *Daily Mail*

Atlantic prize. To his chagrin, he was repeatedly rebuffed—either no one was interested in him, or they had made other arrangements. The rejections had been so thoroughly final he'd given up on the transoceanic flight and was now simply seeking work. This was his first time in the Vickers facility; he had not approached them during his quixotic pilgrimages to other plane makers because the newspapers had never mentioned the firm as a prize contender.

After Ted and his parts-selling friend settled into their chairs in the office of the improbably named Percy Maxwell Muller, Vickers Works superintendent, they were hospitably served tea and made comfortable. The friend was enthusiastically extolling his product's superior qualities when a powerfully built young man wearing greasy mechanics' coveralls burst into the room. Former RAF Captain John Alcock had returned to his old haunts at Vickers/Brooklands the day after he'd mustered out, his enthusiasm for an Atlantic attempt at full throttle. Despite Jack's intense lobbying, the firm's directors remained reluctant to commit. Nevertheless, despite the fact he'd officially been rehired to resume his old test flying duties, they had allowed Jack to put an Atlantic program together quietly. In fact, the company had been interested all along but decided to play its cards close to the chest until they were certain Vickers could supply a winning machine and competent air crew. The late-arriving John Alcock had all along been the key to the project, their best test pilot as well as a man whose judgment and abilities were unquestioned by everyone from top management down to the lowliest spanner turner.

Time had nearly run out, however, and a final decision had to be made almost immediately; Vickers' competitors already had a tremendous lead. Fortunately, in the week since Alcock had been back, he seemed to be everywhere, pushing in the shops as if he'd already gotten the go-ahead. This morning, he'd come to Muller's office to talk about the specialized instrumentation needed on a modified, two-engine *Vimy* bomber—the company's new and much prized long-distance flying machine.

"Look here, Percy," Jack said, brusquely interrupting the parts pitchman. "We have got to have a proper chin-wag about fitting the *Vimy* with the necessary navigation apparatus. I've little idea what we are going to need, much less how to gather it up." Quite forgetting that Vickers was still trying to keep their Atlantic preparations confidential, Alcock kept on blabbing in front of the two strangers. "What's more, I'm at a complete loss as to how to locate an available, qualified over-ocean navigator."

Arthur Whitten Brown's eyes lit up. Could he have heard that right? "I say," Ted blurted. "Are you contemplating a run at the *Daily Mail* prize?"

Alcock looked at Brown as if just discovering there was someone else in the office. He turned to Muller with a "who is this" look.

"Oh, yes," Muller said haltingly. "I suppose introductions are in order." But then he stopped; Ted realized the superintendent could not remember his name.

Brown, who was wearing his RAF lieutenant's uniform bearing his aerial observer badge, stood up and offered his hand. "Ted Brown. I'm an engineer by trade." Just as well to get in a job plug with Muller while he had the chance.

"Jack Alcock," came the reply. The pilot took a moment to size Brown up. "Why did you ask about the prize?"

"Well, it so happens I have been studying the problem of over-ocean aero navigation for the past several years. I had plenty of time for it as a Hun prisoner."

Alcock was intrigued and pulled up a chair, ignoring the parts salesman and Muller. "You don't say? I was an unwilling guest myself." As was his nature, Jack promptly cut to the quick. "Tell me more about navigating across the ocean."

Ted willed himself alert, realizing his main chance may, at this moment, be dropping into his lap. "As I see it, there are five primary aids available in regards to solving the aerial navigation problem. The first is map reading or pilotage—which is, of course, the one you are most familiar with." Brown had just remembered Alcock's prewar reputation as one of Britain's premier aero racers and long-distance flyers. He felt his heart beating faster; he could see he had the pilot's complete attention. To steady himself and have something to do with his hands, Ted pulled out his pipe and sucked on the stem, pacifier-like. "Of course," he said in professorial fashion, "map reading is of no use on an over-ocean flight.

The three primary methods available for use by an over-water naviga-tor are dead reckoning and plotting; astronomical observations of the heavenly bodies; and drift bearing sights to determine ground speed, drift, and wind direction/velocity." Ted chewed on the pipe stem with increasing authority. "As an aside, the fifth primary aid will be directional wireless telegraphy. While that holds great promise for the future, it is impractical at present, especially over the ocean. Very few broadcasting stations are in operation and, anyway, the capability of today's wireless transmitters and receivers are simply not up to the job."

Alcock was hanging on every word as Brown continued to deliver specific and detailed knowledge of the new science of air navigation. Jack looked as though it was too good to be true that this fellow had suddenly materialized. All the known over-ocean British aero navigators capable of the work could almost be counted on one hand and they were already committed to other Atlantic prize entries.

"I might also mention, Captain Alcock, that last year I received my Aero Club pilot license and that has rounded out my education to a considerable degree." He cleared his throat. "In my view, every heavy flying machine requiring a qualified navigator, which I consider myself to be, should understand the pilot's duties and how to coordinate properly with him."

"A viewpoint I'd not thought of before," Jack said, a bit impatiently, "but, yes, it certainly can't hurt."

Alcock's body language told Brown it was essential he get on with things. This clearly was a man who did not suffer fools nor those who would waste his time. "Back to the topic foremost on your mind when you came to see Mr. Muller. In my judgment, the primary navigational and instrument aids on a trans-Atlantic machine are a reliable magnetic compass; the latest aneroid altimeter; a reliable air speed indicator; an inclinometer for machine balancing; accurate chronometer, an RAF pilot's pocket watch will do nicely; a Royal Flying Corps 'RFC Wind Gauge Bearing Plate,' more commonly referred to as a drift bearing plate; an Appleyard course and distance calculator—a kind of circular slide rule; a good sextant; and a Baker navigation machine with a Mercator Pro-jection chart of the North Atlantic that shows magnetic variation—the latter data very important to a crossing. There are, of course, a number of supplemental items in addition to these primary tools." Ted went on to list them in some detail, then paused to let it all soak in.

Alcock had a question he was anxious to ask. "Everything I've heard and read tells me that accurate astronomical observations are essential to the attempt. My over-ocean navigator must be expert in proper sextant use and be able to do the rather complicated computations, often under quite difficult conditions. What say you about that?"

The engineer and mathematician in Ted Brown relished the question. He was convinced he was uniquely qualified in this regard. From what he had learned about the navigators of the other Atlantic prize teams, none had his formal training and background. "I quite agree," Ted responded, as he went on to describe his schooling and technical expertise. "Such knowledge is essential, as use of the sextant is currently the only means to firmly 'fix' the position of the machine over the ocean. All the rest are 'educated guesses.'" He paused for emphasis. "As far as the instrument itself, I kept up observation skills while getting my Club license and still regularly practice."

Feeling more and more comfortable, Ted deftly stoked and lit his pipe, all the while continuing to speak. "I might add I've given this sextant business a great deal of thought. I would use an American-made Brandis & Sons nautical sextant, modified with a spirit level to establish an artificial horizon. You see, Captain Alcock—"

"Jack," Alcock corrected.

"Yes, very well . . . Jack," Brown said with a shy smile and almost imperceptible nod of the head.

Percy Muller leaned back in his chair, watching the two men warming up to each other. He was thinking it just might work out; the best thing he could do at the moment was keep still and listen. What incredible fortune they should have chanced together!

Ted was using his hands to illustrate how a celestial observation was made. "A sailor moving slowly on a relatively stable ship can confidently use the horizon as a reference point when determining the observed altitude of a celestial body." Ted thrust his left hand out even with the floor, simulating the horizon, then drew his right hand up at an angle, simulating the position of the celestial body, creating an angle/altitude measurable in degrees and minutes of arc. "But to do this is much more difficult in an aeroplane; often the horizon is not visible, plus the plane is inherently unstable and most likely bouncing around in rough air. The spirit level I mentioned, an encased bubble similar to a carpenter's level that is attached to the sextant, can create that necessary artificial horizon."

Ted puffed a few more times. He'd noticed Jack's eyes had begun to glaze over. He paused for the pilot to get his bearings.

"Yes, that's all very well and good," Alcock said finally. "But what about the ability to identify the star you wish to observe? I mean, I've a devil of a time trying to tell one dot of light from another."

Ted chuckled. "Yes, I know what you mean; it can be quite confusing. I would select only a few bodies, say no more than six, and learn pat their locations in the night sky. Also, I would make the many precomputations necessary for those bodies prior to the flight. This kind of thing is going to be difficult enough as it is with that half-dozen; it certainly can't be done using the fifty to sixty stars the slow-moving mariners have at their disposal."

Alcock stood up, never one to fuss about when the way was clear. "Well, you've won me over Brown." He turned to Percy for the final decision.

Maxwell Muller's voice lowered, emphasizing the gravity of the moment. "Left-tenant, I must be direct. Think very carefully about your answer—there is a very great deal at stake. Can *you* navigate one of our *Vimy* machines across the Atlantic? And even more crucial, are you willing to gamble your life on it?"

"Yes, sir, I can and am," Ted said, surprising even himself with the force in his answer. "Not only am I absolutely confident in my ability to get the job done, there is nothing in this world I'd rather do then be Captain Alcock's navigator!"

Everyone broke into a wide grin, including the forgotten parts salesman. You could see the joy in the eyes of Brown's companion and read his mind—*I'll have many more opportunities to close a Vickers sale; my good friend Teddie has just landed the opportunity of a lifetime!*

Brown could only sit back, incredulous. An hour ago, the last thing on his mind had been the Atlantic trip. Now, so very suddenly, it was being handed to him on a silver platter.

A smiling Superintendent Muller addressed Brown. "Can you come round tomorrow, say 9:00 A.M.? We need to do the paperwork, get you on the payroll, and so forth. All right?"

"Of course, Mr. Muller. I'll be here on the dot."

And that was that. Alcock and Brown shook hands warmly, then Ted and his friend departed. Muller was about to say something to Alcock when he noticed a cloud had come over his face.

"Something the matter, Jack?"

"Did you see how heavily Brown limped on his way out?"

"Yes, we were talking about that before you arrived. A bad crash in France. I gather it's often quite painful. That walking stick he carries is not an affectation."

Alcock was silent for a moment before he spoke again. "I'm quite certain the fellow has the guts and brainpower. The question is, can he stand up to the rough and tumble of a long and extremely fatiguing flight?"

Ted Brown burst into the house yelling, "Kay! Kay!"

Twenty-two-year-old Marguerite Kathleen "Kay" Kennedy came rushing down the stairs, nearly stumbling off the bottom step. "What *is* it, Teddie?"

Brown realized at once he'd needlessly alarmed his fiancée. "I'm sorry, Kay. What a fool I am for startling you so." He quickly recovered, the joy he felt overwhelming all other emotions. "Wonderful news, darling! You'll never believe what happened." The words tumbled out as he explained the day's incredible events. His encounter with John Alcock had tipped the balance with Vickers' senior management, who'd met late that afternoon—pending successful test flights of the modified *Vimy*, an attempt would be made to win the trans-Atlantic *Daily Mail* prize.

"Oh, Ted, isn't that marvelous? You had your heart set on this, had it snatched away, and now it's popped back again!"

The two talked excitedly for the next hour, only picking at their roast beef and boiled potatoes. Ted was still shaking his head in wonder. All that time studying aero navigation, which just that morning he'd thought had come to naught, was now going to pay off after all. The peculiar fortune-teller he'd encountered only that past January had been right all along! On a lark, he and a friend had gone to see her to have their futures foretold. As he related to Kay at the time, "the lady told me that I should take a long journey across water soon and that I wouldn't go alone." They looked at each other in a manner suggesting it had all been somehow preordained.

Miss Marguerite Kathleen "Kay" Kennedy. (Library of Congress)

"You know, Kay," Ted said dreamily. "I believe that ever since man first thought about the wonder of birds in flight, he has desired to emulate them. The myths and fables of every race have tales of human flight. The paradise of most religions is reached through the air; many gods and prophets have passed from earth to their respective heavens and all the angels are endowed with wings."

Kay smiled, somewhat amused at how philosophically pleased he was with himself. She grasped Ted's hand. "I believe my own earth angel already has his wings and won't require assistance from gods and prophets."

Ted chortled. "My clever little Micki, leave it to you to gently lead me down off Mount Olympus!" Early on, Brown had taken to calling her his Irish "Mick," and the nickname had stuck. He looked into those large blue-grey eyes and ran his fingers through her lustrous, dark hair. "Such a lucky man I am," he said softly, as his hand cradled her lovely pink cheek.

Kay's expression abruptly became serious; in spite of her brave front, she desperately wanted to better understand Ted's deep commitment to flight in general and the Atlantic project in particular. "Ted, dear, won't you tell me more about Lord Northcliffe and why he is so interested in flying? A rich and prominent man like him—I am not certain I understand his motives."

Ted sipped at his richly black after-dinner coffee, a habit that doubtlessly sprang from his American genes, placing his elbows on the table and steepling his fingers. "Alfred Harmsworth, First Viscount Northcliffe, aged I believe about fifty-four years. As you must know, he has been our premier newspaperman for many years, controlling perhaps forty percent of UK circulation. Active in government as well, he just finished a term as the country's director of enemy propaganda, a job I have been told," Ted smiled sardonically, "for which he was particularly suited." Kay giggled appreciatively. "Something of a rake as a younger man," Brown continued, "and possessed of an unhealthy thirst for power, he nevertheless has been a patriot and dedicated to the safety and prosperity of the nation."

"Yes, Ted, I think I know most of that, but what about this flying business?" One of the very few private criticisms she had of her betrothed was that in his earnestness to be thorough, he sometimes had a tendency to assume she was dim about national matters. Now that women's suffrage was finally coming to England, she had taken it upon herself to become more knowledgeable about politics.

Ted smiled apologetically, quite aware he had gone adrift. "Northcliffe is keen on technology and its importance to modern nations. He has long been a visionary about the importance of flying machines—both in commerce and national defense, though of course there has always been the element of selling newspapers." In 1906, Lord Northcliffe had offered a £1,000 award for the first flight from London to Manchester, which Louis Paulhan finally won in 1910 (and witnessed by eighteen-year-old engineering apprentice Jackie Alcock). In 1909, the Frenchman Louis Bleriot claimed a £1,000 *Daily Mail* prize in his personally built machine for the first flight across the English Channel. And then, just prior to the World War, Northcliffe stunned the world with his initial £10,000 Atlantic crossing offer. "Now with peace," Ted concluded, "he's even more anxious for Britain to solidify its lead in commercial aero machines and has renewed the Atlantic offer."

"And you wish to be a part of that great adventure!" Kay summed up.

"Yes, my love, I really do. Both for the exploit and, I must admit, how much my share of the prize would mean to us and our future. You do understand?"

Kay said she wholeheartedly did, though not without making her own point that she sincerely hoped the financial aspects were not *the* deciding factor! There would be no way she could completely push from her mind the great sacrifice they both might be compelled to make. Kay, of course, was the second miracle that had happened to Brown, the first having come with his deliverance from the Swiss internment camp and safe return to the UK. Although officially disabled by his injuries and eligible for separation, he volunteered to continue service as an observer/navigator instructor. However, it quickly became clear Ted could not stand up to the physical demands. It was then he came to the Ministry of Munitions where his new boss in the aero-engine design department was the imposing and nearly unapproachable Irish-born Major D. H. Kennedy. The Major, so everyone called him—as if the title "Major" had been his given name—was a stern taskmaster with very high standards. That had suited Ted to a "T," and as a consequence, he flourished in the department. One summer day, the Major invited Brown and several other favored junior officers to a garden party. Serving as hostesses were his three attractive daughters, with the youngest, Kathleen, the most fetching. The vivacious "Kay" and the handsome RAF flight lieutenant hit it off smashingly; before they could catch their breath, they were a couple. Fortunately for Ted Brown, the Major approved of the courtship. It was very important to the old gentleman that the young man—now a mature thirty-two-year-old—was a talented engineer, well-rounded socially, came from a good family, and had an excellent war record. When Ted and Kay announced their engagement in October 1918—in celebration of Brown winning his pilot's license—the Major went out of his way to publicly announce his approval. Most telling of all, his future father-in-law provided introductions to a number of engineering and manufacturing firms, never mind how they'd all fizzled in the postwar rush.

Ted was lustily putting away Kay's delightful cherry tart dessert when suddenly the double-edged nature of the Vickers decision set in. "Oh my, we can't possibly be married next month, can we?" He became frantic.

"What have I done to your lovely plans? And what about the expenses already incurred?" He put down his fork. "This is dreadful. How shall I face the Major?"

Kay smiled reassuringly, having long since taken the measure of her father. "Oh, darling, he will be thrilled for you. This is a chance of a lifetime and mustn't be trifled with." She squeezed his hand again, a gesture that invariably sent a thrill through Brown. "Besides," she went on, "I understood straight away that it was off for now."

Kay almost laughed when she saw his look of dismay. "Leave the wedding to me," she said firmly. "I shall make new arrangements after what I am sure will be your triumphant return." She picked up her cup of after-dinner tea and clinked it against his. "For then, the day will be all that much the sweeter!"

Ted was at a loss to truly articulate his gratitude in having been granted such an understanding mate, yet knew he *had* to say aloud his deepest concerns. There must be no fog in her thinking about the possible consequences. "Darling, you must know it truly is a dangerous venture. We can't ignore that. There's always a chance—"

Kay would have none of it, putting her finger to his lips to shush him. "I won't hear or think anything but positive thoughts." Drawing herself very straight in the chair, she proclaimed definitively, "You and Mr. Alcock shall be triumphant."

Brown was not nearly as sanguine about his and Jack's chances but let the matter rest. Absolutely nothing would be served by needlessly upsetting his dear Kay nor swaying her from such unconditional support. He was going to need that more than anything else in the world, for it was becoming ever clearer in his own mind this trip was going to be very risky indeed!

Later, the two lovebirds adjourned to the Kennedy sitting room where Kay wound up the Decca gramophone and put on one of Ted's favorite recordings—George Robey's "If You Were the Only Girl in the World." Always the hopeless romantic, Brown decided he envied Mr. Bachelor John Alcock in all but one thing. Ted smiled adoringly at his best girl, remembering a letter he'd written her just before the Christmas hols. He had closed it with, "there is no beauty in the world, save when you are with me to share it."

Brooklands Aerodrome
March 31, 1919

Captain John Alcock's mind was racing as his eyes roamed across the myriad of buildings and flying machines parked around the field—Percy Muller's corner office offered a majestic view of the entire aerodrome. Of the original seventeen trans-Atlantic prize entries (many of which were frivolous) from the US and Britain—all former World War enemy belligerents were banned from the competition and France had no long-range machines to muster. Only four teams, all British aeroplane manufacturing companies, were still in the running. The last remaining American entry—really, the only one that had ever been truly serious—was the giant seaplane *Sunrise,* piloted by Swedish-born Captain Hugo Sundstedt. He had been forced to withdraw earlier in March after his machine crashed in Newark Bay, much to the delight of the English press and public, whose excessive pride in British aviation bordered on jingoism. Of those four UK companies remaining, three were based at Brooklands—Martinsyde, Sopwith, and Vickers—twenty miles southwest of London. Only Handley Page was situated elsewhere, at Cricklewood Aerodrome in suburban northwest London.

Jack learned only that morning that the Sopwith entry had arrived at St. John's, Newfoundland. The Martinsyde machine—he could see its tail section jutting out from one of their hangars at that very moment—was expected to be shipped off any day. As for the Handley Page, though he had no hard news, it certainly couldn't be far behind. Alcock frowned in frustration. It might take another month for the *Vimy* to even be ready for its first test flight.

All three competitor pilots were long-time friends of Alcock. He was closest to Harry Hawker, who would be piloting the Sopwith *Atlantic,* an experimental, long-range single-engine machine designed specifically for the non-stop crossing. Powered by a single Rolls-Royce Eagle VIII engine, it had a range of over 2,200 miles. Originally from Australia, thirty-year-old Harry Hawker was arguably one of the best-known and most fearless British Empire pilots. He had also participated in and won many prewar air races, many of them in competition with John Alcock. Although he did not serve directly in the RAF during the World War, he flew as a test pilot and checked out as many as twelve production-model Sopwith machines a day prior to their being sent to operational units. Along the way, he had set many endurance and altitude records—most still standing. Hawker's navigator, thirty-nine-year-old Lieutenant Commander Kenneth "Mac" Mackenzie-Grieve, was a native of Droxford, Hampshire, and a highly respected Royal Navy ship navigator. The pair's prospects for success looked good—Harry and Grieve had already made a 1,800-mile non-stop test flight around England, nearly equivalent to the distance from Newfoundland to Ireland.

Twenty-six-year-old Freddie Raynham, another of Jack's prewar race competitors, was to pilot the Martinsyde machine. Raynham had received Aviator's Certificate No. 85 and in 1911 became the first man to successfully recover from a spin, though he later admitted he did not understand how he did it. Like Hawker, he was a test pilot during the war, though for Martinsyde. He had selected Captain Charles William Fairfax "Fax" Morgan, a former RNAS navigator, as his crewmate. Morgan had much in common with Ted Brown—he'd also earned a civilian pilot license and had lost his right leg during the war. The two flyers had named their machine the *Raymor*, a modified Martinsyde *Buzzard* long-range escort fighter, which they powered with a single 285-hp Rolls-Royce Falcon III V-12 engine. They too had reason to be optimistic; in a static test, the *Raymor's* engine had operated without stop for a full twenty-four hours, setting aside many concerns all round about making a single-engine attempt. Indeed, Rolls-Royce powerplants were the best in the world and were the engines of choice for all four Atlantic machine finalists.

The huge Handley Page entry was the heaviest and most complicated of the entries; pilots called it the "Super Handley." A modified V/1500 bomber, it was the four-engine big brother of the O/100 twin-engine aeroplane that Alcock had been flying when he was shot down over Turkey. The engines were mounted in twin tandem fashion, a pair to each port and starboard nacelle—one propeller operating as a tractor, the other a pusher. At first glance, the massiveness of the Handley appeared to give it an advantage, but Jack was convinced the Vickers *Vimy* offered better reliability and endurance. He'd calculated the *Vimy* could fly farther—non-stop for more than 2,400 miles—while the Handley, much burdened by its large three-man crew and correspondingly greater gross weight, was good for only 2,100 miles. In the event of serious headwinds over the North Atlantic, it was even possible the Handley might fall short of the Irish coast. With flying machines, everything was a tradeoff between gross weight, engine power, and payload—changing any one of them affected the others.

Alcock knew only one of the three-man Handley crew. Early in the war, Jack had taught the pilot, distinguished twenty-five-year-old RAF Major Herbert "Brackles" Brackley DSO, DSC, how to fly, and they had remained close. Commanding the aeroplane was retired RAF General Mark Kerr, the oldest man in the competition at fifty-five. In 1914 he had become the first flag officer—oddly enough, he was at that time a Royal Navy Rear Admiral—to earn a pilot license. He was also known as the kind of fellow who made heavy weather of nearly every task he took on. RAF Captain Tryggve Gran, born a Norwegian, was the navigator, though he was also a fine pilot—in the summer of 1914, he became the first man to fly across the North Sea. Gran was a real adventurer, having participated in Robert Scott's 1912 expedition to the South Pole and was among the first to find the explorer's frozen body. Overall, the Handley Page had fielded a fine team, but they also played their cards close to the chest; how far along they were was anybody's guess.

Jack Alcock had run into Harry Hawker a couple of weeks earlier at the Brooklands Bluebird Restaurant, what had long been a kind of "officer's club" for the aviators. Jack had been quietly sipping a pint and having a bite to eat. "Hello, Jacko, you old sod," Harry had said breezily, as he pulled up a chair. "A little birdie has it Vickers will enter the *Vimy* in the Atlantic contest." When no comment was immediately forthcoming, Hawker pressed it. "Or is that just another load of hanger codswallop?"

Alcock assumed the guarded stance that all the Brookland aviators had for fear of giving out an advantage. Yes, they were all friends and wartime comrades, but the competition was keen, with much riding in the balance. Besides, Hawker's condescending flippancy had irritated him. "There's been some talk along those lines, Harry," Jack said evenly.

Hawker laughed indulgently. He'd seen the "aeroplane" earlier that day, still largely disassembled amidst piles of spare parts and equipment, men clambering here and there trying to pull it all together. "Yes, yes, of course," Harry said wickedly. Whence he began to slowly turn the knife. "Well, after Grieve and I make the crossing and collect the prize, I shall make it a point to come round the field and watch your first test flight."

Alcock did a slow burn but said nothing. Harry must have realized he'd pushed it too far. He promptly downed the balance of his glass. "Well, cheerio, Jacko. Good luck."

"Luck to you, Harry," Alcock had said rather grudgingly and without looking up from his own Guinness stout. And that's the way they'd left it. Now, Hawker was already at St. John's, and Freddie Raynham was about to sail.

Jack gazed glumly down from Percy's office at the Vickers team racing to assemble his flying machine. The ugly truth was they were very far behind, and unless a miracle happened, they were going to get beat— badly. Jack took heart watching Reggie Kirshaw Pierson, the *Vimy*'s legendary designer, barking out orders while running hither and yon to address this and that. Assigned by Muller to modify one of their production machines as quickly as possible, Pierson was personally directing his horny-handed mechanics, riggers, and carpenters—men so dedicated to their chief they would not have shown slack or given up in the middle of a hurricane.

Dressed as he had been for weeks in greasy coveralls and a tattered soft longshoreman's cap, still as fine a mechanic as he was a pilot, Captain John Alcock stepped down the stairs to join the fellows, determined to be just as resolute.

Brooklands Aerodrome
Good Friday, April 18, 1919

After a series of maneuvers and equipment testing, John Alcock was making a left-hand or counterclockwise circuit around the Brooklands field in preparation for an in-to-the-wind landing. Although Jack was sitting on the right side of the tiny cockpit bench, the accepted standard for side-by-side seating was to have the pilot on the left and the second pilot or navigator to his right. This had not been possible in the *Vimy* due to the yoke's fixed position in a machine designed with a pilot's right-seat orientation, on account of the need for bombardier seating before he crawled into the nose for the bomb run. The original reasons for the soon-to-be universally adopted left-side pilot seating arrangement and left-hand pattern circuits remain a matter of some speculation, in much the same manner as the origins of the term "dead reckoning."

There are some strong suppositions, however. Early twentieth-century studies showed that 80% of people were right-handed, 10% ambidextrous, and the balance left-handed, especially for writing. From the dawn of human history, most activities involving one's hands have manifested themselves in the preferred "handedness" of a specific individual. The vast majority of early warriors and soldiers, for example, wielded swords, spears, and clubs in their right hand. And except for certain regions in central Asia, horses were mounted from the left side, leaving the stronger right hand free to hold a weapon. While riding, the reins were held in the left hand for the same reason. When flying machines were first developed, there appeared to be an instinctive inclination to favor a right-handed person by putting that hand on the most important controls. As the early twenty-first-century British writer L.F.E. Coombs put it, he perhaps the

The modified Vickers Vimy *bomber cockpit. (Science Museum Group)*

most knowledgeable chronicler of this early period, the Wright brothers were heavily influenced, either consciously or unconsciously, by this right-hand bias: "Between the two [side-by-side seats in their early machines] was the principal control, the combined wing-warping and rudder level. The [other] levers controlling the forward 'canard-type' elevator were at the 'outboard' knee of each pilot. This arrangement placed the lever requiring the greater degree of skill . . . *at the right hand of the person in the left-hand seat* [emphasis added]." After the Wright brothers' stunning successes at Fort Myer near Washington, DC, and Le Mans, France, in 1908-09, their design influence in this particular area became so profound it is still used almost exclusively to this day.

The left-hand circuit seems to have sprung from similar predispositions. As early as 1912, the left-hand or counterclockwise landing pattern had already been accepted, though the reasons remain somewhat murky. It was true that racing tracks, ice skating rinks, and other such venues were usually run toward the left. The recent advent of the modern Olympics in 1896 Athens conducted all its events counterclockwise, and that might have been an influence. As the years went by, it was also found that flying machine counterclockwise landing circuits were easier to perform due to observational ease; a pilot sitting in the left seat making left turns was much more in command of his approach and landing.

Alcock leveled the *Vimy*'s wings after the turn to final approach, reduced power to just above best flare speed of 45 mph indicated, waited for the *Vimy*'s wheels to slowly settle on the well-packed sod, and allowed the machine to roll itself to a stop. Superintendent Muller headed a large group waiting for Brown and him to scramble down via wing and ladder the ten feet to ground level. After three weeks of frenzied labor, Percy was beside himself to learn the results of the test flight.

"How'd it go, Jack?" he asked breathlessly.

"Splendid! First rate!" The pilot's smile was so wide and long-lasting it threatened to leave a permanent crescent on his face. His subsequent jubilant summary reduced the Vickers management and mechanics present into giggling children celebrating the last day of school. The Rolls-Royce engines had performed like precision Swiss watches, Jack had reported, the cockpit and engine monitoring instruments registered superbly, and the machine's flight controls operated flawlessly. A bang-on first test flight!

"All except for that bloody wireless," Alcock muttered under his breath as he turned away and gathered up his gear. From the start he'd been against including the heavy transmitter/receiver equipment, but Brown convinced Muller of its importance and Jack had reluctantly gone along.

"I'm sure we can find the fault," Brown offered soothingly. "I'll work with the wireless fellows and fix it straight away."

As was Alcock's way, he promptly cut back to the chase. "Percy, the machine performs so well we don't need to do any more testing. Those fellows in Newfoundland could be on their way any day."

"I entirely agree, Jack," Muller said. "But let's stay by the book and first gather up Archie for a final postmortem." Archie Knight, Vickers Works manager, had overseen all the modifications from the military version of the *Vimy*, literally working day and night with every mechanic, carpenter, and rigger he could lay hands on—the company's still ostensibly secret but very late entry was taxing the entire Vickers flying machine subsidiary to its limit. Nonetheless, the exacting Muller had still wanted to make sure no last-minute stones needed overturning.

The men huddled in Percy's office, shuffling paperwork and sipping tea. Knight started it off by asking Alcock about the structural integrity of the fabric and wood airframe of what had been officially designated the *Vickers F.B. 27 Vimy Mark IV, Serial Number C105,* the modified machine painted in a special new silver-colored livery. The military model had been named in honor of the terribly bloody 1917 Battle of Vimy Ridge near Arras. Alcock and Brown had already decided that, unlike the other prize entries, their machine need not have a "pet" name.

"Rock-solid as the Tower," Jack replied.

"And the two power plants?" Those would be the specially selected Rolls-Royce 12-cylinder water-cooled Eagle VIII engines, rated at 360 hp at 2,035 maximum rpm. Each turned a four-bladed wooden propeller 10 feet, 5 inches in diameter.

"Tip-top." Alcock had been very pleased with their performance. "Ran the entire time without a burp. Took maximum revolutions for the allowed five-minute limit without complaint or overheating."

"Aeroplane performance?"

"We took off at just under 12,000 pounds gross weight, and after thirty minutes, I was able to get a climb rate of 300 ft./min. Coaxed 101 mph indicated airspeed at 5,000 feet level flight. Both marks a bit better than we'd calculated." The *Vimy* was one of the first heavy machines to achieve three-figure airspeeds.

"Any problems with the modifications we made on the military version airframe?"

Alcock shook his head. "We are fine all round. As I'd expected on the landing, a bit more back pressure on the wheel kept the nose clear of the ground all the way through the roll out."

The *Vimy's* basic airframe size had remained unchanged—wingspan 68 feet, length 44 feet, and maximum height above ground 15 feet. The undercarriage consisted of a double set of rubber wheels under each side of the fuselage. For weight and drag reasons, Jack had insisted on removing the nose skid, which had been designed to prevent the fuselage front from plowing into the ground on landing. Alcock had also ensured all fuselage fairings were streamlined in order to gain another mph or two.

The most important of the interior structural changes included installing extra petrol tanks—for a total of seven—in the observer/navigator position at the fore-end of the fuselage, behind the cockpit, and the rear gunner/bomb-spaces. The sixty-five-gallon tank in the rear gunner position was given a turtle-back fairing for streamlining purposes. These changes raised total petrol capacity from 865 gallons to 1,050 gallons, giving the modified machine a range of up to 2,400 miles, or about 23 hours duration.

As a concession to safety in the event of a ditching, one of the smaller gunner/bomb space petrol tanks had been fashioned as a buoyancy raft. Additionally, a small cupboard was fitted into the tail section to hold emergency supplies, the tail presumed to be the last of the machine to sink. They would not carry parachutes; without the raft, they would be lost in any event. Redesigning the pilot cockpit to accommodate Ted and his navigation instruments and facilitate crew coordination had been the most complicated of all the modifications.

Percy and Archie turned to navigator Brown. "Any comments?"

Brown had a wry look on his face. "Well, it's a wonder Jack and I are still speaking, what with all the squabbling over who gets what space in that tiny cockpit."

All four men laughed. During the test flight, there had been no little shouting back and forth over turf, mostly good-natured. The *Vimy's* crew space had been reduced to something less than a small park bench, Jack on the right, Ted on the left—hip-to-hip and shoulder-to-shoulder, with virtually no wriggle room.

"That said," Brown continued, "I think we have most of the kinks worked out. Our compass was well behaved and situated so that both of us could easily read it. The same can be said for the altimeter and indicated air speed gauge."

Their altimeter was a form of aneroid barometer—the first such devices appeared around 1910 when flying machines began rising more than a few hundred feet above the ground—and was constructed to measure the air pressure at any altitude and convert that value to feet above mean sea level. It corrected for temperature using a standard lapse rate decrease of 3.5 degrees Fahrenheit per 1,000 feet of altitude and was good up to 15,000 feet. The earliest air speed "indicator" had been nothing more than a flat plate set against the direction of travel; air pressure bent the plate back and an attached pointer moved across a calibrated scale, indicating the velocity of the machine passing through the air. The *Vimy*'s air speed indicator was by comparison much more sophisticated; a hollow pitot tube, invented by France's Henri Pitot in 1730 for determining ship's speed, measured forward air movement by comparing static fuselage port measurements against into-the-wind pitot tube data with the results reported to a cockpit meter.

Vickers engineers had distributed their cockpit instruments somewhat randomly on what most were calling the "dashboard," presumably after a horse-drawn vehicles' mud or dashboard. In 1910, Elliott Brothers, a British instrument maker, developed what was probably the first integrated instrument array, displaying engine revolutions, altitude, and air speed. In 1913, the British War Department developed the Mk IV package that included altimeter, tachometer, air speed indicator, and stopwatch. This integrated instrument packaging idea was slow to catch on, however. It was not until the mid-1920s that what we might call the first modern instrument panel initially appeared.

"The rotatable drift bearing plate," Brown said, continuing his report, "easily clamps on the left edge of the fuselage next to me, giving a clear view of the earth or sea directly below the machine. Today's wind aloft calculations closely matched measured conditions at the field, confirmation the instrument is properly calibrated. Fuel tank switching went smoothly. The storage compartments under our seats, side panels, and below the dashboard will accommodate our needs, though, of course, it is all very tight and clumsy. Both Jack and I will have to be quite deliberate, as well as patient, with one another!"

That got another round of knowing smiles.

Percy wanted a bottom line. "Is there anything either of you can't handle or are uncomfortable with?"

Both Alcock and Brown shook their heads, with Jack speaking for both of them. "Teddie and I are a good team and ready to go."

Percy Muller looked at Works Manager Archie Knight, who nodded his agreement. Muller made the call. "I'll pass the word along tonight. We'll start disassembling and crating the machine immediately. I'll make arrangements for the next steamer to Halifax, Nova Scotia."

As they filed out the door, Alcock still had something sticking in his craw. Saying to no one in particular, but loud enough for all to hear, he said, "We're ready to go all right, except for that stinker of a wireless, which, mark my words, will only cause trouble and add unnecessary weight to the machine. Even if it does work, I can't see any possible good it would do in the air." He finished his argument with a challenge. "I would much rather have that weight in petrol."

Brown felt he had to offer a rebuttal. "Jack, if we get in trouble, my regular position reports will offer us a real chance of rescue. Even with the wireless, we are going to be well north of the shipping lanes. Someone will have to know where we are."

John Alcock wasn't convinced. Like most pilots, he harbored a deep distrust of the chronically unreliable wireless sets, to say nothing of their supposed future applications for "blind flying" and "direction finding." The long-haired engineers, Jack believed, were always coming up with new gadgets, most of them completely impractical.

Percy ended it. "For safety reasons, the wireless stays."

Aboard the RMS *Mauretania*
May 4, 1919

Alcock and Brown stood silently on the open deck adjacent to the bridge, watching Southampton slip away. The two weeks following the Good Friday test flight had been an absolute scramble getting the *Vimy* broken down, crated, and ready for shipping—to say nothing of the myriad of other loose ends that needed tending. The two flyers had split the work. While Alcock supervised everything to do with the aeroplane proper, Brown rode interference on the ship's navigational and instrumentation needs, along with their personal requirements as aero crew. Due to interminable problems popping up, including serious transportation and port labor difficulties, it was uncertain when the machine could finally be on its way. It had therefore been decided an advance party headed by Alcock would proceed to Newfoundland as soon as possible. For the Vickers men aboard, it was a relief to smell the sea and finally be underway.

Over the past weeks, during those precious few hours they were able to carve out for relaxation, Alcock and Brown had shared their life stories. The conversations were easy and natural from the first, with their new professional association quickly blossoming into a warm friendship. Aviation was a passion for each and, while their individual makeup as men was quite dissimilar, mutual respect and robust senses of humor easily overcame any differences. They were uproariously amused to learn they had both grown up in Manchester, England, very nearly a stone's throw away from the same childhood playgrounds! The six-year difference in their ages explained the lack of mutual contemporaries, but they still had much in common. They were startled to learn that Norman Crossland, a founder of the Manchester Auto Club, had employed Alcock as a mechanic in 1911. Crossland had been a boyhood friend of Brown's. It was pleasant for both to recollect that earlier time, and Ted always believed it served to bond them more quickly and solidly.

Just a few yards away, Captain Rostrom continued to boom out orders as his mighty Royal Mail Ship, the running mate of the ill-fated RMS *Lusitania*, was tugged out to open sea. Rostrom, his 800-man crew, and 2,200 passengers were bound for New York via Halifax, Nova Scotia. The Vickers advance team was pleased to learn the captain had taken a special interest in them, offering Alcock and Brown the run of the mighty four-funneled superliner. Percy Muller had tapped three of the Aviation Department's most responsible executives to accompany Jack and Ted: Ernie Pittman, foreman of the mechanics and carpenters; Bob Dicker, a flying controls expert and trusted prewar friend of Jack Alcock's; and Gordon "Monty" Montgomery, who was to boss the erection of the crated *Vimy* after it arrived by freighter, hopefully no more than a fortnight behind them. The machine itself would be accompanied by seven additional workmen, all of whom would be under Montgomery's direction.

A few evenings before the team left London for Southampton, Brown had taken his Micki to a West End show; they both greatly enjoyed the theater. After returning to the Kennedy home, Kay presented him with a tiny mascot for the flight, a black cat doll she had named Twinkle Toes. The black cat was purposeful, Kay knowing Mr. Alcock embraced rather than was frightened by the traditional superstitions. She had learned the "ace" pilot particularly liked to poke a finger in the eye of Friday the 13th, which he proclaimed, "my lucky day." Of course, when Alcock learned of Twinkle Toes, he was not to be outdone in the talisman department. Jack went out the next morning and purchased his own, much larger black cat mascot, which for reasons Ted never discovered, he dubbed Lucky Jim.

On the quay before departure, everyone had been smiling and in good cheer, despite the fact that the competition had such an enormous jump-start. Ted was so exuberant he blurted loudly to Kay just before kissing her goodbye, "I've a hunch we're going to win!" It had been a jarring moment; all within earshot looked at one another with varying forms of a you-must-be-kidding-me expression. Although it had remained unspoken, everyone at Vickers knew it was going to take an Act of God for the *Vimy* to have any chance at all of overtaking its rivals. Second thoughts about the increasingly risky financial gamble the firm was taking had also been clearly visible on several senior faces.

Still, the company continued to project an optimistic public front. A few days earlier, London's *Evening Standard* broke the news with a bold headline:

NEW ENTRY FOR ATLANTIC FLIGHT—VIMY!

Jack took a long drag on his Gold Flake cigarette before resting his forearms on a *Mauretania* bridge rail. "Well, Ted," he said, as if it had just occurred to him. "We're off."

Brown was dreamily puffing on his newly favorite briar, filled with fresh Bond Street tobacco. The beautiful Kaywoodie had been another *bon voyage* present from Miss Kennedy. "It's a new model just out," she had said breathlessly. "I ran to Harrods to fetch one home before they were gone!"

"Indeed, we are," Brown replied to Jack. "Hopefully we shan't be waving at Hawker and Raynham as they pass over going the other way." The Sopwith team had been in Newfoundland for over four weeks; the Martinsyde crowd for three. It was a wonder to both Alcock and Brown that one or the other, or both, hadn't yet made an attempt.

The immense preparations had brought the Vickers aviation people to the limit of their endurance. Nearly the entire department had worked eighteen hours a day, meticulously disassembling the *Vimy* and carefully crating it, the engines, the bulky radiators, and all the support equipment for transport to Newfoundland. The plain truth was Vickers had taken too long to make up its mind and was now paying a heavy price. The tension had been intense; even the normally affable John Alcock became surly under the pressure. Ted began giving him an understanding wider berth, trying his best to take some of the stress off the man upon which so much was riding.

Perhaps the most crucial aspect of the preparation stage had been the selection, care, and feeding of the Rolls-Royce Eagle Mark VIII engines. R-R had designed the first version of the Eagle in 1915; by war's end, 4,000 of the 200-hp version engine had been manufactured. In 1917, when much larger multi-engine bombing machines were appearing, the company developed the more robust 360-hp Mark VIII Eagle. By the time the Armistice was signed, it was universally agreed that Henry Royce built the world's best aeroplane engines—all four of the remaining Atlantic prize entries were using his power plants.

Jack had spent two days at Rolls' Derby headquarters, located some 120 miles northwest of London, rigorously testing the two Eagles he'd specially chosen. With company head Claude Johnson at his side, Alcock systematically examined every detail and aspect. Johnson, very much aware of Captain Alcock's experience and reputation, accommodated the pilot's requests at every turn. He knew that Jack was widely respected as an expert mechanic, unlike nearly all other flyers. Alcock, who had intended all along to personally liaise with the R-R spanner-turners, continually dazzled them with his grasp of engine technology and willingness to get his own hands dirty. At length, Alcock informed Johnson he was well-satisfied with both Eagles and asked they be shipped to Brooklands as quickly as possible.

"Oh, by the way," Johnson had almost casually added. "As a courtesy, we are offering at our cost one of our best engineers to accompany your team." In fact, he'd made the same gesture to the other British competitors, determined to show no favoritism while ensuring Rolls engines remained the talk of the aviation world. Johnson motioned over a cheerful-looking, redheaded fellow. "Jack, I want you to meet Bob Lyons. He'll be looking after your pets for as long as you need him." Birds of a feather, Alcock and Lyons hit it off immediately, to the point Jack had insisted that Lyons accompany the Vickers advance team on the *Mauretania*, bringing that party to an even half-dozen.

During this same period, Ted Brown concentrated on his many duties. There was the matter of arranging for the procurement and shipping of oil and petrol, along with those annoying meetings at Burberry trying to make properly work the electrically-heated flying coveralls and getting Jack to cooperate on a fitting date. Brown had been mostly worried about how much help he could expect from the Admiralty and Air Ministry, especially regarding the loan or sale of the necessary celestial height observed (HO) tables, nautical daily almanacs, and various instruments.

To his amazement, Brown discovered the government stuff-shirts were unaccountably skeptical of all heavier-than-air flying machines and didn't want to cooperate. "If we were balloonists," a head-shaking Ted later told Jack, "they'd of made a present of the stuff!" It had taken considerable doing for the unknown former observer to establish his bona fides as a serious air navigator. In the end, and not without a little help from his well-connected future father-in-law, Major Kennedy, Ted finally received everything he needed, either through a government loan of an instrument or convincing Vickers to buy the necessary item.

It could not have hurt that it was becoming more and more clear the Atlantic competition was of benefit to everyone. Both private aero companies *and* the British government had much at stake—business was fascinated by the profit potential in rapid over-ocean commerce, and four years of costly war had convinced the military of the importance of long-range aero machines to national defense and offensive warfare. Parliament's support had been made all the easier by Northcliffe's insistence no government financial help be allowed. The uncanny prophesies of Lord Alfred Tennyson, as expressed in his famous 1842 poem "Locksley Hall," were on many minds:

> *Saw the heavens fill with commerce, argosies of magic sails,*
> *Pilots of the purple twilight, dropping down with costly bales;*
> *Heard the heavens fill with shouting, and there rain'd a ghastly dew*
> *From the nations' airy navies grappling in the central blue.*

It was widely understood that all four of the remaining *Daily Mail* prize team navigators would be *de facto* pioneers, operating separate air "laboratories" that sought answers to problems yet unsolved. As a matter of fact, the navigation issues were perceived to be larger obstacles to overcome than the technical capability of the pilots and flying machines themselves. The key to accurate aerial navigation had come down to the same common denominators faced by mariners for centuries—how to successfully travel from Port A to Port B, only now much faster and through the air. The definitive answer rested, as it had for mariners, with knowing the precise latitude and longitude of both A and B.

The problem of determining latitude had been solved, at least reasonably so, a half-millennium earlier. Northern hemisphere sailors in particular—where nearly all of the world's commerce was conducted—had discovered that with the use of such tools as astrolabes and the more primitive cross-staffs, the angle they observed between the horizon and the sun's height at local high noon was effectively equivalent to their latitude. At night the Pole Star, or Polaris, remained rigidly fixed (essentially) and was equally of value in establishing latitude lines. Longitude, however, remained stubbornly unsolvable without complex observations of the stars, planets, sun, and moon, all followed by extensive mathematical computations—something only scientifically trained shore-bound experts could perform. Certainly, such efforts were beyond the capability of ship captains or their lieutenants. Seamen had to continually deal with not knowing how far along they were on their course line, which inevitably led to becoming either hopelessly lost or winding up a wreck on suddenly appearing rocks and shoals.

It wasn't until early in the eighteenth century that real progress came regarding firmly "fixing" a ship's position. The English Astronomer Royal, John Flamsteed, labored for forty years to produce the first complete and technically precise map of the heavens. Published posthumously circa the 1720s, his 3,000-star catalog, *Catalogus Britannicus*, and a companion star-atlas called *Atlas Coelestis* "cemented the positions of the fixed stars on the celestial clock dial," as writer Dava Sobel has put it.

Around 1730, armed with Flamsteed's priceless "maps," the American optician and inventor Thomas Godfrey and the English mathematician John Hadley independently invented the reflecting *octant*, which replaced the primitive astrolabe. It was later refined in the 1760s by the English instrument maker John Bird. A handheld device first conceived by Sir Isaac Newton, the octant used reflecting mirrors that pivoted along a graduated arc that enabled an observer to measure the angle in degrees and minutes between a celestial body and the horizon. In the eighteenth-century Royal Navy, the instrument became known as "Hadley's Quadrant," the misnomer likely resulting from a general misunderstanding of the nature of its mirrored construction. In any event, the instrument revolutionized the observation process—very precise latitudes could now be ascertained.

Still, there was one last giant piece of the puzzle left unresolved—how can a ship reliably find its longitude anywhere on the Seven Seas? Simply stating the problem, during an observation, one must know both the precise time on the ship and the precise same time at a prime meridian, a designated longitude baseline. This—the most difficult navigation problem of them all—was at last solved in the late-1700s by the Englishman John Harrison when, after another four-decade-long effort (circa 1730-1770), he invented an accurate, under-long-voyage-ship-conditions chronometer, or watch, as it was first called. After a contentious battle with a number of unscrupulous British astronomers with their own agendas, including the then-Astronomer Royal, they who insisted on promulgating a much more complex and often unusable technique called the "lunar distance method," Harrison finally prevailed. Captain James Cook's brilliantly successful Pacific voyages in the 1770s, using Harrison-type watches, settled the matter conclusively in favor of John Harrison and his collaborator-son William. Parliament finally, though reluctantly—the matter remained stubbornly political—awarded them all of their £20,000 prize money (nonetheless, the historically misunderstood King George III still had to personally intervene to ensure the Harrisons actually received payment).

From then on, with the knowledge of the correct time aboard ship as calibrated from the Prime Meridian—the accepted zero longitude starting point established in 1884 at Greenwich, England, by the International Meridian Conference—both latitude and longitude could be determined by trained sailors using precomputed nautical daily almanacs and height-observed (HO) tables. Ted Brown and his fellow Atlantic flying machine navigators were on the verge of successfully adapting those proven marine navigation techniques to the even more complex problems associated with three-dimensional, over-ocean aerial flight.

John Alcock soon learned Arthur Whitten Brown completely understood these and other aerial navigation problems, deferring to him regarding all navigational aids and instrumentation needs. Further, they had agreed that only Ted would be allowed to do the cockpit installations of their instruments. Brown was not only a skilled navigator and trained engineer, but an excellent technician to boot. It would be Ted's job, coordinating with Jack, to place and install each of the dashboard's necessary dials, meters, knobs, levers, electrical wiring connections, and so forth while the machine was being modified at Brooklands. Despite the fact much could be carried over from the military version cockpit, the alterations still presented significant challenges.

The conversion from a military single-pilot cockpit to a civilian dual pilot/navigator station with special long-range needs had to be difficult no matter how careful the planning—after all, the thin leather-cushioned seating bench and dashboard just an arm's length away were only four feet wide. In this ridiculously tiny space, Ted would be seated on the left, Jack to the right. Alcock's automobile-like control wheel could not be recentered squarely in front of him, remaining where it was, slightly staggered to his left. It was an irksome circumstance that would prove to compound an already heavy pilot fatigue load. Brown's cherished wireless set—headphones, line jacks, transmitter key, and lowering antenna reel with weighted lead ball on its end—was installed on his left side of the cockpit. Powered by a dry-cell battery, the wireless was recharged by way of an eight-inch diameter wind-generator airscrew mounted on the lower wing under the starboard, or right, engine. An identical wind-driven generator airscrew under the portside engine independently powered the dashboard instruments and petrol pump.

Ted's portable navigation equipment had to be carefully positioned in such a manner so as to be readily accessible during the flight. Both men were painfully aware that some activities that were easy enough to perform on the ground would be next to impossible to accomplish in the air. It is hard to appreciate how very difficult it is to even hold a pencil and write something down when hands are freezing, the wind is whistling by just overhead at 100 mph, the machine is bouncing around so violently even forward vision becomes a blur, and it's raining inside the cockpit. Further, trying to actually shoot a star accurately and be able to *read* the measurements off the sextant scale *in the dark* represented an enormous challenge. Or, in those same conditions, attempt to take a drift and ground speed reading off the rotatable drift bearing plate through breaking clouds while desperately attempting to hold the course reticule steady on an ocean white cap or Very pistol flare for the necessary seconds needed for an observation, then *somehow reading* those measured results in all the murk. A remarkable device used in both World Wars, the Very could send visual messages by way of variously colored flares. It was invented by a US Navy ordnance officer, one E.W. Very.

Ted had modified his American-made Brandis & Sons marine sextant by embedding an Abney spirit-level in an attached mahogany vertical strip that provided a reliable artificial horizon. Invented by Sir William Abney circa 1870, the level was intended for use by surveyors, but by 1919, aero navigators had recognized its application to their celestial navigation problem. At altitude at night, often with lower clouds below, it was often impossible to see the actual horizon, to say nothing of the problems caused by other technical issues in any non-bubble aero sextant. The Abney level, at least, compensated for the worst of those difficulties. Brown had considered using an octant, Hadley's Quadrant, if you will, but decided its field of view was too narrow for comfort—the sextant offered sixty degrees field of view, or one-sixth of the sky; the octant only forty-five degrees, or one-eighth. With the inevitable weather and machine instability problems, coupled with the obstruction of the *Vimy's* upper wing, using an octant would make it that much harder to locate a specific celestial body. He would sacrifice the additional marginal accuracy for observational assuredness.

Brown's navigation equipment would be stored in the small compartment under his seat or at his feet on the cockpit deck. As Ted had decided in the Swiss internment camp, he would rely on a rolled Mercator Projection chart installed in his Baker navigating machine—to be accommodated on his lap while en route. Invented by Commander T.Y. Baker, Royal Navy, the instrument eased chart handling and simplified the procedures necessary to lay down the correct fix locations and position lines on the chart.

The Baker also accommodated two sets of star transparencies that could be overlayed atop the Mercator chart. The first set bore precomputed so-called "Sumner circles" dedicated to Brown's half-dozen chosen celestial bodies *for all times of the day and night*; the second, another precomputed set of six Sumner circles for those same celestial bodies *based on calculations from the Height Observed (HO) Tables*. Developed by the nineteenth-century American mariner, Captain Thomas Sumner, these lines were also called "circles of equal altitude." Only a small portion of a Sumner circle needed to be drawn on the chart, which effectively was a straight line. Later, navigators of all stripes would settle on the term "lines of position," or LOPs.

Alcock and Brown watched the tugs turn back toward their South-ampton berths. Both men were taking special delight at hearing the powerful throbbing of the *Mauretania*'s engines as the vessel came fully to life. They had already sensed the enormous pride Captain Rostrom and his crew had in their ship and were looking forward to the *Mauretania* upholding its reputation as both an East and West *Blue Riband* winner— awarded to any vessel that holds the record for the fastest time in either direction across the Atlantic. The great ship would soon be steaming toward North America at its usual 25 knots, about 29 mph.

Ted gazed up at a flock of gulls still stubbornly trailing them and recalled his earlier remark about watching their competitors pass over-head. Almost to himself, he said, "I expect we ought to decide what should be done in the event we are beaten."

Alcock shuffled his feet. "Yes, I've given that some little thought." He took one last drag on the cigarette and flipped the butt in a nearby ash container. "Vickers has put a lot of money and time into our machine. It seems to me everything should be done to help them recoup. What would you say to making the jump anyway? I mean, after all, it's quite possible we could fly farther than the winner—that would be worth something, eh? I've all along believed we have the longest endurance machine." He gazed out to sea for a few moments before continuing. "It would show the world what a fine, reliable aeroplane the *Vimy* is, good publicity for Vickers." Jack paused, turning to look directly at Ted. "Or is that all just rot, a tom-fool idea?"

Ted found himself a bit astonished. His pilot was willing to risk all even if there was little or no chance of any personal reward. Brown's regard for his new friend had been high before, but now it soared. The idea was extraordinary; it was one thing to take a risk for a friend or comrade in trouble or even to win a great prize as they were doing, but to do so merely for sake of the well-being of an inanimate company that was under no obligation to reciprocate in kind? Ted wondered if he would have had the selflessness to make such a suggestion.

"Interesting idea," Ted said, noisily rolling the pipe around against his false teeth as he thought the matter over. No matter how bad things had gotten during the war, he'd never shown yellow or failed to back up a flying mate. He and Alcock had become crew and were in this thing together. All the way. No matter what. "I'll go along with whatever you decide, Jack," he said softly but firmly.

The two men remained silent for a time. Ted's thoughts returned to the flight; whatever his private concerns about their chances to win had not allowed his concentration to waver. Four to five more days of sailing remained before the *Mauretania* docked at Halifax; what more could he do to profit the mission in the interim?

Brown authoritatively tapped the tobacco grounds from his pipe into the ash container. "Jacko, I think I'll have a go with Captain Rostrom. He has offered to pass along a few tips about Atlantic navigation."

Although he wouldn't fully appreciate it until later, that spur-of-the-moment decision became extremely important. The many hours Brown spent with the captain—who during the crossing put Ted through an authentic and most demanding competition with the *Mauretania*'s chief navigation officer—provided many valuable insights about the North Atlantic that became extraordinarily useful and in one or two cases, perhaps even decisive.

After arriving at the Halifax, Nova Scotia, harbor late on May 9, the Vickers party gathered themselves and their luggage into motor-taxis and departed for the city's railroad station. The team's final destination was still nearly 1,000 miles to the northeast and could only be reached by locomotive and ocean ferry. While glad to be on the "other side," none of the men were looking forward to several more days of what promised to be unpleasant travel, especially after the near-luxurious accommodations they had enjoyed on the *Mauretania*.

Alcock and Brown's taxi had no more than pulled away when Ted glanced out a window and did a double take. "Look there, Jack!" he said excitedly, pointing at two huge flying boats moored in the harbor.

Alcock's eyes widened. "It must be the Americans! Stop, driver!" After studying the aeroplanes for half a minute, he suddenly exclaimed, "Something is wrong. Ship's news reported yesterday that *three* machines had departed New Jersey."

The driver could not help but overhear the conversation. "Right you are, sir," he said. "One of them had to land in the sea. According to our morning newspaper, those two fellows in the harbor are waiting for the other to catch up."

The much-heralded US Navy flying boats were indeed poised to launch for Europe via the Azores and the Iberian Peninsula. The NC-1 and NC-3 were moored alongside their depot ship, the USS *Baltimore*. The NC-4 had been forced down by engine failure off the Massachusetts coastline and had taxied into a naval air station near Cape Cod. The NC designation had been derived from the combination of "N" for US Navy and "C" for the Curtiss Aeroplane and Motor Company. The American government tasked the first four aeroplanes off the factory line with the over-ocean effort (the NC-2 had been given special modifications that proved impractical, and it was dropped from the effort). Too late for the war, the NCs had been quickly repurposed when the embarrassed US realized it would be unable to field a credible entry for a non-stop crossing—the relatively tiny *Daily Mail* prize so dear to Vickers, Alcock, and Brown meant nothing to the all-out American national effort. The three machines had begun their journey at Naval Air Station Rockaway Beach, New York, on May 8, 1919.

These Curtiss biplane flying boats were giants by any measure of the day, each *twice* the size of a Vickers *Vimy*. From a distance, they looked majestic, but up close, each was transformed into a forest of motors, spars, bracing wires, and struts—in aviator-speak, it was a dirty, high drag machine, and its very complexity made it trouble-prone. The NCs were powered by four 400-hp V12 Liberty engines (1,600 total horsepower compared to 720 for the *Vimy*)—three tractors with a fourth pusher mounted tandem-fashion behind the centerline tractor. Upper and lower wingspans were 126 feet and 94 feet, respectively, compared to the *Vimy's* 68 feet wingspan, and 28,000-pound maximum takeoff weight to the *Vimy's* overloaded 13,500 pounds. All that heft and payload capacity, however, came at a steep price. The NC's maximum cruise speed was about 85 mph, and its published maximum range was 1,470 miles (fuel consumption 85 gph versus 46 gph for the *Vimy*)—at least 500 miles less than needed to even hazard a non-stop Atlantic crossing. The effort had the complete backing of the US Navy, including an astounding armada of some fifty-five destroyers strung across the Atlantic from New Jersey to Europe as marker buoys (the NC navigators were not trained for long-range over-ocean work), as well as five strategically placed battleships that served as weather stations. Their final jumping-off point from North America was to be Trepassey Bay, pronounced Truhpass-ee, by the Newfies, 70 miles south of St. John's.

While the experimental flying boats were not capable of a non-stop flight, much American face could still be saved by making the first journey from the New World to Europe by air. All the same, the slow-moving NC boats could never have met Lord Northcliffe's specifications of no government support and completing the flight within the allowed 72-hour time frame in the same machine (Northcliffe had *not* specified a non-stop flight, but even a several-stop trip was not possible in so short a time using the navigationally challenged and trouble-prone NCs). In the end, the Navy flyers encountered many difficulties, including an inability to deal with severe "blind" flying conditions, compass problems, and multiple mechanical emergencies. Only one of the flying boats completed the journey from Newfoundland to England, and it took fifteen days.

The sudden emergence of these flying boats came as a shock to the British. In contrast to their efforts, all funded by private concerns, the American seaplane contingent enjoyed full government support at all levels. There was still the matter of British prestige in what could only be called the aerial version of a *Blue Riband* competition. Further, the American flight was certain to grab the newspaper headlines, to the detriment of the English competition; the layman on either side of the Atlantic having little to no appreciation of the degree of technical difficulty between the two programs. In sum, then, the British teams in Newfoundland, at least initially, regarded the American effort as nothing short of an outrageous poaching of their rightful place in aviation history.

The taxi driver finally lost patience with all the gawking and jawboning—it was costing him money! He abruptly shifted the car into gear and sped away. Brown would've liked to have huddled a time with the American crews to discuss the navigation problems inherent in their unprecedented voyages, but he and Alcock had a train to catch and time wouldn't allow. Once the driver was again on his way, and with the counter running, he calmed down, even becoming a bit loquacious. "I'm told those Yanks expect their friend to join them sometime today," he shouted over his shoulder, "and then leave for Newfoundland tomorrow." The motor-taxi was older and clearly needed a replacement engine silencer, which probably had added to the drivers' irritation about all the flying boat kibitzing. "The newspapers claim the weather on their planned southern route through the Azores is much better than the North Atlantic, which is what seems to be holding up those fools in St. John's."

Both Jack and Ted stifled guffaws. The taxi driver sat alert and glanced at his rearview mirror, noticing one of the men was in a RAF uniform. "Hah!" the fellow blurted. "I'll wager your fare the two of you are here to join that crowd." He looked again at their faces and victory-grinned his suspicions. "Personally, I think you're all daft!" A very tired Ted Brown was beginning to wonder if there wasn't some truth in what the man said.

By train from Halifax, the Vickers party journeyed to North Sydney on the tip of Cape Breton Island, crossed by ferry to Port aux Basques in southwestern Newfoundland, and boarded the narrow-gauge Reid Railway to St. John's. Ted and Jack thought they had been transported back to the English Midlands of 1850; the journey dulled them to stupefaction with unaccountable delays, excruciatingly slow speeds on apparently untrustworthy tracks, and endless stops at places bearing such unlikely names as Codroy Pond, Kitty's Brook, Gafftopsail, Tickle Cove, and Come-by-Chance. Thoroughly frustrated, they could only attempt to sleep away the hours. After nearly four days of seemingly endless slow-boat-to-China travel, they arrived at St. John's, the capital. In 1919, Newfoundland was still an independent dominion within the British Empire, even of Greater Canada. As for St. John's, Brown would soon come to think of it as something between a large town and a small city.

At least they had stumbled partway back into the twentieth century. Although there were perhaps 300 to 400 motorcars operating in the city and much evidence of electrical service, no motor-taxis were visible. The Vickers team finally found two horse-drawn Victoria cabs, which, after cramming in all six men and their luggage, transported them to the Cochrane Hotel. Jack Alcock had inquired of lodgings at the rail station and was informed the Cochrane was the only one of consequence in the city, but "it was always full up." Still, there was no harm in trying, the station agent said, adding rather sardonically, "Perhaps the Dooley sisters will have a spot of straw in their stable."

The venerable four-story Cochrane, which had also lodged Marconi two decades earlier when he established the first North American wireless station on nearby Mount Pearl, was a relic of the Victorian age. Local musicians played the old standards in the lobby surrounded by faded but heroic nautical scenes, paneled walls of glittering cut glass, and the obligatory potted plant forest. Ted Brown half-expected to run into Mr. Dickens himself, sitting in a corner quietly conducting close observations of the human condition in preparation for his next novel about the downtrodden.

Fortunately for the Vickers team, Miss Agnes Dooley, in charge at the hotel's reception desk that late-night evening and who had initially turned them down cold, never before had encountered the likes of Captain John Alcock. After listening to his long-winded, passionate appeal to reconsider, delivered in his most ingratiating manner, she threw up her hands in surrender. "Enough!" she exclaimed. "Lord save us from more flying people." She gave Jack a saucy look. "Especially those with a gift for the blarney." She slapped a set of keys in Alcock's hand. "It's the smoke room for you and yours, and ye can be grateful for that!" When Jack tried to give her a big kiss, a flustered Agnes fled to the kitchen where, unbidden, she put together a surprisingly generous plate of supper leftovers, which the ravenous Vickers men happily devoured. It was past midnight before they finally stumbled into bed. Brown, the last to turn in, wrote a hasty letter to his dear Kathleen with the latest, closing it, *"I am coming back soon to claim you—and to live happily ever after! All my love, Teddy."*

* * *

Two of the English flying teams already in Newfoundland were breakfasting in the Cochrane's dining room when Alcock and Brown strode in the following morning. Jack and Ted had known the others were there and, because of their own almost embarrassingly tardy arrival, had decided to put on a brave front. Both were freshly shirted and tied; Brown was wearing a nicely fitted ensemble of laced boots, riding breeches, and Norfolk jacket. Despite his habitual indifference to dress, Alcock had taken pains to fit himself out rather smartly in breeches, though without Brown's sharp creases, and a heavy tweed coat—an all-out before these old pals and former aero racing competitors.

Harry Hawker was the first to spot them. "Jack!" Both he and Kenneth "Mac" Mackenzie-Grieve leapt from their chairs, with Freddie Raynham and Charles "Fax" Morgan right on their heels. The crews of the Sopwith *Atlantic* and the Martinsyde *Raymor* ostentatiously escorted Alcock and Brown to their table, pulling up additional chairs and signaling a Dooley sister to set two more places.

The short but reliably feisty Hawker, who only moments earlier had been quite blue over the disappointments of the last few weeks, bubbled over—Jack's presence had reinvigorated him. "So, Vickers mustered their full after all!" He shook his head in wonderment. "Still, it's a bit jarring to have you suddenly turn up."

Trading glances with both Harry and Freddie, Jack said, "Not half as surprised as I am to see you two still nested here in St. John's!"

Before Hawker could respond, Grieve intervened. "First things first, Jack. How about introducing your friend here?"

Ted Brown felt himself blushing. He'd never before met any of these famous flyers and, much to his surprise, found himself a bit "starstruck"— as he'd heard his Brooklyn relatives describe their own emotions when glimpsing the likes of such US cinema players as Mary Pickford and Douglas Fairbanks.

"Sorry, chaps," Jack said with a contrite little laugh. "This is Ted Brown, my navigator. Was an observer in the war, shot down a couple of times, prisoner—all the usual, that. Trained as an engineer and has done a splendid job of teaching himself over-ocean navigation." He looked at Grieve and Morgan, shaking his head in newfound respect. "Teddie has convinced me I've much to learn about that subject!"

Everyone chuckled while nodding in vigorous agreement. All six men knew they were flying into great danger, attempting a navigation feat that a few years before would have been, they now knew, certain suicide. The pilots had learned from their experiences during the war that, never mind their earlier ridiculously inadequate flying machines, they could not possibly have succeeded in a transoceanic attempt without a highly trained "Magellan" to guide them.

Ted glanced around the table and, in his courtly manner, said, "How do you do? Jack has told me a good deal about you fellows, and I'm quite excited about being a part of this adventure."

Fax Morgan cocked his head. "Say, Ted, from where in the Commonwealth do you hail?" Morgan had picked up on Brown's "not quite

British" accent. It was something he'd never heard before—properly refined yet not posh, certainly no hint of a stuffy public school.

Ted flushed once again, though he wasn't quite sure why. He reached for his pipe, always a comfort at such moments. "Actually, though Jack and I were both born in Manchester, my parents are Americans." He added hastily, "of British ancestry." Brown briefly filled them in on his war experience and background. His willingness to renounce his American citizenship and swear allegiance to the Crown impressed the others. He hadn't had to do that; the US was not to go to war for another two and a half years—and then he probably could have found a way to stay out of it altogether. They could see the man had paid a heavy price; no one could miss his heavy limp and walking stick. He and Morgan would soon bond; the war had taken Fax's right leg and his prosthetic limp very nearly matched Ted's own. In the evenings to come, they would often ponder why the Gods of War showed such a capricious inclination to maim observers.

Ted lit his pipe and indulged in a few puffs before continuing. "Over the years, I've lived with relatives in the States. I expect a bit of their lingo and manner has rubbed off." In his usual smooth manner, he steered the conversation away from himself and back to matters at hand. "You know, Jack and I did think you fellows were dead certs to have already been on your way."

Both Hawker and Raynham's faces clouded over. Freddie spoke first. "Bloody Newfoundland weather!"

Harry was more eloquent. "The average Englishman associates St. John's, Newfoundland, with cod liver oil and wood pulp. We now know their staple product is fog."

Freddie Raynham picked it up from there, just as their eggs, bacon, and toast arrived. "Harry and Grieve arrived on March the twenty ninth; Fax and I on the eleventh of April. Each of us has been ready to go for weeks but, the wretched weather has thoroughly flummoxed us." He leaned into Jack, who was hungrily digging into his eggs. "Let me tell you, Alcock, one cannot believe the ugly weather at this place, to say nothing of miserable North Atlantic conditions. Despite any number of hopeful mornings, every one of them has so far turned a dud."

Raynham had not been exaggerating. Over the coming weeks, Jack and Ted would see the continuation of that same daily, drearily poor visibility. The Air Ministry's aerologist at St. John's, RAF Lieutenant Laurence Clements, would later write that a typical forecast of a 1919 Newfoundland spring day would look something like this:

St. John's—Dense ground fog.
    Intermittent sleet and rain.
    Very limited visibility.
    Gusty winds.

North Atlantic—Risk of fog.
    Strong westerly winds.
    Intermittent snow.

"To say nothing of usable aerodromes," Hawker had continued to relate at that first breakfast. He looked at Jack rather grimly. "This is the worst imaginable place for launching flying machines. Hills, gullies, rocks, mountains, scrub forest—almost no level ground anywhere. One imagines himself trying to build an aerodrome in the Swiss Alps."

Alcock's attack on his eggs slowed dramatically, his face beginning to pale. Hawker read his mind. "Yes, you are going to have a devil of a time finding a field to operate from. Freddie, I, and the just-arrived Handley Page bunch have locked up what little is available, and I can tell you even those grounds are nothing to write home to mum about."

Jack asked where everyone had located their machines. Freddie said, "Fax and I have settled on a spot a half-mile away called Quidi Vidi. It was the local cricket field."

Fax Morgan broke in with a knowing grin. "The early eastern Canadian 'frogs' apparently named the place. The locals call it 'Kiddy Viddy.'"

Ted Brown laughed softly while tapping out pipe grounds. Plays on words always amused him.

"Kiddy Viddy has little to recommend it," Raynham added, "other than it's just long enough for a fully-loaded *Raymor* to takeoff and only a half-mile from our H-Q here at the 'Cockroach Inn.'"

Ted chortled once again. Two plays for the price of one!

Hawker moved things along. "Grieve and I parked the *Atlantic* at the Glendenning Farm about six miles away. It took no little effort to carve out a 400-yard stretch, but we've made it serviceable."

"What about the Handley Page?" Alcock asked.

Harry Hawker looked at Freddie before offering a careful answer. "It seems our esteemed colleague, Admiral Mark Kerr, preferred to strike out on his own. They've located some sixty miles north of here, along the coast at Harbour Grace. Of course, the Handley Page V/1500 is a massive four-engine machine and needs more field than the rest of us. Perhaps the ground is better up there." Hawker's tone suggested there might be other reasons but let it go at that.

John Alcock and Ted Brown looked at each other. The mystery of why there was still a competition had been solved, but the already long odds against their own success now looked even longer.

While another of the Dooley sisters cleared the breakfast dishes, Harry Hawker deftly steered the conversation back to the subject he was most interested in—the current status of the Vickers machine. With the weather providing such an intractable obstacle, it was possible for Alcock and Brown to become real competition. While lighting a cigarette, he casually asked Jack, "Has the *Vimy* arrived yet?"

Alcock knew Harry well enough to understand what he was about, but there was no point in prevarication. "Labor strike in London has held everything up. We hope they are able to get away in a few days." Alcock didn't think it was necessary to mention that Vickers had been doing an all-out crash job just getting the machine that far. No point in giving him any more of a leg up in the morale department.

Hawker attempted to put on a show of commiseration but was unable to hide his schadenfreude. "Bad luck, old man," he said, nearly allowing an evil grin to escape. Good friends, they were, but that didn't mitigate the intense competition between them.

"By the way," Ted Brown said seemingly offhandedly, but actually as an attempt to head the conversation away from possible unpleasantness. "On the ninth, we saw the American NC flying boats in Halifax harbor. They appeared ready to go. Have you chaps heard anything?"

Harry smashed a clenched fist to the table, rattling the crockery and wrecking Ted's diversion. He may have been a teetotaling, nonsmoker, but the diminutive Hawker had the kind of fiery temper one sometimes finds in men of his size. "Damn them! Who do those bloody Yanks think they are! They come waltzing up here just in time to upstage our efforts with a cheap stunt. What does it prove to hopscotch across in those wallowing 'Nancies'?" Ted and Jack later learned that Hawker had been foaming at the mouth for days about the US Navy's flying boats—what he and others derisively labeled Nancies. Although an Australian himself, Harry was firm in his belief the Atlantic was a "British Lake."

Grieve answered Ted's question, mostly to give his partner time to cool down. "In a word, Ted, no. Haven't heard a thing. However, if they'd left, we certainly would have been alerted. There are hordes of US and European newspapermen mucking about, both here and in Halifax." He smiled rather grimly. "I dare say most of those fellows are secretly hoping to write a few obits in order to spice up circulation."

Fax Morgan snorted; Harry had gotten his own wind up. "Those flying boats will rarely be out of sight of a ship, what with a US Navy vessel marking the way at 50-to-100-mile intervals. The Americans might just as well fly the English Channel fifty times; what they are doing proves nothing."

Hawker mumbled something unintelligible, and the conversation withered. Ted thought Morgan had given too harsh a judgment on the US effort—after all, crossing an ocean in any manner was an unprecedented feat and was sure to generate a great deal of worldwide interest in intercontinental travel. In the end, wasn't that what this entire business was all about? But Brown said nothing. He slid his chair away from the table, fumbled for the walking stick, and made motions to stand up. "Well, fellows, I think Jack and I had better call time on breakfast. We certainly have our work cut out."

Everyone took Brown's cue and stood as well. "We're off as well, chums," Raynham said. "Our steed awaits." He turned to Alcock and Brown and said with feeling, "Best of luck on your search for a field. We'll see you tonight unless, of course, a miracle occurs and the weather brightens, which the Admiralty assures us will not happen."

Over his anti-American tirade as abruptly as it'd come, Hawker echoed the *Martinsyde* pilot. "Right, off we go. Luck to us all." He put one hand on each of Ted's and Jack's shoulders and, with a squeeze, said in a much softer tone. "Keep your fore-noses down in the turns." In pilot-speak, Harry was telling the fellows to be careful while in the air. And in this, he was completely sincere.

Cochrane Hotel
Friday Evening, May 16, 1919

A weary Jack Alcock parked his newly purchased motorcar in front of the hotel and trudged to his and Ted's room to change for supper. His persistent sweet-talk to Agnes Dooley had finally resulted in the Vickers men getting their own rooms, much to everyone's relief in having escaped the overpowering smells of the crowded smoke room. Ted had returned earlier from the Admiralty's Marconi wireless station near Mount Pearl and was nearly dressed. It had been from St. John's in 1901 that Guglielmo Marconi had transmitted the initial Morse-coded signal from North America to Clifden, Ireland—for the first time, communications between North America and Europe had been reduced from a week or more via trans-Atlantic steamer to just minutes by radio encryption. Brown had spent the day with Mount Pearl's station commander, RAF Lieutenant "Birdie" Clare, lamenting the *Vimy*'s chronically cranky receiver/transmitter and discussing ways to make practical flying machine ship-to-ship and ship-to-shore communication a reality.

"How'd it go?" Ted asked.

Alcock shook his head. "More useless tramping around. A bloodhound couldn't pick up the scent of an aerodrome in this godforsaken wilderness. I must have run up a hundred miles in that ruddy excuse for an automobile."

Shortly after arrival, Bob Lyons, their Rolls-Royce engine colleague, had steered Alcock toward a secondhand American-made Buick Tourer for sale. The seller had pointed to the odometer, which showed just 400 miles, a practically new auto, so the man had said with a straight face. Jack's suspicions were quickly confirmed; the actual mileage was closer to 40,000, the speedometer having been cleverly manipulated. In any event, it didn't matter; Alcock had little choice. Other than a mule or horse, St. John's had almost nothing in the way of transport for rent or sale. He'd reluctantly paid the necessary truck out of his ever-dwindling Vickers expense allowance.

While wrapping his tie into a not very tidy Four-In-Hand, Alcock further elaborated on his day's travails. "Harry and Fred were not kidding. This place has the roughest, rockiest, uneven ground I've ever seen. When finally, the stones give way, the marshes take over. And everywhere are steep hills and even low mountains. The farmers are the real sharpies; they see me coming a mile away. Ready to sell or rent a few feet of their precious meadow for a thousand pounds, they are, and make me grateful for their generosity to boot!" He shook his head in disgust.

Ted frowned. "What are we to do?"

Jack shrugged his shoulders, still grumbling, "Keep looking—what else can be done?"

Brown could see his mate needed shoring up. "Well, there is plenty of gloom all round. Agnes Dooley tells me it was another day of discouragement for the Sopwith and Martinsyde teams. More mechanicals added to this Newfoundland weather, which simply will not yield." Ted's voice suddenly firmed. "Damn it all to blazes, Jack. All of that leaves *us* an opportunity. We simply must persevere!"

Jack Alcock had been watching Brown in the mirror. "Right you are, Ted," he said smiling, himself suddenly buoyed by his partner's optimism. "Can't give up, must keep pushing—that's the stuff!"

"Oh, yes," Ted said as he put on his evening coat. "Almost slipped my mind. Left-tenant Clare told me today, with great amusement, I might add, what happened to the US Navy's C-5 airship on the shore of Quidi Vidi Lake." In addition to their NC flying boats frog jumping across the pond, the Americans mounted a last-ditch attempt to beat the British on a non-stop flight using one of their lighter-than-air machines. At the outset, it wasn't as outlandish an idea as it might have seemed. The nearly 200-foot-long hydrogen-filled blimp manned by an aircrew of four had successfully flown non-stop the 1,000 miles from Montauk Point, New York, to St. John's, arriving only the day before. However, despite the glowing American press announcements, US Navy Lieutenant Commander Coll had confided to Birdie Claire that "it was the roughest trip I've ever experienced."

Despite the pride he'd always maintained in his American heritage, Ted sounded as amused as Lieutenant Clare had been over what followed earlier in the day. "Mount Pearl intercepted the American dispatches. It seems while servicing the blimp's engines and refueling, the winds began gusting to over forty knots, and before anyone could do anything about it, she broke loose her moorings and sailed out to sea. The two men aboard jumped in the nick of time. Several injuries reported, though none serious. The gas bag itself has disappeared into the ether."

Alcock was human enough to openly laugh at the US Navy's misfortune. "They flew the bally thing all the way from Long Island," he said, "and now it's on its way to Ireland without a soul on board!" He did not know any of the American flyers and, like all the other British airmen, considered the Yanks unwanted interlopers in this business of being the first to fly the Atlantic.

As had now become custom, it was all jolliness and camaraderie among the three British aircrews when they sat down for their nightly suppers. This evening the Dooley sisters had prepared a Newfoundland specialty dish called "fish and brewis," baked cod served with a stewed hard bread crust/milk porridge gravy. It came on a bit strange to the men's taste, but in the end, it went down satisfactorily. Mid-meal, Jack brought up a subject he'd been thinking about all day.

"Say, Harry, you and Freddie have been here for some time. What does one do about this restriction on strong spirits?"

Hawker responded with a fiendish grin. "So, you've been introduced to this quaint New World custom!" Canada and Newfoundland had followed the US lead into national prohibition just that spring, and in many quarters, including St. John's, there was a great deal of grumbling over the inability to secure even a gentle pint at the local pub. After several minutes of making Jack and Ted believe they would have to remain dry during their time in St. John's, Harry declared victory and explained the way out of their dilemma. At the time, Hawker did not know the question was important only to Alcock; Ted Brown was indifferent to alcoholic beverages.

Leaning into the table quite conspiratorially, Harry said, "The procedure, my dear friends, is to approach the right physician and outline your needs. For the customary fee of one Canadian dollar, the good doctor will write a 'scrip' to the local pharmacist, which will authorize that fellow to sell you a bottle of 'Tonic Waters,' which I have been reliably informed satisfies every requirement. One may repeat this procedure over and over ad nauseam." Harry smiled broadly, quite pleased with himself.

Nearby, an ever-growing evening throng of newspapermen had been straining to overhear every word the flyers spoke, always hoping for any kind of story. What with all the weather delays, some of the print men were getting desperate for nearly anything to send to their increasingly impatient editors. At just that moment, a young reporter from one of the New York papers decided to take matters into his own hands and approached Raynham's navigator.

"Mr. Morgan, sir," the eager beaver blurted, "my readers keep asking just how is it you propose to navigate the 2,000 miles to Europe with nothing on the surface to guide your flying machine?"

Fax Morgan, who was an accomplished practical joker as well as a descendent of the infamous buccaneer, Henry Morgan, was up to the moment. "Why, young man," he said with a wide smile, "that's a bit of a secret, but because you have caught me at a weak moment and I like the cut of your jib, I'll let you in on it." He gave a come-hither finger gesture and lowered his voice. The reporter whipped out his notebook and licked the tip of his pencil.

"You see, I've six crated homing pigeons whose home is in Ireland near our first landfall. Once we're 300 miles out from St. John's, I'll release the first pigeon. The bird will fly straight for its home, and we'll simply alter course to his direction." Fax's voice became even more conspiratorial. "Every 300 miles, I'll release another bird. By the time the last one departs, we will ourselves be 'home free!'"

Morgan leaned back smartly, putting a period on the explanation of his clever navigation aid. The reporter uttered a rushed thank you and bolted for the Mount Pearl wireless with his scoop. The door had no more than closed behind the fellow when the aero men burst into laughter, as well as several of the more seasoned reporters who had overheard the tale.

As the merriment died down, a still chuckling Fax Morgan leaned into Ted Brown and, almost as a throwaway change-of-subject question, asked, "Any luck finding an aerodrome?"

Alcock, who was under increasing strain due to his so far unsuccessful efforts and who had *not* joined in on the fun, overheard the remark and, for whatever reason, took it as an effort to rub salt in their wound. "Oh, bugger off," he snapped, staring stonily at Freddie's navigator, who looked as startled as the proverbial deer caught in a bright light.

Ted was instantly alarmed and stepped in. "Thanks for your concern, Fax. It's slow work, to be sure. Still, we have word the *Vimy* and the balance of our party will sail shortly, and upon their arrival, we think we shall have found suitable grounds." He puffed rapidly on his pipe, adding what he hoped was a friendly smile. "We have no intention of letting you fellows off the hook so easily, you see." Alcock said nothing, though his brassed-off expression did slowly dissolve.

"Which reminds me," Hawker said, after the tense moment had passed. "Freddie and I have been talking. We think instead of continuing this nonsense of everyone sneaking about in the dead of night trying to get the jump on the other fellow that we ought to establish a gentleman's agreement. If any one of us decides to depart, we agree to give the others as much advance notice as possible, at the very least one hour. Of course, the Handley Page bunch would have to be exempted from our arrangement due to time and distance considerations. What do you say?"

There was a general murmuring of agreement. It was an eminently practical solution to an increasingly disagreeable aspect of what had otherwise been a friendly competition. There had been entirely too much amateur intriguing going on, especially among the mechanics, carpenters, and riggers. Of course, Harry and Freddie had the least to lose with the new arrangement. The daily weather reports were improving, and a window of opportunity almost certainly had to soon present itself. Among the four competitors, including the still-unready Handley Page, they had the only two machines primed to go. A glum John Alcock, who had not said a word since his exchange with Fax Morgan, nodded faintly, though he seemed indifferent to the arrangement one way or the other.

Portugal Cove Road
Three Miles West of St. John's
Sunday Evening, May 18, 1919

Still on the aerodrome hunt, Alcock and Brown were returning to the Cochrane after another frustrating day bucketing over rough back roads when their Buick was hailed to a stop by a St. John's acquaintance/hanger-on going the other way.

"Have you heard?" the man shouted over the idling engines of both motorcars. Brown had a queer feeling the fellow had come looking for them.

"Heard what?" Jack asked with annoyance. Did the man think he was clairvoyant?

"Hawker was off this afternoon. It's believed all is well."

Jack and Ted looked at each other as if to say, "it was bound to happen; what took so long?"

The man spoke again. "Mr. Raynham was immediately alerted, and he and his mate readied the *Raymor*."

When, after several seconds, nothing more was forthcoming, a thoroughly irritated John Alcock felt like taking a cattle prod to the fellow, a man apparently so dim he needed five sheets of paper to work out the time of day. "Yes? Yes?"

"I'm afraid, sir," he said with a long, grave face that somehow looked insincere, as if getting some black enjoyment out of the telling, "Mr. Raynham and his machine have shot their bolt. They cracked up just as it lifted off the ground, both men hurt rather painfully."

Jack ground the Buick's shift into forward gear and engaged the accelerator, leaving the informant in his dusty wake. The lobby of the Cochrane was still in a whirl when they arrived. A half-hour later, Raynham arrived from hospital, swathed in head and arm bandages. Fax Morgan remained behind under intensive care; he'd been more seriously injured and was expected to lose an eye. Greatly relieved to see Alcock and after several men got him settled into an overstuffed chair with a large glass of "tonic water" in hand, Freddie Raynham's story tumbled out.

"What a bloody day, Jacko!" He was still short of breath and was having difficulty collecting himself. "Smashed up like some sprog pilot!"

"Easy, Fred," Jack soothed.

Raynham brushed the comment away with a wave of his hand, determined to exorcise the awful moment. "You'll recall how enraged Hawker became last night when we learned one of the American Nancies landed safely in the Azores. It was no consolation to him the other two fell short and the American Navy had to fish them out of the drink. This morning his mood was even worse. He was completely horrified the Americans were now sure to be the first across—'a terrible blow to British prestige,' he kept saying. I tried to reason with him that it wasn't the same thing, that they, as he himself had said, were only making a series of supervised hops. What's more, the sole machine still flying had yet a long way to go, but he was not to be mollified."

Raynham paused for a refill of "tonic water," breaking into a coughing fit when he took too much at one time. When that was over, he ploughed on, still a bit breathless. "After you and Ted left for the hinterlands early this morning, Harry informed me that if Mount Pearl could muster any kind of a reasonable forecast, he and Grieve would depart as soon as they could get to Glendenning Farm. Because of the Yanks' roundabout course through the Azores, Spain, and so on, he thought he still had a chance of beating them to England. By that time, Harry had succeeded in working steady old Grieve into a proper snit, and they both determined to take off today, come Hell or Noah's Flood. And wouldn't you know, Birdie rang up with a conveniently improved weather bulletin, much to all our surprise. Harry and Mac were gone in a flash."

Raynham was administered yet another dose of script anesthetic, and this time he took it more deliberately. "Naturally, Fax and I gathered up our own fellows and made for Kiddy Viddy and the *Raymor*, knowing full well that with any serious delay, Hawker and Grieve would be difficult to overtake. Of course, I knew the wind was a bit ticklish, but still . . ." Fred allowed one of his mechanics to mop his face. It was clear he should have been promptly put to bed, but nothing was going to deter him from telling his story; the disaster simply had to be purged from his system before he could rest.

"Oh yes, Jack," Fred said in a frantic aside. "Admiral Kerr and your friend Major Brackley got wind the game was on and hurried down from Harbour Grace to watch Harry lift the *Atlantic* off. They said little about their own machine, but the long faces spoke volumes."

Raynham paused, looking peculiarly at Alcock and Brown. "Do you know what Hawker said to Kerr just before he waved goodbye?" Fred didn't wait for a reply. "He said 'tell Raynham I'll be there to greet him when he lands in Brooklands.'" Raynham snorted in mock disgust. "Cheeky bastard! Even with an hour lead, there was still a good chance we could overtake him after nearly 2,000 miles." And then, speaking as if his flying machine was still intact and poised for takeoff, he said, "Our little *Raymor* is a good 20 to 30 miles per hour faster than the *Atlantic*."

The injured pilot suddenly jerked his head up, as if having just come to. "Any news? Are they all right?"

Ted Brown responded. "I spoke to Mount Pearl only moments before you arrived. As far as Birdie Clare knows, though, he hasn't received any wireless signals. Hawker and Grieve are proceeding without incident."

Freddie Raynham nodded, genuinely relieved they had apparently gotten safely away. And then, all at once, tears streamed down his face. "I should have taken Harry up on the offer he made last night. He said that if he left first, I was free to ferry my machine from Kiddy Viddy to Glendenning Farm, top off with petrol, and start from there." He looked painfully at John Alcock, saying pilot-to-pilot, "Kiddy Viddy had a strong crosswind today, what turned out to be a veritable hurricane. Harry's field was pointed straight into the gale. The problem was I didn't think I could afford taking all that extra time getting over there and lose whatever chance there might be. . . ."

Alcock rested a hand on his friend's shoulder, understanding Fred's deep anguish was not only about losing his chance and dazzling scarlet/

yellow machine but causing such grievous injuries to the already muti-lated Fax Morgan. It took Fred a minute or two before he could recompose himself.

"I advanced the throttle on the Falcon engine, and we began trundling away. I, of course, had the controls leaning into the crossing wind using full deflection and seemed to be managing. A moment after we broke ground, however, a vicious side gust struck. Within seconds, I ran out of aileron and, with that, so went any more ability to compensate. Just before we impacted, I did manage to get the wings level, thank God, but we still hit sideways with a terrible shattering, tearing off the wheels like nothing and nearly turning us turtle. Our only luck was the petrol didn't catch fire. That, of course, would have been curtains."

Jack Alcock could see his crestfallen old friend was now completely exhausted and took charge. "That's quite enough for one day, Freddo. It's off to bed with you." Too weak to protest, Raynham allowed himself to be led away by two of his mechanics.

Later, around the hotel feeding table, Ted Brown tried to console both Alcock and himself. "Harry and Grieve well on their way, Freddie and Fax in smithereens, and you and I still sans field or machine. Rotten luck, all way round," Brown finished gloomily, his attempt to buck up their joint spirits having died aborning.

Jack picked idly at Agnes Dooley's supper of salt fish, pea soup, and several types of unknown but tasty bread as the two men finally got around to what they had both been thinking. Ted spoke first, suddenly determined not to give up.

"We'll know if Harry was successful sometime tomorrow. Let's put off any more idle speculation till then. Meanwhile, I say business as usual. First thing in the morning, we're off again in the Buick."

Jack smiled weakly and slowly nodded agreement. He was enormously grateful for his partner's steadiness under such trying conditions.

Monday morning, afternoon, and evening came and went, but ominously, there was no word on Hawker and Grieve. It had been nearly thirty hours since they'd departed; everyone knew their petrol could have lasted little more than twenty. At midday, the Handley Page trio came down from Harbour Grace to vigil jointly with Alcock and Raynham—all three teams had planned to drink a toast to Harry and Grieve once word came of their successful arrival in Ireland; though still in hospital, Fax Morgan was feeling better and in as good as spirits as could be expected. Freddie's state of mind had so improved he was making noises about rebuilding the *Raymor,* somehow finding another navigator, and perhaps making a long try at London itself. As the hours continued to slip by, however, that kind of talk faded. The silence from Europe about Hawker's fate grew increasingly ominous.

About 8 P.M., Lieutenant Birdie Clare strode slowly into the dining room. Everyone came instantly alert in hopes of good news. The grim-looking Clare had nothing of the sort. "I have to report that neither Mount Pearl nor Cliveden, Ireland, has heard anything on the wireless from Hawker and Mackenzie-Grieve."

When the RAF officer paused to let that sink in, Ted quickly whispered to Jack, "Mac told me he was having a devil of a time getting wireless reception on their practice flights. He thought the engine magnetos might be to blame. Fortunately," Ted added, in a deliberate attempt to allay Jack's own shaky confidence in the *Vimy's* radio, "we do not have the same issue."

Birdie continued, his long face advance-telegraphing what he was about to say. "I've also just received a communication that says the *Daily Mail* front-page headline for tomorrow is expected to be 'HAWKER MISSING, Presumed Lost At Sea.'" He looked up from his flimsy. "Sorry, lads, that really is all I have. Let me assure all here you shall be the first to hear of any new dispatches."

After Clare left, a hush descended over the Cochrane's dining room, each man lost in his own thoughts. At length, Alcock turned to the Handley Page's pilot, his former student Major Herb Brackley. "Do you mind, Brackles, if I ask how far along work is on your machine?"

The major looked at his boss, Admiral Kerr, who nodded a rather reluctant okay. Kerr was the stranger among this tightly bound group of aero men, not sharing with the others a longtime association or wartime RAF camaraderie. "The V/1500 is a large and complicated aeroplane," Brackley began, "but our men are working very hard to have it assembled by first of June." He shrugged his shoulders. "After that, all, of course, depends on flight testing and this abominable weather. As you no doubt already have discovered, due to a pitiful lack of facilities, we are all forced to work out in the open or under tents and on rude scaffolds."

After a moment of reflection, Brackley decided that turnabout was fair play. "When is the *Vimy* to arrive, Jack?"

Alcock turned to Gordon Montgomery, the Vickers man who would direct the reassembly of the flying machine. "What's the latest, Monty?"

Lost in his own thoughts, Montgomery had been sitting at a side table along with other support members of the three teams, and it took him a moment to realize he'd been addressed. "The Southampton strike appears to be finally settled," he replied, "and so we are hopeful the *Vimy*, carpenters, and mechanics will sail shortly. Arrival here at St. John's on or about May 26." The *Vimy* would be coming directly to the shallower St. John's harbor in a much smaller and more versatile vessel than the *Mauretania*.

Worn out from another fruitlessly long day, Jack flashed his annoyance. "That's all well and good, of course, but the trouble is we haven't any place to even set up the machine!" He had already learned the Glendenning Farm owners were immediately reclaiming the field used by Hawker, unhappy their spring/summer plans had already been badly upset by the unforeseen weather delays.

A still heavily bruised Freddie Raynham abruptly looked up from his spiked coffee cup. "Say, I don't know why I didn't think of this before." Everyone looked at him strangely, as if he wasn't already thoroughly overloaded with enough thoughts. "There's plenty of room for the *Vimy* at Kiddy Viddy," Fred went on, "next to where I have decided to put together *Raymor II*, a.k.a. the *Phoenix*." Raynham's face may have been purple-blotched and half-caved in, but his inherent sense of good sportsmanship had remained intact. "You can assemble your machine alongside while searching about for your own aerodrome." As with Glendenning Farm, the larger Vickers machine could not make a maximum weight takeoff out of the restricted space at Kiddy Viddy, but there would be enough room to assemble and test-fly it.

The six Vickers men brightened. Alcock spoke for all. "Good show, Freddie!" he exclaimed with great warmth and a wide smile. "This comes as a great relief." Raynham had once again confirmed he was a consum-mate British gentleman. The gesture just at that moment was especially meaningful; only hours earlier, Alcock had directed subtle hints at Admi-ral Kerr in hopes of a similar consideration at the larger field at Harbour Grace, but the admiral had rather bluntly changed the subject. Ted Brown had recently written his Micki that, "*With one exception, there is the best possible feeling among the small colony of British aviators congregated here.*"

"Mind now, Jacko," Freddie chided good-naturedly. "Don't be think-ing you can take over the place and push me aside. The damage to the *Raymor* was not as extensive as I first believed—and I've sent several wire-less messages to London in search of a new navigator. I'm not out of the hunt yet!"

"Bravo, Freddie Raynham," Brown thought while joining in on a scattered round of applause. He greatly admired Raynham's extraordi-nary pluck and was surprised to discover he had to suppress an impulse to root for him!

Cochrane Hotel
Alcock and Brown's Room
Monday evening, May 26, 1919

Newspapers in North America and Great Britain screamed out the headline:

ALL HANDS SAVED ON SOPWITH MACHINE!

A week after Hawker and Grieve were given up for lost, a miracle had occurred. A British steam freighter, the SS *Mary*, had sailed into the Butt of Lewis on the Outer Hebrides, Scotland, with electrifying news. Not equipped with a wireless set, the ship's master sent visual signals to the famed Lewis Lighthouse informing the world he had rescued the lost *Atlantic* flyers several days earlier. A Royal Navy destroyer, the HMS *Woolston,* was sent to pick up the two men and take them to Scapa Flow, the United Kingdom's chief naval base. Hawker and Grieve were now en route to London, where King George V was expected to lead an enthusiastic welcome home.

After wrinkling his nose at the reportage, Brown handed the St. John's *Evening Telegram* to Jack. Alcock hurriedly glanced through the text. "What slosh! They haven't the foggiest notion what they're talking about. Hopefully, we'll get a proper accounting from Vickers." He paused, catching himself. "The important thing, of course, is that Hawker and Grieve are safe." He glanced one last time at the item about the *Mary*, shaking his head in wonder. "My God, what fortune to have cracked up in the middle of a vast ocean directly next to a steamer!"

The English-speaking press could not get enough of Hawker's "epic adventure;" by all accounts, the British Isles were agog in adulation. At one point two days later, it became too much for John Alcock, and he turned churlish. To Ted Brown, he growled, "England's hands are so blistered clapping Harry Hawker's back, we'll be lucky to get a languid hand!"

The two men spent all that Monday looking for a proper aerodrome and had only just returned to the hotel. The past week had been one wild goose chase after another. It was not for lack of leads—nearly everyone in St. John's was aware of their field hunt and willingness to pay hard cash. The flyers had at last thought they were onto something of value when around noon, a man approached them about an "ideal aerodrome" near Harbour Grace. After making the long trek to the north, it turned out to be a 150- by 300-yard "postage stamp" hayfield. Adding salt to the wound, the owner had demanded a thirty-day £5,000 rent plus damage indemnity. On the way back to the Cochrane, Alcock had marveled, "What cheek! We could purchase half of St. John's for that sum!"

There was a knock at the door. Before Jack could utter a "come in," Bob Lyons, the Rolls-Royce engine expert, burst into the room. "The *Vimy* has arrived on the SS *Glendevon*!" he said breathlessly. "Pittman, Dicker, and Monty have gone down to help with the unloading and transport." The three men bolted for the Buick and raced toward the

Mr. Charles Lester's tandem wagon transporting the Vimy's *fuselage from SS* Glendevon *to Quidi Vidi field. (The Rooms Provincial Archives, St. John's, Newfoundland)*

docks. Halfway en route, they met the oncoming Vickers transport train, led by one Charles Lester, a carter by trade. Following in trail was a growing army of local civilians and reporters from America, Britain, and Continental Europe. Hawker's flight had utterly galvanized public interest in the *Daily Mail* competition, and suddenly, the flyers were the hottest story on both sides of the Atlantic.

Alcock gave the drayman a hearty greeting. "Good evening to you, Mr. Lester!" A less exuberant Ted Brown said nothing, having sized the man up as self-important and suspecting him of being a bit too eager for any new opportunity. Lester had rather boisterously introduced himself when the Vickers advance party first arrived. "I safely transported Mr. Hawker's and Mr. Raynham's machines to their respective fields," the St. John's native had proclaimed to Jack, "and I can do the same for you and at a fair price!" After speaking to Harry and Fred, Jack Alcock promptly hired him.

On this day of the *Vimy*'s arrival, Alcock's smile slowly turned into a worried frown after he noticed how laboriously Lester's horse teams were working to make their way up and down the hilly, cluttered, and narrow streets of St. John's. The drayman, an alert fellow, caught his look. "Now, see here, Skipper. I've been successfully plying these parts since you were in nappies. I'll get your precious kite to its nest, don't you worry, as well as ready for all your playing around in the morning." With that, the caravan of men on foot and horses pulling wagons continued to slowly wend its way through St. John's.

* * *

Eight-year-old Ralphie Moyst was coming home from school when he heard a loud commotion ahead of him. People were shouting and running helter-skelter, which sent a dozen dogs into a barking frenzy. When a young woman hurried past him, Ralphie scrunched up his nerve and yelled after her, "What is it, Miss?"

Over her shoulder, she shouted back, "It's an aeroplane! Coming straight down the road!"

Little Ralphie was completely confused. "But," he yelled after her, "if it's an aeroplane, why is it using the road?" The young lady didn't hear him, and he was left to puzzle the mystery out for himself.

Very curious, the sickly, pale-skinned boy limped off in the direction of the running people. Ralphie had contracted polio when he was very small and for a long time had to use crutches to get around. He had since gotten stronger and was proud he'd recently graduated to a walking stick. Ralphie still had to wear special boots and, while his brothers and sisters had good eyesight, he could not see much without his thick glasses. Once, when he asked his mother why he was so different, she comforted him by saying, "Ralphie, my dear boy, it's because you are special."

The little fellow managed to squeeze into a small opening in the crowd lining the road—two gentlemen on either side had unobtrusively created enough space for him. Like everyone else, Ralphie waited expectantly for the parade to pass by.

The boy had been lucky; he'd arrived just in time. Ralphie immediately recognized Mr. Lester leading the teamsters. Walking alongside him were several strangers wearing fancy English clothes. Someone said the flying machine was in the crates on the wagons, all in pieces. Two of the men were said to be the flyers, but Ralphie didn't see how that could be so as nobody had on helmet and goggles. His eyes strayed to the fifty-foot-long, rectangular-shaped crate straddled atop two wagons linked together as one. The big load was being pulled by Mr. Lester's prize brace of Morgan and Percheron draught horses. Although the unmatched pair was not so pretty, it was generally agreed they were the strongest team in St. John's. Ralphie had admired the huge animals for as long as he could remember—the Moyst house was located only blocks from Mr. Lester's pasturage near Mundy Pond.

The wide-eyed little boy watched spellbound as the horses pranced by only a few yards away, their nostrils flaring, muzzles blowing away foam, and eyes rolling white while laboring mightily up an incline. The train's teamsters were flapping reins, cracking whips, and shouting encouragement constantly—Ralphie pretended he did not hear the bad words.

More teams and wagons followed, filled with machinery, wood crates, and all manner of strange and unfamiliar objects. The boy heard a man ask another, "Where is it they are going?" He didn't know, but a nearby elderly lady overheard the exchange. "I clean rooms at the Cochrane," she offered, "where all the birdmen stay. Mr. Raynham, the pilot of the machine that crashed after Mr. Hawker left, has allowed Captain Alcock—he was that fellow in the cabby cap walking 'longside Mr. Lester—to set up his flying machine on the land Mr. Raynham leases at Quidi Vidi field."

* * *

True to his word, Lester arrived at Kiddy Viddy with his cargo unscathed and soon had it unloaded. Across one entire side of the field, under temporary canvas, laid the two precious Rolls-Royce Eagle engines, drums of oil and petrol, the fifty-foot-long fuselage encased in a single crate, wing sections packed in twelve- and thirty-foot containers, two huge engine radiator assemblies, tools aplenty, and scores of wood boxes filled with hundreds of parts—the sum of which, when assembled, would be transformed into the noble Vickers *Vimy*.

At midnight, after ensuring that all was accounted for and posting two men as night guards, Jack led the Vickers working party back to the Cochrane. Agnes Dooley, who appeared to be developing a soft spot for that "rogue English pilot," held open the kitchen to feed Jack's men— all together now numbering thirteen, including aero crew, supervisors, mechanics, rigger/carpenters, a radiator expert, and a general handyman. Just before bed, Alcock messengered a wireless dispatch to Lieutenant Birdie Clare at Mount Pearl, addressed to Vickers Brookland:

Glendevon arrived safely. Machine assembly begun. Cable Hawker Grieve logs and experiences important to learn what they encountered en route. Weather here unreliably reported in England. Weather conditions St. John's very poor be patient. Tell press no one more anxious to go than we flyers.

Alcock and Brown had been receiving increasing criticism from home about not getting on with it. No one in Britain seemed to appreciate the enormous difficulties the aero teams were encountering in Newfoundland and had become restless at the lack of progress. And no wonder— the weather in Britain was beautiful, blue skies from horizon to horizon. The *Daily Mail's* competing London newspapers were leading the jackal feeding parties, with the foreign pressmen at St. John's, especially the Americans, happy to play along. Jack decided enough was enough and had put his foot down with the cable.

The Vickers response came the next morning just after breakfast:

Logs and other detail on Hawker flight to follow. Undercarriage was successfully dropped, engine normal, weather good on departure. Wireless inoperative due to magneto interference. First four hours at 10,000 feet normal. Encountered heavy fog, unable climb over. Engine radiator cooling water temperature began running high. Reduced power but unable to sustain altitude. Returned normal power, temp rose again. Hawker thinks solder or rust blocked water filter. Finally engine running so hot had to reduce power, lost altitude. Next two hours machine rose and fell in desperate struggle to balance altitude and engine temp while all while dodging rain and cloud. Grieve could not get a star fix until finally hit clear spot. Discovered they 150 miles south of desired course. Was blessing, they were along steamship route. Search began for a ship while Hawker desperately clung to sky. Finally at last minute he spotted Mary *and landed next to it with Grieve firing Very pistol red flare. Crew sat in small emergency dingy until rescue boat arrived.* Atlantic *machine recovered.*

Jack handed the wireless to Agnes as he and Ted walked out of the dining room. "Pass this along to the chaps, won't you, love?"

Ten minutes later, Alcock brought the Buick to a stop at Kiddy Viddy field. All the men were hard at work, prying open crates and erecting tents and lean-tos for weather protection. The construction would begin with laying out the main fuselage assembly. The work was going to be that much more difficult due to the unavailability of mechanized cranes and winches—everything had to be moved, lifted, and lowered by block and tackle or raw muscle power. The *Vimy* was too large to fit into the hangar tent/warehouse that had been erected, and as a result, the flying machine would have to be assembled out in the open. To protect it from the worst of Newfoundland's notoriously cold and blustery spring, a large stiff canvas screen was stretched out between poles against the prevailing northwesterly winds. Unfortunately, little could be done about the rain, and all too often, work would have to be stopped and the aeroplane covered with tarpaulins.

Alcock sharing Gold Flake cigarettes during the Vimy's *assembly.*
(Alamy Stock Photo)

The work began, but matters were not progressing fast enough to suit an increasingly restless Jack, giving Ted Brown an idea. Borrowing the Buick, he hurried back to the Cochrane and rounded up every newspaper reporter he could locate; lacking anything about the aero race to write about, most of them were lounging about the Cochrane devising schemes to extract more "tonic water chits" from the local apothecary.

"Gentlemen," Brown began, "I am aware of a certain unrest concerning the lack of news to report. We at Vickers also lament that deficiency, which naturally reflects on our own lack of progress." Ted puffed affably on his pipe. "May I put forth the idea that if the *Vimy's* assembly can be accelerated, it would be that much the sooner something newsworthy could be reported." He paused, looking about to be sure he still had the news hawks' attention. "Now, we are rather short of mechanized equipment, and everything is moving frightfully slow. If you good fellows could see your way to lend a hand, literally may I add, I should think it would be that much the sooner that newly fresh and entertaining copy would be available to your newspapers." He puffed out one last immense blue cloud for emphasis. "What do you say?"

It was a clever appeal. The competition had now come down to only Vickers and Handley Page, with the latter fully mired in unforeseen assembly difficulties that came built-in with their four-engine giant. What's more, due to the enormous stir created by the Hawker/Grieve rescue, American and European public interest in the race had greatly intensified. Frustratingly for all concerned, little was happening, and the press had so far been unable to satisfy the public appetite for news.

Brown jammed five of his newly impressed reporters into the Buick Tourer; a half dozen others followed in another motorcar. Alcock didn't say anything when he saw Ted's fresh labor detail, but his wide smile spoke volumes. Monty Montgomery was more demonstrative. "Kippers, Teddy! You're a bloomin' snake charmer!"

Ted smiled appreciatively but his mind had already shifted back to the many technical issues that still had to be dealt with. There was one item in particular—MacKenzie-Grieve's problems with his radio. Jack had made no comment on that portion of the dispatch from Brooklands, but Brown knew it gave another point in Alcock's favor toward chucking the *Vimy's* entire wireless apparatus. Ted rolled the empty pipe around in his mouth for a full minute—he'd been smoking relentlessly all day, and it'd left an unpleasant aftertaste—before an additional precaution came to him. He would remove the wireless assembly from its crate straight away and set it up on the roof of the Cochrane, where in the evenings, he could conduct extensive testing with Lieutenant Birdie Clare on Mount Pearl. He determined to perform these tests as discreetly as possible, so as not to further arouse the English bulldog that resided within Mr. John Alcock.

The following morning could not come soon enough for the Vickers team. As they threw themselves into the work at Kiddy Viddy, Alcock had all he could do to wrest himself away from his Mistress *Vimy* and attend to all the other loose ends. He was striding to the Buick to get on with the endless aerodrome search when the always enterprising Charles Lester hailed him from across the street.

"Ahoy, Skipper, can you spare a moment?"

"Always have time for yourself, Mr. Lester," Jack said equably.

"I'm wondering how much acreage your machine needs to take flight?"

Alcock really didn't have time for curious chatter, but Lester had done a good transport job and deserved a bit of humoring. Jack said, "Kiddy Viddy has a clear run of about 300 yards. That was good enough for Hawker and Raynham's smaller one-engine aeroplanes, but the *Vimy* is a big two-engine machine with more robust requirements. With only a light load, I can test fly at Kiddy, but with the full oil and petrol bag-gage required for the big jump, I will need at least a 400-yard run and preferably a bit more." He barked a bitter laugh. "I am coming to believe there are no such places left within a hundred miles of this hilly corner of Newfoundland!"

A thoughtful-looking Lester scratched his chin for a moment and said, "I have a horse pasture that might fit your bill. Would you like to take a look?"

Jack was dumbfounded. Surely Lester had heard of his search before this moment—every Tom, Dick, and Harry in and around St. John's that owned a patch of green had already made certain they had something for Mr. Alcock to look at.

"How is it, Mr. Lester," Jack asked, his head cocked to one side, "that you've only just now come to me on this? The word on my needs has been common knowledge from the moment of our arrival."

Lester looked surprised. "Fact is, Skipper, I pay little heed to the local gossip, closed my ears to it long ago." He went on, sounding a trifle miffed. "I'm a hardworking stiff, your noble sir, with no time for pub talk."

Jack gave Lester a measured glance, doing his best to hide a deep skepticism that the man was not a master at keeping his ear close to the ground. For whatever reason, he was only just now bringing his offer forward. "My dear sir," Alcock said, "if you think you might have something for me, then by all means, let us have a look!"

Mr. Charles Lester brightened. "We're off at once then; my horse pasture is close by."

It certainly was; after less than a ten-minute drive to the southwest, the two men arrived at a field near a small lake called Mundy Pond. On the way out, Jack had been more than a little nonplussed that the seemingly mythical aerodrome he had so long sought could actually be right under his nose. Of course, the more he thought about it, the more the idea took root and, despite realizing exactly what was happening, allowed his hopes to rise.

"Here we are, Skipper!"

Jack groaned softly, that old sinking feeling coming on once again. The pasture was a jumble of hillocks, gullies, and small spruce trees—its surface littered with large and small rocks, with not a few granite boulders. And if that was not enough, neatly bisecting the tract was a drainage ditch with an accompanying waist-high stone flood dike.

"Mr. Lester," Alcock said deliberately. "If I tried to take the *Vimy* off from your field, I would wreck it and myself before halfway along."

Lester was unperturbed. "As it lays at the moment, true enough. But before I give my full thoughts on that topic, let's you and I pace it off to be sure we have something to talk about in the first place."

Alcock shrugged. He'd come this far and had nothing to lose but a few more minutes. Surprisingly, it was longer than he'd first thought—the irregular terrain had fooled him. There was indeed 400-plus yards, a solid 1,200 feet of potential straightaway, though much of it was at an incline, and the rock/gravel soil was firm enough to accommodate the *Vimy*'s very heavy gross takeoff weight. That, however, was the full extent of the good news. Lester stood silently off to one side while a deep-in-thought John Alcock sized it all up.

The field's surface itself was a mess—it took a good deal of imagination to picture it even remotely serviceable. Further, the pasture sloped downward from west to east, which meant a takeoff roll to the west would be uphill. The north-south axis was much too dangerously steep, in fact out of the question for the attempt. Fortunately, the prevailing winds were westerly, making a takeoff in that direction the most likely, though an east departure—in the direction of Europe—would certainly be preferable.

Jack eyed Lester hard, saying, "I would be most interested to hear your thoughts on how this field could be made serviceable."

Charles Lester was equal to the challenge. "Cap'n Alcock, this ground can be cleared of all the rocks, trees, and shrubbery, then leveled off. We can remove a section of the dike and, at least temporarily, fill in a portion of the drain ditch. I have a fine bunch of young, strong lads who are used to hard work." He paused a moment. "I think we can make a proper surface suitable to your needs in about ten days."

John Alcock stared at the man. Was he serious or simply cunning? Could what he proposed be done and, more importantly, what did Lester have in mind as payment—Alcock's expense budget from Vickers was decidedly limited. Charles Lester, like that enterprising fellow who had offered the "ideal aerodrome" near Harbour Grace, might be thinking he had found his main chance.

"Well, sir," Jack responded. "All of it sounds perfectly boffo, of course, but what would it cost me?"

Lester was indignant. "Excepting for the necessary provision of a modest daily wage for my men, not a ha'penny, sir!" He paused, perhaps giving Alcock a few moments to let the remark sink in, understanding anyone would be suspicious of such apparent generosity. "Well now, Cap'n, perhaps there is one thing you could do for me in return." Ah yes, Jack's expression seemed to say, here it comes.

"Should you be successful in your aim," Lester continued, "which I and all my acquaintances are certain you will be, and afterward gain the ear of those London worthies who can make or break a man's reputation, perhaps you might find it in your heart to mention that Mr. Charles Lester of St. John's, Newfoundland, made a cheerful and important contribution to your success and remains eager to help others engaged in similar Atlantic endeavors."

Alcock was astonished. Even with the rather impertinent request for him to head up a London branch of the Lester Drayage Advert Office, it was nevertheless a most generous offer. "Mr. Lester," Jack said grandly, "you are a prince among men. I accept your offer! We will rename this place 'Lester's Field,' forever commemorating it as the first trans-Atlantic aerodrome!"

Later, back at their Cochrane Hotel room, Alcock laid out to Ted the amazing turn of events. "Why," Jack said, "Mr. Lester held out so long on this field we'll probably never know, but I'm not one to look into mouths of gift horses!" An abashed Brown told Jack of his earlier misgivings and that he felt bad he'd so misjudged the man.

And so it began. While the *Vimy* was being assembled at Kiddy Viddy just a few miles away, Lester and his thirty laborers set to work landscaping the Mundy Pond pasture. Boulders were dynamited to smithereens and dumped into gullies and crevices, along with an almost endless supply of smaller rocks. Horse-drawn graders leveled the hillocks to at least acceptable tolerances, and fences and shrub trees were removed. A one-hundred-foot-wide section of the stone dike was pushed into the drainage ditch and leveled off. A small corral was constructed nearby to temporarily accommodate Lester's half-dozen draught horses.

As the men labored, they sang a Newfoundland work song with an improvised chorus:

Oh, lay hold Jackie Alcock, lay hold Teddie Brown,
Lay hold of the cordage and dig in the groun'
Lay hold of the bow-line and pull all you can,
The Vimy *will fly 'fore the Handley Page can.*

Whirling Dervish Jack spent the next several days happily flitting between Lester's Field and Kiddy Viddy, coordinating both efforts. Sixteen-hour days for all hands became the order of the day, with the team leader and pilot always in front, setting the example. No detail was too small, no task too onerous for Captain John Alcock.

Cochrane Hotel
Saturday Evening, May 31, 1919

Alcock and Brown adjourned early to their room, skipping the usual Saturday night sing-alongs and high jinks. Ted had been pressing his pilot for days for a sit-down regarding all the flight issues they were going to face. It hadn't been easy; Alcock had been so immersed in the reassembly of the *Vimy* he'd kept off-putting Ted to the point Brown finally had to put his foot down.

"Now, Jack," Ted said rather firmly on their way up the stairs. "We are going to devote the evening to planning, specifically on coordination between the two of us and details on how I plan to conduct the navigation. And we are going to accomplish that tonight if I have to lock you in the room!"

A subdued Alcock raised his palms in submission. "Sorry, Teddie. You're quite right. The mechanic in me has gotten the upper hand." He suddenly flashed that old Jackie Alcock grin and bowed submissively, sweeping his right arm toward their door. "Lead on, MacDuff!"

Both men burst out laughing and, after ensuring a hot pot of tea and plenty of tobacco were at the ready, got straight to work.

"This," Ted began, placing his Baker navigation machine with the rolling map on a small table, "is our route chart. I want you to spend some time studying it. You see these knobs on either end? You can turn the map either forward or backward. I've plotted out the entire flight with the planned course line. I'll be slowly scrolling it forward to match our own actual position as the flight progresses." Ted demonstrated, going over the courses, proposed flying altitudes, and scheduled celestial observations. "The chart is called a Mercator Projection, but we shan't dwell on

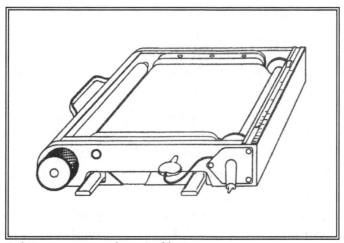

Baker navigation machine. (Public Domain)

that. There are only two things I want you to remember about it. First, you'll note the true course I've drawn, 078 degrees, is the same throughout our entire route. We are going to follow what is known as a rhumb line, or as the ancient Greeks called it, a 'Loxodrome course,' which on our Mercator chart allows us to cross every longitudinal meridian at the same angle, as expressed in degrees. The downside to this approach is that we must fly a bit farther, something on the order of 30 to 50 miles, than if we took a Great Circle course, the shortest possible route. But with the Loxo approach, we won't have to worry ourselves with continual course corrections, something that would be problematic in the *Vimy* in any event."

Jack barked a laugh. "Why, Teddie, are you saying I can't hold a heading?"

Ted suppressed a smile at Jack's flippancy. "You know what I mean. It will be hard enough as it is to stay within five degrees of whatever heading I give you. We will have to trust your ability to average it out."

Brown re-lit his pipe. "Now pay attention, Jack; this is important. The second thing you must understand about this Mercator projection is magnetic variation"—he thumped his finger on the chart's wavy black lines—"and how dramatically it will affect our compass headings—much more than anything you've ever experienced before."

Variation is the difference between the compass reading, *i.e.*, the magnetic North Pole, and the true geographic North Pole. It was at its most extreme in the high northerly latitudes. A century earlier, the very idea the earth might have an identifiable magnetic field was just being grasped. The polymath Alexander von Humboldt, arguably the greatest scientist of the early nineteenth century, was the first to attempt to map this field. In a paper in 1804, he invented "isogonic lines," which connected points with equal magnetic variation from true north. Brown's nautical Mercator chart included the North Atlantic's curving isogonic lines.

"Here, Jack, let me show you how it will work." Ted used his pipe stem as a chart pointer. "St. John's has 30 degrees of west variation. My laid off true course will be 078 degrees, which is East by Northeast. We must then factor in plus or minus degrees of drift. After applying that drift, we can use the handy memory refrain, 'Variation East, Compass Least and Variation West, Compass Best,' which tells us to *add* the 30 degrees of west variation for a compass heading. To say it another way, our desired true course throughout the flight will be 078 degrees. Assuming an initial drift of nearly zero degrees, which seems likely given the prevailing due westerly winds, our true heading would therefore be the same as true course. Adding 30 degrees west variation to true heading gives us a departure magnetic/compass heading of 108 degrees or East by Southeast." Ted's procedure stated as an equation would read: TC (True Course) plus/minus drift = TH (True Heading) plus/minus variation = CH (Compass Heading). For his pilot's benefit, Brown had used the chart to graphically illustrate the idea they would appear to be flying *southeasterly* on the compass rose rather than what would seem to be the correct *northeasterly* heading.

Alcock, who had remained silent during Brown's discourse, said evenly, "You want to be sure I won't be startled when you give me a compass heading that appears to have us headed for the African Sahara." There was a twinkle in the man's eye.

"Precisely," Ted said, wondering why he'd felt compelled to offer such a long-winded, patronizing explanation. It was easy to underestimate John Alcock—though unpolished in so many ways, he had a formidable intellect. Brown continued checking off items from his neatly drawn up list. "Now then," the navigator said, pausing to sip from his teacup, "during those minutes when I'm taking drift sightings and celestial observations, it's very important you hold steady the compass heading and altitude. You'd be surprised how such little things can throw off a final result. I'll signal when I'm ready to start and do the same when finished."

Jack smiled indulgently. "Ted, old man, as you said earlier, that's a tall order with the *Vimy*!" He sighed. "Of course, I'll certainly do my best to accommodate."

"That's all I can ask," Ted said understandingly. "In summary then, in addition to my pilot assisting duties, I'll be responsible for our compass headings and estimated time to landfall in Ireland. We'll use dead reckoning as our primary means of navigation, supplemented by the drift bearing sights I take off ocean whitecaps, Very flares, or perhaps even the odd iceberg that might present itself. For the hard 'fixes,' which I sincerely hope will come with some regularity, we can only count on sextant observations. Those occurrences will depend on the amount of cloud above us, which our good friend Captain Rostrom of the *Mauretania* regrettably assured me we'd find abundant over the North Atlantic." Brown shuffled a few papers on their small table. "Would you like to see the two sets of precomputed transparent Sumner overlays for the six celestial bodies?"

Alcock held up both hands. "Spare me, Lord, from those blessed overlays and your infernal computations! I've seen you juggle those incomprehensible numbers hour after hour, and I want nothing to do with them!"

Brown laughed. "Fair enough." He looked thoughtfully at his pilot— here was the moment to establish the final trust between them. "I'll make you a bargain, Captain Alcock. If you don't trifle with the headings, requests for altitude changes, or estimated times I give you, I won't advise you on the operation of the machine."

"Done!"

For the next hour, they thrashed out the last of the details on the airborne work they would share. They were coming close to wrapping things up when Ted said, "Just to be clear, you want me to monitor on no less than an every-fifteen-minute basis the temperature and revolution gauges on both engines?"

"Righto," Jack said. "With those gauges located outside the cockpit on the engine cowlings and because we'll be flying in darkness some of the time, do keep your electric torch close at hand. Even with the dials having radium illumination, there still could be trouble making out the numbers."

The two men briefly discussed the long-duration drag issues caused by the *Vimy*'s distinctively bulky engine cowlings. Octagonally shaped in the front, they gradually tapered rearward to a feathering point. Company wind tunnel tests had shown that particular configuration offered the least air resistance for a body with a flat face, which the *Vimy*'s huge radiators presented, though no one could quantify exactly how much it would help. The Vickers workmen, of course, could not resist giving the unique-looking engine nacelles a nickname, calling them "power eggs." Alcock finally declared the drag issue moot, as nothing could be done about it.

Ted paused, then asked, "Jack, I'm not entirely clear why you want me to so closely monitor the Petrol Overflow Gauge on the center-section strut?" The meter was located about three feet above their heads.

Alcock explained. "The gauge is essential to knowing whether the petrol flow to the engines is within certain limits. Too little and those eight Claudel-Hobson carburetors will starve; too much and they'll flood—either circumstance would not be conducive to our continued good health."

Ted, suppressing a chuckle at the masterful understatement, nodded his agreement.

Alcock thought he should further elaborate. "The fuel flow on this machine can sometimes be erratic, especially under difficult flying conditions like heavy turbulence, icing, heavy rain—that sort of thing. We are going to be asking a very great deal of the old bus, and the rate of petrol to the engines is a critical point of vulnerability."

Jack abruptly changed the subject. "Have you had a chance to test our cockpit communication and the electrically-heated Burberry flying suits?"

"Yes," Ted responded. "In fact, this afternoon, I did a complete check on all the electrical systems. Our telephone system is functioning normally, which hopefully will allow us to speak and hear each other better over the engine noise. The power from the portside wind screw generator will handle the full load needed for the heating suits and dashboard instruments—the aneroid altimeter, air speed indicator, clock, aperiodic compass, and cross-level inclinometer."

The flying machine air speed meter, an idea inspired by the earlier mentioned Henri Pitot, was invented in 1912 by the Englishmen Alexander Ogilvie and Eric Clift (patented separately). The device utilized a two-sensory system to measure the speed of the machine through the air—the air pressure taken from a hollow pitot tube usually located on the leading edge of a wing facing into the machine's forward motion was compared to the pressure measured by a static port mounted at a ninety-degree angle from the pitot, usually on the fuselage's side, with the results converted to miles per hour and displayed on the meter. Brown could take this *indicated* air speed and, after entering the *Vimy*'s altitude and corresponding (adiabatic lapse rate calculated) outside air temperature into his Appleyard course and distance calculator, determine his *true* air speed.

Using that same handheld Appleyard, Ted could then calculate wind direction, velocity, and true heading. He first applied the already calculated true air speed to the left or right drift observed on the earth's surface (expressed in degrees), which was read off the *vertical* reticule on his drift bearing plate, formally known as an RFC (Royal Flying Corps) "Wind Gauge Bearing Plate." To get the ground speed, he'd again line up the drift bearing plate on a surface feature (land or water) and then, using his 1916 British Mark V Military Pocket Watch, time in number of seconds how long it took for two of the drift bearing plate's *horizontal* reticules to pass over the same ground object. After further interrogating the Appleyard with this combined data, the true heading and ground speed of the machine can be calculated. After applying variation, the navigator now knew what his compass heading should be and could calculate an estimated time of arrival (ETA) to his next checkpoint.

One of the first of these extremely useful drift bearing devices was developed during the Great War by RAF Major H.E. Wimperis while working on a truly useful bombsight. The drift bearing plate, as he described it, "enabled the velocity and deviation [drift] of the wind to be [accurately] obtained whilst in flight." The later-developed optical drift meter became so effective a navigation aid it was used until the dawn of the twenty-first century and might still be in limited operation in a few remote localities.

The Great War-inspired aperiodic compass was so-called because it was without "a period of confusion," that is, after a turn, the pointer would stay directly on the new heading without back-and-forth oscillations. (The American NC flying boats used simple boat compasses prone to come loose from their mounts in rough air and give erroneous readings.) The cross-level inclinometer, which showed when the wings were level, was a spirit level comparable in concept to the Abney level Ted would use with his modified Brandis sextant. The inclinometer and altimeter were the only cockpit instruments Jack would have that could assist him when in blind-flying conditions.

Brown had also satisfactorily checked out his precious wind-screw/battery-powered wireless set but said nothing to Jack about it—why wave that red flag in front of the Alcock bull? Ted was still at a loss as to why Jack had so much antipathy toward the device. As accomplished a pilot as he was, Alcock had a tendency to reflexively disparage innovative new flight aids, especially those of an electrical nature or any that suggested his natural piloting skills could not measure up. "The good pilot," he'd once snorted, "can tell the attitude of the aeroplane by the feeling in the seat of his pants, the way the wind whistles through the wing bracing wires, and his own well-developed, innate sense of balance while in cloud or fog."

"Ted," Jack said, he having a few crew coordination issues of his own. "I've worked up a petrol usage schedule for all seven tanks. We'll switch them based on gallons per hour consumption rates as measured on the dashboard clock. While it's not accurate enough for your sextant, it'll be fine for fuel management. I'll count on you to keep the timing and to make the actual tank changes."

"Yes, of course," Ted assured him. "I'll watch them like a hawk."

Of course, none of this was new to either of them, but it was absolutely crucial each man understood precisely what was expected of him. Even one small mistake or misunderstanding could be fatal.

The two men lapsed into a thoughtful silence. Finally, Brown said, "What else can I do to help you?"

A somber Jack hesitated for a moment before replying. "Teddie, the *Vimy* is a very difficult plane to fly, which I may have to do for up to twenty straight hours. I won't be able to take both hands off the wheel at any time. All my thoughts will be concentrated on ensuring the engines keep running, the aeroplane stays in the air, and I can hold your headings." Like nearly all flying machines of the day, the *Vimy* was inherently unstable, meaning to fly it "hands off" even for a few seconds would result in immediate loss of control. "I'll need you," Jack continued, looking Brown straight in the eye, "to keep that in mind constantly from takeoff to landing."

Brown nodded, wearing an equally grave expression. The same had been true for the smaller machines he was familiar with during the war, but those flights were only of three- or four-hours duration and certainly not in as massive an aeroplane as the *Vimy*.

Alcock looked at his watch. Brown yawned mightily and Jack reflexively did the same. It was nearly midnight.

"Time," Jack said softly.

"Time," Ted agreed.

Both men were snoring fiercely within minutes.

* * *

Earlier that same day, and to great fanfare, US Navy Lieutenant Commander A.C. Read and his five-man crew arrived at Plymouth, England, in their NC-4 Curtiss flying boat—completing the first trans-Atlantic flight from mainland North America to mainland Europe via Halifax Harbor, Nova Scotia; Trepassey Harbor, Newfoundland; The Azores; Lisbon Harbor, Portugal; Ferrol Harbor, Spain; and on to Plymouth. Fifteen days had elapsed since their departure from Newfoundland. Despite the scores of US Navy ships marking the way, the NC crews and their machines were not really up to the task. Owing to faulty compasses, an inability to deal with blind flying conditions, and poor dead reckoning navigation, both the NC-1 and NC-3 got lost and were forced down in the Atlantic, just a few score miles short of the Azores. Fortunately, all twelve of the heartbroken crewmen were rescued. Among the survivors were future World War Two Admirals Marc Mitscher and John "Jack" Towers. Only the NC-4 commanded by Commander Read arrived at Horta Harbor, The Azores, safely, barely escaping disaster—five minutes after landing, the port was so clogged with heavy fog it would have been impossible to locate.

Commander Read and his men were given a rousing welcome at Horta, something that would be repeated with ever-increasing gusto at each of their European stops. Newspapers around the world lavished glowing praise on the great accomplishment. In America, the public went mad with joy in "being the first to cross the Atlantic." Newspapers were unanimous in their belief that the flight would be remembered on the same footing as Columbus and his 1492 first landing in the New World. Two weeks later, Britain would erupt in similar delirious joy after Alcock and Brown arrived in Ireland. The English newspapers strained themselves, reaching for even greater superlatives in an attempt to outdo the American upstarts. Not a soul in western Europe or North America would have believed that *both* flights would be virtually forgotten a century later.

Cochrane Hotel
Late Sunday, June 8, 1919

A flight test of the *Vimy* at Kiddy Viddy was planned for the morrow. Alcock and Brown asked Monty Montague, carpenter foreman Ernie Pitman, and Rolls-Royce's Bob Lyons to join them for an important meeting, never mind a social evening that spontaneously arose among their own Vickers fellows and the ever-increasing number of newspaper reporters that had signed up for Ted's labor pool. Alas, Brown's clever ploy had worked too well—they were now oversupplied with men! Plus, the newshounds had been getting bolder by the day and were becoming a nuisance—both at Kiddy Viddy and the Cochrane. Jack and Ted realized they'd arrived at a critical point, and the time had come to stage-manage the first flight test, perhaps find a way to rein in the newsmen, and realistically assess their chances against Admiral Kerr's team.

It'd been an arduous late May and early June all the way round. With Jack in overall charge of the aerodrome construction and flying machine assembly, he could not be spared for anything else. To Brown, then, had fallen the responsibility for final cockpit instrument and navigation equipment installations. When Ted was not monitoring weather conditions with Lieutenant Clements or working on his own chart planning, mathematical celestial computations, and log/course work, he too was camped out at the field, pitching in uncomplainingly with more than his share of the physical work and despite the excruciating pain in his left leg. Either Alcock or Brown, both highly skilled mechanic/technicians in their own right, were continually around the aeroplane, making sure nothing had been left unfinished or poorly done. Further, Mr. Lester—God bless him!—had been true to his word; the pasture near Mundy

Pond, now called Lester's Field, was ready to accept flying operations. If the test went well tomorrow after takeoff from Kiddy Viddy, the machine would be landed at Lester's Field for the final arrangements.

This was not to say any of it had been easy. The Vickers crew, forced to work out in the open, had been continually plagued by combinations of rain, sleet, snow, and high winds for days on end, which very often slowed work to a crawl. It was small consolation the Handley Page fellows were suffering the same conditions at Harbour Grace, and neither team would gain any advantage over the other from the adverse weather. Alcock's men still had to grit their teeth and persevere through miserable sixteen-hour days, interrupted only by the tedious canvas covering/uncovering of the *Vimy* as the St. John's precipitation regularly mandated.

While Alcock, Lyons, Monty, and Ernie Pitman's gang of mechanics and fabricators were reassembling a machine they were intimately familiar with, nearly all of Brown's navigation work had been quite literally uncharted territory. In the early days at St. John's, Ted had discussed over-ocean navigation with both Grieve and Fax Morgan, incorporating those elements of their ideas he thought useful and modifying or dropping others to suit his own needs. Such a process naturally required a very careful anticipation of potential problems—what some flyers were calling "staying ahead of the aeroplane"—so as not to be surprised over the ocean under difficult, perhaps even irredeemable, circumstances.

Brown's mentally demanding work occurred in the evenings while the others rested or used up their pharmaceutical scrip on "medicinal tonic." It was then that he labored, always painfully—Ted so very fearful of becoming over-reliant on his secret supply of opiate painkillers. He only used them when it was absolutely necessary; all of it had been much harder on him than even Alcock knew. While Ted's blue eyes still burned with youthful fire, they were surrounded by old man's crowfeet, his once glistening brown hair now speckled with more than a little gray, and only half his teeth still his own—all of it courtesy of the damnable war.

Over the last several days, he'd been consolidating his celestial strategy, by far the most difficult discipline of all his navigation aids. Ted understood, as no one else on the Vickers team fully appreciated, that successful observations of the heavenly bodies were absolutely crucial. If he could not firmly "fix" his position at least once or twice mid-ocean, any dramatic wind shift or major instrument malfunction would almost certainly sweep them into oblivion. As he'd long ago decided, it was quite impossible to use the Royal Navy's entire inventory of fifty to sixty navigational celestial bodies. He had firmly decided on his favored six, they among the most easily recognizable objects in the northern hemisphere—Polaris, or the Pole Star; Vega; Jupiter; Venus; the Sun for daytime; and the Moon, for day and night. The work on the two sets of Baker navigation machine transparent overlays for each of the six bodies had been completed, they that formed the basis of determining his Sumner lines. Ted had decided to stop calling them Sumner lines in deference to Jack, instead using the clearer term "lines of position," or LOPs. The calculations themselves were based on data obtained from the Admiralty-published Height Observed Star Tables and the Nautical Almanac, a centuries-old bible of daily timetables anchored to the Prime Meridian at Greenwich, England. Brown still would need to make last-minute computations based on the actual day and time of the observations.

Again, the Baker navigation machine, the box-like apparatus that was to rest on Ted's lap while he used it in flight, was specifically designed to accommodate Sumner transparencies. As the Vimy moved through the sky, he would turn a knob and that part of the rolled-up map indicating his estimated current position would crawl into view—opposite knobs unrolling and rolling up accordingly. After Brown took a sextant observation (to determine the body's altitude in degrees and minutes above the horizon) and noted the exact time, he would complete a final set of calculations and plot those values on the observed body's dedicated "time of day/night" and "height observed tables" transparencies, which were already superimposed atop his rolling Mercator chart inside the Baker machine. The combined resultant would show a line of position, or LOP, on the chart, upon which he would know he was somewhere located. In order to get a true "fix," that is, determine *exactly* where he was, it would be necessary to take at least one more celestial observation, as close to a right angle as possible to the first shot, and repeat the procedure. After the observations were further reconciled to one official observation time—to account for distance traveled between shots, the *Vimy* could be "fixed" where the two LOPs crossed on his chart.

Ted had no illusions about what he was up against. As he had repeatedly reminded himself, the work was laborious enough sitting in a dry and comfortably heated hotel room; to accurately observe and plot celestial sightings in an open-cockpit machine with darkness, obstructive upper wings, clouds, turbulence, freezing temperatures, and precipitation all scheming against him promised the most difficult, extended physical activity he would ever undertake.

"What about the compass?" Jack had asked Ted at that Sunday evening meeting as Monty Montague brewed up a fresh pot of tea. The early part of the get-together had been filled with a much too lengthy handwringing over the status of the Handley Page, and it was time to get back to their own problems. "I heard about your little fit this afternoon while installing it. I hope there's not a problem." Alcock was more than a little uneasy it had been necessary to leave so much of the crucial cockpit work to Brown.

The entire team understood the machine's most critical flight instrument was the aperiodic compass. Six inches in diameter and alcohol-damped—the type would soon be referred to as a "whiskey compass"—it also had a special radium-etched pointer for night readings. With more than a little physical difficulty, Ted had installed it face-up on a raised wooden ledge in front of Alcock's right knee. It was Royal Navy Captain F. Creagh-Osborne who, in 1909, introduced the first practical aircraft magnetic compass—a self-contained apparatus filled with a mixture of alcohol and distilled water. The *Vimy* would be using an improved version of the Creagh-Osborne compass developed by RAF pilot and scientist Keith Lucas early in the Great War. Unfortunately killed in a crash in 1916, Lucas's pioneering work ultimately led to the first real *precision* aero compass. Coupled with the combined efforts of others, his device provided a much more accurate directional heading that was calibrated to account for inherent turning and gravitational errors, also eliminating the unstable swaying back and forth of the pointing needle while in and after turns. Such problems had long been seriously annoying. Now, with pilots undertaking over-water flights of much longer distances that greatly increased chances of becoming lost, those dangers were becoming potentially fatal (what very nearly happened to the American NC-3 flying boat).

"It did give me a bit of a go, Jack," Ted allowed, forcing a tight smile. "Simply the usual gripes one makes when everything doesn't promptly go his way." Brown didn't mention the unusual positions he'd been required to assume had been so painful he at one point nearly passed out. There still remained, he was quite certain, a lingering question as to whether he was physically up to it all and, for a man of Brown's determination, *that* had to be fought off at every turn.

Montgomery set his teacup down rather firmly, as if to say, "enough of all that."

"Right, I suggest we continue down the list, each item one at a time, and make sure we've a full accounting. If Jack is to test fly tomorrow, we don't want any stumbles." He shuffled his own notes before asking Ted in a manner suggesting he would rather have avoided the subject, "What's the latest on the wireless?" Everyone was aware of Alcock's annoyance over the entire assembly—"a bloody extra hundred pounds we could well do without!" he'd again complained only the day before.

Ted responded with assuredness. "I've just completed a transmission test with Birdie at Mount Pearl. Excellent results." Brown sincerely hoped the set's infernally chronic bugs had been finally worked out.

"Overall, is the cockpit ready, Ted?" Alcock asked, not taking up the wireless bait. "I'm damn sorry to have left that all to you."

"Don't give it another thought. You've got all you can handle, and after all," a grinning Brown said as he rattled his cup and saucer in Jack's direction, "navigation and instrumentation are my cup of tea." The group chuckled, and Ted's leg momentarily stopped throbbing; his play on words having produced a pleasant placebo effect.

Ted continued with his navigator station update. All the fixed instrumentation had been installed and tested. He'd assembled his personal navigation kit—a supply of #2 lead pencils; a Bigsworth plotting protractor—the best available; marine dividers for measuring and walking off distances; the Appleyard course and distance calculator, a circular slide rule with heading and drift solutions that were developed during the Great War by the Admiralty's Rollo Appleyard; a handheld prismatic compass for checking headings from sight bearings off surface features, the moon, and the sun; his Mark V pocket stop and second-setting watch; and a small note/logbook. Blank spaces in the log were left to pencil in actual conditions and other remarks while en route.

Bob Lyons of Rolls-Royce was next. For the big jump, he'd calculated the two Eagle engines would require 64 gallons of radiator cooling water, 40 gallons of Castrol lubricating oil, and 1,050 gallons of Shell B petrol. "Your total oil consumption," Lyons said, "will be one gallon per hour; your petrol consumption 48 gallons per hour." For Alcock, it went without saying those numbers assumed optimum conditions, something that rarely happened. Still, Jack reassured himself, there should be sufficient safety margin. "Maximum speed at 5,000 feet at a cruise power setting of 1,900 revolutions remains the same as our Brooklands test flight—101 miles per hour, but we are strongly recommending you maintain a less engine stressful cruise of 1,500 to 1,600 revolutions—maximum of 1,700, sacrificing if you must a few miles per hour. I am calculating a service ceiling of 10,500 feet pressure altitude, though local conditions and the lack of an updated ground reported altimeter setting could cause a reading to be in error by up to four or five hundred feet either way from the actual absolute altitude." Lyons paused and looked hard at Alcock and Brown. "I must be very clear—I've rechecked the calculations with Monty and Bob Dicker. In order to ensure you can get all the way across, the *Vimy* must depart St. John's nearly 1,000 pounds heavier than its design maximum of 12,500 pounds."

Alcock whistled softly—a 13,500-pound gross weight takeoff! As if to steer the conversation away from the ugly prospect of a dangerously overweight launch from a rough, short field, he turned to Ted and asked, "What about the 'compass swing?'"

"I've asked Birdie to help with that tomorrow morning," Ted replied. "He's setting up a cardinal direction pointer next to the machine."

While a final "swing" would be necessary just before the actual attempt, a dress rehearsal was important to get the procedure down pat. For without a precise calibration of their magnetic compass just prior to takeoff, the two men might just as well put a pistol to their heads as attempt a 2,000-mile trek across a trackless ocean. Fortunately, the procedure was not complicated, though attention to detail was crucial. Lieutenant Birdie Clare would mark off the four cardinal directions—North, South, East, West—on the ground nearby the *Vimy*. The machine would be maneuvered into each of those four positions and the cockpit compass read. For example, if the compass read 005 degrees on the North marker, either an iron compensator would be installed, or a screw adjustment made on the compass to correct the reading to 000 degrees. Accordingly, the other three cardinal directions would be compared and adjusted to 090, 180, and 270 degrees. While these "swings" could not be made perfect—there were simply too many technical variables—Ted Brown was confident the result would fall within his tolerances.

After the group discussed a few more items, Alcock thought to mop up. "Anything else?" When the responses came back negative, Jack said, "Good, then that's that. Furthermore, I find myself suddenly thirsty!" By general agreement, it was decided they join their mates in the dining room for a communally sponsored "nightcap."

Later, when the Dooley sisters began gathering the last of the glasses and tableware and everyone was departing for their rooms, the Vickers radiator and cooling expert hesitantly approached Alcock.

"A moment, Cap'n?" The fellow looked troubled.

"Certainly, Davis." Jack ushered him over to a couple of empty chairs. "What is it?"

Davis spoke haltingly; a man comfortable only with his fellow shop men and fabricators, he was not used to speaking to persons of authority. "It's about the *Atlantic's* radiator, sir." He cleared his throat of phlegm. "I'm hearing reports Mr. Hawker has blamed rust particles for clogging his radiator water filter and that it was responsible for the machine's engine overheating and failure." Davis mustered his full resolve. "Sir, I do not believe that was the cause."

"Do go on, Davis."

"Right, sir." Emboldened by this encouragement from the nominal leader of the Vickers team and anxious to protect the good name of British radiator specialists, the man ploughed on. "I spoke at length with Mr. Hawker's engine cooling men—his ground crew has not yet left for home—and they mentioned the gentleman's unfamiliarity with the engine radiator-shutter control lever. On at least two separate test flight occasions, Mr. Hawker placed it in the wrong position." The shutters operated much like a venetian blind—the open position allowed in the maximum amount of cooling air; closed offered the least. "I fear that for some reason, he may have become confused and reversed the proper procedure."

Jack Alcock looked at the ceiling for a long moment, nodding ever so slightly.

"Thank you so much, Davis, for bringing this to my attention," he finally said. "That indeed is a cautionary tale. Nevertheless, I'm quite sure Harry performed in his usual stalwart fashion, and it was only bad luck that did him in."

"Naturally, sir," Davis replied obediently.

"I will discuss this important subject with Left-tenant Brown—you have done the right thing bringing it to my attention. We, of course, have similar shutters on our own Rolls engines and will take heed of your warning."

"Thank you, sir."

"Meanwhile, Davis, I think it best we not mention this to the reporters, who of course will not understand such purely technical matters."

"Of course, sir."

"Wouldn't want to cast any aspersions on Harry's magnificent achievement, would we?" Jack continued. "After all, both Grieve and Hawker feel bad enough missing their main chance, yet we must remember they set a record for the longest distance flight over the ocean yet attempted." Jack gave Davis a wide comforting smile.

The Vickers radiator man murmured his complete understanding and retired in obvious relief, having sated his conscience without jeopardizing his own status within the team. Later in their room, before switching off the electric light, Alcock related Davis' story to Brown. "Knowing Harry and his impulsive ways as well as I do, it has the ring of truth to it."

First Test Flight
Kiddy Viddy Field
Noon Local Time, Monday, June 9, 1919

The Vickers men broke out their sack lunches, thoughtfully prepared by the Dooley sisters earlier that morning, with Agnes having personally assembled Captain Alcock's, she insisting, "I'll never hear the end of it if that man gets even one crumb of dry bread." Ted Brown, who had spent the late morning confabulating with Mount Pearl Station Commander Lieutenant Birdie Clare and RAF aerologist Lieutenant Laurance Clements, settled onto a wood bench next to Alcock, who was happily munching on a ham sandwich. Before Brown even sat down, Jack bubbled, "Lyons, Monty, and Pitman have given the final nod. You and I are to take the machine up directly after feeding our faces." He took another big bite. "If all goes well, we are to land at Lester's Field and prime the *Vimy* for the big trip."

"Good show, old boy!" Ted said. "I've got everything ready on my end. Can't see why it won't go swimmingly." Ted nudged his flying comrade mischievously. "Still remember how to pitch it about, do you, Jacko?" It had been many weeks since Alcock had been at the controls and, indeed, such a long spell earthbound did make a man rusty. The heavy demands of operating a flying machine, the veteran pilots had learned long ago, took constant and regular practice to stay safe and proficient.

Alcock grinned. "Like riding a bicycle—once one learns how, you never forget!"

Several automobiles suddenly appeared at the field, disgorging a mob of reporters. Closely behind were more autos, at least a score, along with

The fully assembled Vimy *just prior to first "Kiddy Viddy" test flight on June 9. (The Rooms Provincial Archives, St. John's, Newfoundland)*

a number of horse-drawn carriages. Bringing up the rear of the train was a long line of bicycles and pedestrians.

"Bollocks!" Alcock sputtered. "We did everything possible to keep a lid on this test and still wind up with half of St. John's in our lap."

"No matter, Jack," Brown said soothingly. "Monty and the fellows will keep them at bay. Besides, the people here get very little excitement—who are we to deny them?" Ted glanced at the clear sky above. "Look at that, would you? At long last, the weather has gone on its best behavior for our first hop."

And so it had, and so would the *Vimy*. Captain John Alcock smoothly lifted the machine off Kiddy Viddy and promptly put it through its paces. As Brown would later write, "Under Alcock's skillful hands, the Vickers *Vimy* became nippy as a scout. We headed directly eastward and passed over the sea for fifteen minutes."

The flyers were struck by their first aerial view of that part of Newfoundland, indeed the first aerial view that humans had ever seen of the city, with the possible exception of Hawker and Grieve during their harried departure some three weeks earlier. Alcock flew over South Side Hills and beyond Cape Spear before circling back around the city. The unprecedented sound of heavy motors thundering directly overhead brought hundreds, if not thousands, of people out to the streets and nearby meadows, all oohing and ahhing while craning their necks in an effort to follow the flying marvel. Brown would later write, "The day was so unusually clear the sea was reflecting a vivid blue. Near the coast it was spotted and streaked by the glistening white of icebergs and whitecaps. Trial observations of my navigation instruments proved them to be okay. The machine and engines seemed in perfect condition." Then, with chagrin: "But not a spark could be conjured from the wireless."

Jack turned the *Vimy* back toward land, crossing St. John's at 4,000 feet. The two men were astonished to observe the area around the city looked even bleaker and more forbidding than it did from the ground. More disconcerting was the crew's inability to locate Lester's Field, lost in the myriad of unrecognized hills and dales below. At last, the ground men realized the flyers' plight and touched off "a smudge-fire as a signal." Alcock made a disciplined approach, followed by a smooth uphill landing. What happened next confirmed to Ted he was in the hands of a master aviator. The *Vimy* had touched down in good shape, but in the restrictive confines of the field, they quickly ran out of pasture and, "after topping a brow," found themselves heading for a stone fence. The *Vimy's* only braking capability was to pull back hard on the control wheel, raising the nose and lowering the tail, which increased drag on the bentwood tail skid. However, it immediately became apparent that wasn't going to be enough. At that instant, and with great authority, Alcock manipulated the large knob on top of the single throttle lever in such a way the port engine went to idle and the starboard to near full throttle. In an instant, the differential breaking whirled the machine ninety degrees left, in a manner some pilots were calling a "ground-loop." Although the *Vimy* took on a punishing side load, with the wheels skidding sideways, no damage was done. Forward momentum melted away only yards short of the stone fence.

Monty Montgomery and his men, who'd already motored over from Kiddy Viddy, pushed the *Vimy* to a sheltered part of the field where they could peg it down against the elements. The Vickers' ground team leader also had the aeroplane immediately roped off; a horde of frenzied spectators began hurrying to Lester's prairie once they realized the flying venue had changed. While usually well-mannered, the excitement of being a part of the epic trans-Atlantic race had become too much for many, and fears had grown within the Vickers camp that the crowds might turn mob-like. Still, feelings on this point remained mixed; it was most gratifying to see how solidly the citizens of St. John's were backing "their *Vimy*" against the "Handley Page archrivals" at Harbour Grace, in the manner, Ted supposed, of rabid football fans cheering on the home team.

Bob Lyons shouted up to the cockpit after the propellers stilled. "How did they run, Jack?"

Alcock was grinning from ear to ear. "If your Rolls-Royce engines were skirts, I'd become a bigamist and marry them both!"

Brown chimed in as the two men dismounted the machine. "The entire flight went splendidly, Bob. Everything worked as expected."

Jack's smile had disappeared by the time he was on terra firma. "Well, not everything," he said to Montgomery, who had been standing next to Lyons. He went on with surprisingly less malice in his voice than might have been expected. "I have been saying all along that bloody wireless is a needless addition of, what the bloody hell is it, a hundred and fifty pounds of useless ballast?" The total weight of the radio equipment increased with each succeeding rant. "Tell them, Ted." He stomped off to join the mechanics.

An embarrassed Brown was at a loss to explain. "I haven't the foggiest why it wouldn't work, Monty." He fumbled in a pocket for the comfort of his pipe, adding, "but I'm sure we can fix it."

Montgomery had all along been a supporter of the wireless, principally for its safety aspect, but now even he was beginning to wonder if Alcock didn't have a point. "Well, Teddie," he said with some finality, "let's hope so. We are almost ready to sign the machine off for the flight." Later that evening, Brown would take the apparatus to the Mount Pearl station. He and Lieutenant Clare quickly located the fault, made the repair, and Ted quietly reinstalled it in the *Vimy*.

A much more serious matter arose. Ernie Pitman, the mechanics foreman, walked up to Alcock wearing a downcast expression. "What is it, Ernie?" an alert Jack demanded before the man could open his mouth.

"Jack, I'm afraid we have a problem with the fuel supply. Let me show you." Pitman led Alcock, Brown, Monty, Dicker, and Bob Lyons to a makeshift tent housing the fuel barrels. One of the mechanics poured a sampling into pans from each barrel. "As you can see, it's precipitated," Pitman explained. Jack and Ted dipped a finger into each pan to inspect the peculiar fluid, none of it looking or feeling like normal petrol. "When it dries out," Ernie said, "it's reduced to a powder." He shook his head. "I've not seen anything like this before."

Jack was too nonplussed to say anything. "Feels like a soft resin," offered engineer Brown. "Sticky, with I think something of the consistency of India rubber, wetted by petrol."

"Whatever that mixture of the original petrol and benzol has become," Bob Lyons made clear, "it's out of the question to feed it to the Eagles. At a minimum, the stuff would clog the carburetors and lead to immediate engine stoppage." Here it was, that bugbear of every flyer since the aeroplane had been invented some fifteen years earlier—contaminated fuel! In an effort to make the fuel even more efficient—an attempt to go from 98% outstanding to 100% perfect—the additive had completely mucked up the works. Lucky it was Pitman had made the discovery before someone had begun refueling, which would have completely fouled the innards of the *Vimy's* magnificent engines and indefinitely delayed anymore flying. But still, with no useful petrol available, the entire project was suddenly dead in the water.

If that was not enough, the mood of the Vickers team instantly became even more down-in-the-mouth when the mighty hum of the Handley Page's four engines were at that very moment heard approaching from the northwest. The great ship made several lazy passes over the city, a demonstration that struck everyone as even more powerful than the *Vimy's* circuits only an hour earlier. It seemed obvious to even the citizens of St. John's that the Handley team was also well into the final stages of preparation, and the race must now be a dead heat. It could only be imagined Alcock's emotions as he watched Major Brackley at the controls, a man he'd taught to fly just a few short years earlier, on the cusp of snatching away what Jack sensed even then would be the greatest achievement of his life. Admiral Kerr would release a statement later that day to the press, stating "everything worked most satisfactorily" and that "another test flight would follow." He closed with "present favorable conditions are becoming disturbed, so that the date of the trans-Atlantic flight is unsettled," leaving the general impression that he was not ready to go despite the brilliant show of his machine. The admiral was a cautious man; too cautious, Handley Page executives would later ruefully discover.

That evening, and without mentioning the competitor's apparently successful over-flight of the city, Alcock would send the Vickers' directors a positive summary of the *Vimy*'s test results, ending it with an upbeat: *Machine absolutely top-hole!* To his dismay, he received the following cold response: *Weather perfect here. Please cable reason for non-start.* A thoroughly deflated Captain John Alcock wordlessly showed the wire to Brown and the others, who could only shake their heads at the continuing lack of comprehension among Vickers, Ltd. top executives regarding the horrid weather conditions in Newfoundland.

With the sky clouding over a darkly setting sun, a matching gloom accompanied the team on their drive back to the Cochrane Hotel. Agnes Dooley had been primed to give a bit of his own devil back to Jack Alcock, but when she saw the look on his face, she wisely said only, "Your suppers are ready, gentlemen. And Mr. Raynham decided to wait up for you."

The Vickers bunch plopped down tiredly next to Freddie, who it soon became clear was not in a particularly good mood. Ted picked up on that first, he a man who was particularly sensitive to physical suffering. Brown surmised Raynham's crash injuries affected the man more than he let on.

"How is it going, Fred?" Brown asked sympathetically.

"Not so good, Ted," Raynham replied, ignoring the implied reference to his personal condition. "Simply can't scare up a new navigator anywhere, and the old *Raymor* was brutalized worse than I first thought." Raynham made an effort to straighten up and act cheerful. "Still," he said, looking about, then realizing a heavy wince that suddenly passed through him would give the lie to it all, "don't you chaps start singing hymns over me quite yet!"

"Never dreamed of it for a moment, Freddie," a wan-looking Jack Alcock offered.

Fred Raynham was not so far gone he hadn't picked up something was wrong. "What the matter, Jacko? Got a blister on your big toe?"

Monty Montgomery stepped in. "Fred, we've just discovered our entire petrol supply has become contaminated. Useless even for further testing."

Raynham scratched a cheek, looking thoughtful. "Before you added those fancy mixtures, your Eagles used the same foundation fuel as my *Raymor*, correct?"

"That's right," Bob Lyons said. "Shell B."

Fred leaned back in his chair, looking brighter than he had all evening. "Well, as it happens, I have a spare quantity of Shell B that I can place at your disposal for any final tests," Fred added, the fatalistic tone in his voice a telltale sign that a part of him had indeed given up on his own effort. "It should be enough until your replacement petrol arrives."

Ted and Jack looked at each other. Alcock's old friend and competitor had once again pulled their chestnuts out of the fire in the manner of the American frontier cavalry riding to the rescue of under-siege settlers. None of the Vickers team would ever forget Mr. Frederick Raynham's gallantry in Newfoundland; he had not the need to draw from his own pocket a single shred of "tonic water" scrip for the balance of the evening. *Vimy* flight tests recommenced immediately the next morning.

A few days later, additional stock consigned to the *Vimy*, including plenty of fresh petrol, arrived at St. John's by direct steamer. The ship also bore the trilby-hatted Mr. Percy Maxwell Muller, Vickers Works superintendent. With the prize now within the Aviation Department's grasp, Muller had felt compelled to personally oversee the final stages in what had become a highly publicized, much-at-stake match race. The team welcomed his presence; unlike many senior managers who sometimes tended to stifle an otherwise smoothly running operation, Percy always bore an infectious optimism that raised spirits. Alcock and Brown had another reason to welcome him; their unpaid bills were beginning to cause some grousing among St. John's merchants. They could turn that unpleasantness over to the super.

Even better, the Newfoundland weather was finally showing signs of sloughing off its spring tantrums and settling into more sedate summer fare. Further, the *Vimy's* preparations were nearing completion, with perhaps just another day or two of testing before everyone would be satisfied the aeroplane was ready. Ted and Clements had already put themselves on a twenty-four-hour weather watch, looking for the right combination of decent weather conditions at St. John's and an acceptable forecast—crude as it had to be—over the North Atlantic.

* * *

Ralphie Moyst was thrilled to learn the Vickers *Vimy*—he had made it a point to learn the machine's name—had been moved to Mr. Lester's horse pasturage. Ralphie's home was just a few blocks to the east of the field, and he was able to get over there nearly every afternoon to drink in all the excitement. He would always remember the sounds and smells—Captain Alcock starting up the mighty motors and the propellers creating such gale force winds that anyone behind the flying machine had to gasp to catch his breath; the odors of gasoline, oil, and road apples from Mr. Lester's horses mixing into a unique scent that even into old age he would associate with those magic days. The animals themselves had been corralled into a small corner of the field and were having to live off what was left of last year's hay crop, a condition they were acutely aware of after sniffing at the fresh, green summer growth just out of reach.

A few of Captain Alcock's hired workers were Mr. Lester's local men, but most were strangers who spoke with what Ralphie presumed were English accents. These men did not like Ralphie and his friends hanging about and were always shooing them away. One man, in particular, they learned to stay clear of. "'Ere you," he would say, wildly waving his arms and running at them as if to disburse a pack of adolescent wolves, "out of the wye!" And they would scatter, only to re-form at another spot a few minutes later.

However, one Englishman did not seem to mind the children, had even once smiled at Ralphie when he caught the boy staring at him. He always wore a nice suit or his military uniform and was usually addressed by the mechanics as "Left-tenant Brown." After wondering for a moment if there was such a thing as a Right-tenant, Ralphie had noticed something else—the man walked with a limp and carried a walking stick, *just like he did.* Which meant, as Ralphie knew from his mother, that the man was special.

One afternoon, to Ralphie's great surprise, Left-tenant Brown approached the children and stopped in front of Ralphie, saying with a smile, "Hello, old fellow." Pointing his own nicely polished cane at the boy's homemade stick, Brown continued. "Now there's a fine, stout-looking piece of walking equipment."

"Thank you, sir," Ralphie stammered. He did not think it was near so fine as the Left-tenant's but kept that to himself.

"What's your name?" Brown asked kindly.

The boy's tongue suddenly felt like it was covered with thick moss. He finally spit out, "Ralphie Moyst, sir."

"Well, Ralphie, are you having a good time watching us prepare our flying machine?"

"Oh, yessir!" The boy had noticed straight away the man sounded more like a Canadian or maybe even American, though not quite that either. "Very much so, Left-tenant Brown!"

"Oh ho, so you know my name! You must be a clever chap." Brown guffawed extravagantly. "Say then," he said abruptly, as if something interesting had just occurred to him, "let's give that cleverness a test. What is it, do you think, I'm to do on the flight to assist Captain Alcock?"

Ralphie lowered his eyes, too ashamed to admit his ignorance.

Brown laughed sympathetically. "Well, Ralphie, as a matter of fact, there is no reason you should know, is there?" The boy brightened as Brown continued. "I am to point the way for Mr. Alcock, so he may steer us on a course directly to Ireland."

Ralphie wasn't sure what all that might involve but thought he had the general idea. "Like the man who looks at stars on a steamer?"

"Exactly, my boy! Spot on!"

Ralphie was thrilled to learn that Mr. Left-tenant Brown, who was so like him physically except all grown up, had such an important job. He supposed it was this wonderful knowledge that made him special. A thought occurred to Ralphie. Could he not also become a man who guided aero pilots through the skies?

Brown's look turned serious, seemingly reading the boy's mind. "What do you want to be when you grow up?"

"I don't know, sir." Looking through thick glasses, he reflexively glanced at his crippled leg and special boots.

Brown instantly sized up the situation. "Now, you listen to me, Ralphie. Don't worry yourself about that leg. As you get older, you'll find that it is just something you must get used to and not let it get in the way of things. Set your mind on a goal and stick hard to it. If you do, why, you should be able to do almost anything you want." He paused, giving the boy an encouraging smile. "Will you remember that?"

The boy stared back, not saying a word. Brown pressed the matter. "Do you believe me, Ralphie?"

"Yes, sir," the boy mumbled as he stared at the ground. Then suddenly, a moment later, he raised his head, "Oh, sir, I want to believe you." Another moment passed, and then his face lit up. "I do believe you!"

"Good fellow," Brown said gently, letting his hand rest on the boy's shoulder. "I'm very glad." Then his voice turned businesslike. "Now, my boy, I've got to get back to work. Perhaps I'll see you another time before we go." He gave Ralphie's shoulder a tender squeeze, then stumped back to his mates and the *Vimy* flying machine.

Ralphie watched him and the other men for some time longer before making himself go home to supper. On some level, he understood this encounter would become one of the most important moments in his life. To himself, he kept repeating over and over, "I believe you, Left-tenant Brown. I can do most anything I want."

* * *

Alcock and Brown were convinced the *Vimy*'s window of opportunity was rapidly closing. Two days earlier, Jack had made one last, surreptitious attempt to pump information out of his old friend Major Brackley when he and Ted journeyed to Harbour Grace to watch the Handley Page make another test hop. But Admiral Kerr had imposed an ironclad gag order, and an uncomfortable "Brackles" could only silently shake his head. When he returned to St. John's, Alcock told his team to be ready on a moment's notice; if necessary, the *Vimy* would take off at the first hint the Handley Page was about to depart.

Alcock did note one very important detail that gave him a bit of comfort. His keen, professional eye as a mechanic and self-taught engineer had told him the complicated four-engine monster was giving the admiral's men more problems than any of them were willing to acknowledge.

During the second test flight that Thursday morning, and to Ted's enormous frustration and utter embarrassment, the wireless packed it in yet again. The apparatus had worked for a time, but then the transmitter insulation failed, giving Brown a violent shock. Mercifully for Brown's eardrums, Alcock's expletive-filled tirade had been largely drowned out by the drumming Eagle engines. Uncharacteristically, the pilot was still upset after finishing their prescribed test regimen thirty minutes later, and the subsequent landing was not one of his best. Neither man could bring himself to mention the wireless during the otherwise positive postflight discussion.

While the tension and stress had continued to mount, Superintendent Percy Muller was nevertheless pleased with the project's progress. Muller was especially proud of the marvelous effort the ground men were making—a month, earlier he'd not thought it possible the *Vimy* could be ready this soon. Yes, his executives had been the day-to-day decision-makers, but it had been Westcott, the general handyman; Davis, the radiator specialist; Potter and Crouch, mechanic/riggers; and Humm, Wand, and Chick, the carpenters, that had literally done the heavy lifting. Bob Dicker recalled years later: "What a grand lot of lads we had—never a moan or grumble despite the fact that conditions were far below home standards."

At this point, the eastern coast of Newfoundland was busting at the seams with flying fever. The public had become as nearly "air mad" as the aviators themselves. In addition to the numerous curiosity seekers and reporters, the Atlantic race had also attracted a number of notable foreign aero men. Not long after Hawker and Grieve were rescued and the *Vimy* leapt to the top rank of remaining competitors, Ted Brown had the opportunity to meet a young US naval aviator named Lieutenant Commander Richard E. Byrd. The American had come to Newfoundland to observe the NC flying boats launch for Europe, his interest accentuated by having recently built a "bubble sextant," a specifically designed aeronautical sextant with a built-in "level bubble." L. B. Booth of the Royal Aircraft Establishment at Farnborough was developing a similar instrument, what became the RAE Bubble Sextant Mark VI, but it was not yet available. The periscopic sextant would be developed much later, beginning in the late 1940s. It mounted through the overhead of a *pressurized* transport or bomber where it could safely be inserted and retracted, clear of obstructions, eliminating the plexiglass dome and its distortions. With the advent of higher jet speeds, this streamlining advance became essential.

Brown would later write, "[Byrd and I] had an interesting talk on the problems and difficulties of aerial navigation." At the time, Ted wondered if he might secure a Byrd sextant for his Atlantic flight. Byrd agreed, wiring the US Navy in Washington asking them to send one. The Navy obliged, "but unfortunately, owing to transportation difficulties, it reached St. John's after our departure." Brown was nevertheless appreciative of the gesture, and in the end, it took away a bit of the underlying British animosity, at least in Ted's eyes, toward the American flyers. Brown would later reflect when he read of Byrd's 1920s exploration triumphs in the polar regions how much easier it would have been to have had either a Byrd or RAE bubble sextant rather than his jury-rigged Abney level/Brandis.

With the *Vimy* fully assembled and the machine in its final testing stages, many of the Vickers men found themselves with more spare time. Evenings were spent playing cards or visiting the neighboring film cinemas. When circumstances allowed, Alcock and Brown sometimes joined in. In order to talk privately with one another or simply play tourist, Jack and Ted enjoyed exploring the hilly streets of what they both considered a quaint New World fishing village. Ted once gave a local reporter a glimpse into their stress-relieving jaunts. "We are able to recognize parts of [St. John's] with eyes closed and nostrils open. The closer we are to the quays and wharfs, the stronger the scent of drying, very dead cod."

Increasingly, there were problems with the local rubberneckers, some of whom appeared to have no other occupation than to pester the flyers, spending hours each day leaning against the fence and ropes the team was forced to erect around the *Vimy*. It wouldn't have been so bad if it had just been benign curiosity. Alcock caught one fellow inexplicably holding a lighted cigar against a wing. When Jack shouted at him to stop, the man began shouting obscenities. Others felt compelled, when the Vickers men were distracted, to cluster next to the lower wing's trailing edges and manipulate the ailerons. Another favorite trick was to test the firmness of the machine's fabric by poking at it with the point of an umbrella. A few were determined to pass along their advice. One morning, Monty Montgomery was asked in rather high-handed fashion if it was true Alcock and Brown intended not to drop their undercarriage after takeoff. When informed that was so, the man harrumphed, prophesying that such neglect was sure to lead to catastrophe.

Nevertheless, rain and wind remained the primary enemy. It was a bit easier now that the heavy work was finished, but the *Vimy* had still to be left out in the open. Most of the work those last days had been centered on ensuring the machine was properly serviced and maintained for the test flights. In addition to carefully filtering the petrol and engine oil, the radiator water for the two Rolls-Royce engines also had to be filtered and boiled to remove impurities. One afternoon, this latter procedure gave Jack a long-overdue opportunity to indulge his joy in pranking.

"What is it you are boiling there, Mr. Alcock?" asked a particularly annoying bystander.

With a wink at Teddie, Jack turned to address the little man. "Why, I thought it was common knowledge that one must boil aero engine petrol in order to remove all the water and other impurities."

The fellow nodded sagely, then decided to let these high-handed Brits, with all their fine talk, know just how much he really understood about flying matters. Pointing at the midsection of the fuselage, he stated, "Now, Mr. Alcock, is that not where you store the gas to make the machine lighter?"

Alcock had all he could do to control himself. Brown and the others turned their faces away and waited for it.

"Right you are, sir!" Jack exclaimed. "We managed to cobble together a supply of precious hydrogen from none other than Count Zeppelin's personal reserves, hidden somewhere in Germany. You mustn't breathe a word now—His Majesty's government would be most embarrassed."

Of course, the fellow could not return to his circle of friends fast enough to share this valuable intelligence. All the Vickers men within earshot ducked behind the *Vimy* and broke into convulsions. It was that kind of thing that Alcock always managed to pull out of his hat to relieve the enormous strain within the team.

* * *

Later, that Thursday evening of June 12, back at the Cochrane, Alcock and Brown would give a serious interview to the handful of newspapermen who'd pitched in to help ready the *Vimy*. It was a special reward the fellows would appreciate; the race to be first across the Atlantic had become the most important story in the English-speaking world.

New York Times reporter: "Captain Alcock, could you explain to our readers why you are so willing to risk your very life on such a hazardous venture?"

Alcock, smoking a rare pipe: "You must understand that nearly ten years ago I chose to devote my life to advancing the science of flight. That takes a total commitment—all in, you might say. As opposed, that is, to a factory worker, clerk, or advertising office man who is able to check his cares at the shop or office door each evening. This flying gets into and stays within one's bloodstream. Once infected by the flying bug, it becomes incurable." He grinned, a turn of phrase having occurred to him. "You might say we pilots fly to live, not live to fly."

Brown: "Then too, gentlemen, you must understand most of us in this game have spent years at war and have come to view the Grim Reaper as an old acquaintance. While one never gets 'used to' danger, in the classic sense, one learns to manage his emotions so that great goals and new breakthroughs in the human endeavor may be achieved."

London Daily Mail, not fully satisfied with those answers: "Yes, of course, we all are quite aware what brave fellows you are and your commitment to the flying machine. However, during the war there was no choice but to risk life and limb. Now that, somehow, you've survived that horrible slaughter, one would think that life had become so dear you'd shudder at the idea of risking all merely for glory and prize money."

Alcock bristled: "It isn't the money or glory that ultimately drives us, though of course we are human enough to want recognition for work in our field of endeavor, just like any other man. Human beings have, I think, a built-in instinct to explore the unknown, to solve big engineering problems that have vexed man since the time of Noah and his Ark. A few of us are chosen to be the point of that spear, to lead the way. By definition, such a role is usually the most physically dangerous." Unusually eloquent that day, he paused to further collect his thoughts. "As for the prize money, you must realize that Vickers and ourselves have incurred many financial obligations to our creditors and to our faithful workmen, carpenters, and mechanics."

Brown, chiming in with a sly smile: "Of course, Jacko and I *are* hopeful there might be a guinea or two left over for a new flying adventure and perhaps even a couple of West End shows!"

General laughter, with even Alcock grinning.

Manchester Guardian: "Your hometown readers are, quite naturally, very proud of you both. There is one thing. Many have written us wondering . . . How shall I put it?" He struggled to frame the question before finally blurting, "How it is you fellows are to deal with calls of nature?"

After a round of raucous laughter, Alcock responded. "Well, that's no problem at all. Teddie and I have decided we shall just hold it!" More laughter. "You see," Jack deadpanned, "we flyers have special powers of concentration." It took a couple of minutes for everyone to pull themselves together after that one.

Chicago Tribune: "You Brits seem to be far ahead of everyone else in this non-stop flying business, though of course the US Navy has, in fact, already made the first actual crossing. Still, America's machines haven't demonstrated the long-distance capabilities England appears to have. How do you account for that, and what do you see coming in the future?"

Fielding the question for both men, Brown's mien turned suddenly serious: "As I think most of you gentlemen are aware, I was born an American and have always retained a very soft spot for my home country."

Adding in a rather emotional aside, he said, "When the war came to Britain, I felt compelled to serve what had become my treasured adoptive country, a nation where I had grown to manhood. That decision, however, came at much personal cost. Emotionally, it was very hard to give up my American citizenship."

Ted regained his composure, reflexively slipping back into his customary professorial tone. "The United States, frankly and despite the aeroplane having been invented there, was quite tardy in getting serious about flying machines. This was demonstrated most clearly during the war. Very few US manufactured planes ever arrived on the Western Front; the great majority of American wartime pilots flew French machines. Again, very frankly, while the crews of the US Navy flying boats made an especially gallant and important contribution to the advancement of over-ocean navigation, non-stop Atlantic crossings by American machines are currently not feasible. Having said that, however, I am quite certain US aviation will soon catch up. It simply is inevitable, what with your enormous technological capability and know-how." He allowed himself a sardonic grin. "I daresay our long-distance British flights will thoroughly arouse your red-blooded American flying fraternity!"

Another appreciative round of laughter by the American correspondents, forced smiles from British Empire scribes. Even the newspapermen were feeling the national competition tension. Alcock announced they had time for one last question.

Toronto Star: "What are your plans if you make it across?"

Alcock, snapping at the fellow: "You mean *when* we make it across." Although the man quickly corrected himself, Alcock continued in a cold monotone, making clear this was indeed the last question. "Left-tenant Brown and I have given almost no thought to anything other than working as hard as we can to win this race. We shall simply have to let matters take their natural course once we arrive in Ireland. Thank you, gentlemen, and good evening."

* * *

With Lieutenant Birdie Clare's tireless assistance that same Thursday afternoon, Ted Brown once more repaired the wireless connections, with the two men conducting a series of successful follow-up tests. Brown fervently prayed the maddening glitches were behind them. While he and Alcock were on their way back to the Cochrane to talk to the reporters, he'd found himself chuckling over an incident that happened moments before the *Vimy* took off earlier that morning. Jack had taken notice of a group of giggling young girls just behind the roped-off area, the same who had been following the flyers around for some time. It seemed the teenagers could not make up their minds whether their intentions should be provocative dares or outright flirtations, and in the end, it became something of an in-between soup. Just before the flight test, and in between shared squeals, they began shouting near-taunts.

"Oh, look, girls," exclaimed one anonymous female voice. "Is Mr. Al-COCK finally ready to give us a thrill?" Screeching laughter was still hanging in the air when the huge four-bladed propellers turned over and the engines came to life. Jack, who had heard every catcall, winked at Brown and shouted in his ear, "Grab hold of something solid, Teddie. I'm about to give them their thrill!"

With that, the pilot manipulated the top throttle knob, advancing the port engine to maximum revolutions and leaving the starboard at idle. The *Vimy*'s nose whipped viciously to the right, lining it up in the takeoff position and conveniently putting the giggling bevy directly in trail of the machine. Almost in the same motion, Jack returned the knob to both engines at full ahead, sending a hurricane-force gale past the aeroplane's stern. The girls' hilarity instantly turned to shrieks as dresses billowed up over heads, exposing entire arrays of underpinnings. John Alcock could barely manage the takeoff, he was laughing so hard.

By the time the sun settled low in the sky on that Thursday, June 12, the Vickers team had declared themselves satisfied the *Vimy* was ready for the Atlantic attempt. After Alcock and Brown returned to the Cochrane and had finished their interview with the correspondents, they began besieging RAF Lieutenant Laurence Clements for local and north Atlantic weather reports. Besides those official duties, Clements had also volunteered to assume the duties of the absent Major Partridge—for reasons never made clear—as the official starter for the Royal Aero Club. It would be Lieutenant Clements's duty to affix the club's official seals on the *Vimy* just prior to departure, ensuring the crew could not cheat by flying from Newfoundland in one aeroplane and landing in Ireland in another, no matter such a feat in the 72-hour time frame allowed with the same crew would be a more extraordinary achievement than the one they were attempting!

The weather reports were quite encouraging, which had the odd effect of making a very fatigued Alcock and Brown even more apprehensive. Only hours earlier, information had arrived suggesting the Handley Page at Harbour Grace was also ready to go, though there were also unconfirmed whispers of new and serious radiator problems. It was indeed going to be a restless night.

6:00 a.m. Local Time,
Friday the 13th, June 1919

A courier had just brought Alcock and Brown encouraging weather reports from Lieutenant Clements at Mount Pearl—a virtually clean bill of health for St. John's and the mid-Atlantic. That was enough for Jack. "Teddy," he said excitedly over a hurried breakfast of eggs and toast. "It's a topping morning, and this is our lucky day!"

The two men hurried to Lester's Field and issued a flurry of instructions. Working at breakneck speeds, the aperiodic compass was carefully swung one final time. Brown's Appleyard course and distance calculator, sextant, dead reckoning kit, drift bearing plate, and Baker navigation machine with Ted's Mercator chart overlays were placed inside the storage compartment under the crew bench. Emergency rations were loaded into the tail's store cupboard. Ted would keep a battery-powered electric torch and Very pistol, armed with red and white flares, within easy reach. Food and drink were to be placed in the cockpit just prior to takeoff.

News of Alcock and Brown's imminent departure spread like an American prairie fire. By 8:30 A.M., a huge crowd of perhaps two to three thousand locals milled around Le Marchant Road and in the small meadow between Campbell Avenue and Mundy Pond, where just to the west rested the *Vimy* on Mr. Lester's prairie. All were greatly excited, indeed enthralled, to be eyewitnesses to a world-watched event. No longer would their remote city be a backwater, but instead, the gateway to intercontinental air travel!

As the day wore on, however, it became clear Alcock had been much too optimistic about getting away that day. To begin with, it took all morning for several men to fill the petrol tanks. And then Bob Dicker, who had been

The large crowd at Lester's field on Friday, June 13. (The Rooms Provincial Archives, St. John's, Newfoundland)

standing with Ted Brown casually observing the refueling, realized with mounting horror that the *Vimy*'s starboard dual-wheels were giving way. Dicker had no more than shouted a warning when that right-side undercarriage shock absorber collapsed under the added weight of the petrol, and the machine promptly sagged to one side. All work stopped instantly as everyone looked on in stupefaction. Alcock was the first to recover his senses. "Right, there's nothing to be done but lighten the machine and replace the shock. You men," he pointed at the mechanics pumping petrol, "start drawing it off." Curtly cutting off the groans, Jack barked, "Everyone hop to it smartly!" It would take most of the afternoon to finish the repair and install new elastic shock absorbers on both undercarriages.

Montgomery told Alcock he would use the extra time to give the aeroplane a last coat of "dope." A type of clear lacquer, dope was applied over all fabric-covered flying machines to stiffen the canvas-like material and render it waterproof. "The delay is a bit of a silver lining, Jackie. I didn't want to lay down another burden—you were so determined to leave today, and I was prepared to let it go. But the *Vimy* really did need another coat. I'll breathe easier now."

Smiling tightly, Alcock gripped Monty's shoulder appreciatively. Jack had once told Teddie that problems with flying machines were like bananas—they came in bunches. One had to learn to roll with the blows or he'd go crackers. Only the night before, Alcock had finally been told the buoyant lifesaving suits ordered from the United States, specifically designed for use in emergency water landings, had not yet arrived. Long afterward, it was discovered the suits had been misdelivered to the Bank of Montreal labeled as typewriters and put into cellar storage! Fortunately, Percy Muller's foresight mitigated the situation. On a whim, the superintendent had brought along two wartime Mary Evans Grieve lifesaving waistcoats with inflatable tubes, which had been developed for torpedoed ship victims and named after the inventor.

Alcock and Brown went to bed at 7 P.M. on Friday evening. The already desperately overworked mechanics and riggers volunteered to remain with the *Vimy* all night to not only act as guards but to get the machine fully prepared by morning. Pure cooling water had to be poured into the two engine's radiators, the Rolls' oil reservoirs filled to the brim, and all seven petrol tanks completely refueled—a laborious and time-consuming process. The Shell B was pumped from barrels through a double-filtered funnel of chamois and a fine copper wire mesh to catch impurities. While tedious, the careful procedure eliminated the need for dedicated engine petrol filters. The ground crewmen worked by the light of several motorcar headlamps, supplemented when needed with paraffin flares. When Jack and Ted arrived back at Lester's Field at 3:30 A.M. on Saturday, June 14, the *Vimy* was ready to be positioned for the start.

"Well, Percy, how do we look?" a still-yawning Alcock asked. Not surprisingly, both flyers had a restless night and were still a bit groggy.

"Everything's ready with the machine, Jack," Muller said, speaking for assembly boss Monty Montgomery, foreman carpenter Ernie Pitman, Bob Dicker on flying controls, and Rolls-Royce's man Bob Lyons. The entire senior staff of Vickers aviation had arrived an hour earlier to make absolutely sure every "I" had been dotted and "T" crossed. "But I must tell you," Percy continued, "I am quite concerned about weather conditions." A gusting wind of increasing strength had been sweeping across the field for over an hour.

Those words had no more than left Muller's mouth when an astonished-looking Monty Montgomery barked out a "Good Lord!" He was pointing at a large black cat, its tail held high in a question-mark curve as it strutted across the nose of their flying machine.

Jack chortled. "Marvelous! A fine omen! We needed something positive to offset our inability to takeoff on Friday the Thirteenth."

Querulous looks flew Alcock's way. Brown stepped in. "Gentleman, allow me to explain. Captain Alcock considers thirteen his lucky number, especially when it falls on a Friday."

After allowing a few delicious moments for the others to ponder such heresy, Ted continued. "Our Jackie first became obsessed with flying at age thirteen. He entered and won his first air race in 1913. Jack was awarded the Distinguished Service Cross at aged 2 X 13, or 26. He was freed as a prisoner of war after thirteen months of confinement. The two of us reached St. John's on May 13. The *Vimy* arrived in St. John's on 2 X 13, or May 26. Alas, we had hoped to depart for Ireland on Friday the Thirteenth." He brightened. "But now, of course, the black tabby has redeemed all!"

After the laughter died down, a rather smug-looking Brown put a period on it all. "Furthermore, as you must know, we have our two insurance policies in place." Teddie was referring to their "good luck" black cat doll mascots. He later described their appearance: "Lucky Jim wore an enormous head, an untidy ribbon, and a hopeful expression; whereas Twinkle Toes was dainty and diminutive, and, from the tip of her upright tail to the tip of her stuffed nose, expressed surprise and anxiety." Brown would tuck Kay's feminine kitten—he could not help but think it was so like her—inside his flying suit, while Jack's alley cat, Lucky Jim, found himself bound to a wing strut above the cockpit, a windswept aerial sailor lashed to the mast.

Earlier, during the hour before Alcock and Brown had arrived at Lester's Field, Monty Montgomery and Davis, on behalf of the mechanics, had surreptitiously placed delicate bouquets of Newfoundland white heather in the cockpit. Mechanics Potter and Couch had tacked a horseshoe under Alcock's seat for luck without it ever occurring to either of them how angry Jack would've been if he knew two more pounds of

Mascots Lucky Jim (left) and Twinkle Toes (right). (Science Museum Group)

deadweight Percheron horseshoe had been added to his already critically overloaded flying machine!

At 4:30 A.M., weather expert Lieutenant Clements gave Brown a chart showing the expected strength and direction of the Atlantic winds aloft, informing the flyers that "overall conditions were favorable" for the attempt. However, he noted, surface winds at Lester's Field had gotten stronger overnight, with variable gusting from the southwest and west. It was clear an immediate departure risked encountering a sudden, strong crosswind, the very circumstance that had led to Freddie Raynham's ruin. The decision was made to wait a few hours in hopes the wind would die down.

Alcock was too excited to remain idle in the interim. The pilot climbed into the cockpit and, with the wheels chocked solidly in place and the mechanics holding tightly to the wings, ran up the engines. It was odd, Ted pondered, as he watched the propellers whir, what went through a person's head at such a moment. He was thinking of one morning at breakfast when he and Jack had gotten into a discussion with Bob Lyons about the origins of the now universally accepted word "cockpit." For once, John Alcock held the upper hand in the long-hair department. "It dates from the 1700s. The man who steered a boat sat in a shallow, pit-like opening in the sailing vessel's lower deck and was called a coxswain [pronounced KOK-suhn], a term aviators morphed into the word 'cockpit.'"

Alcock shut down the engines and bounced down from the cockpit like a ten-year-old boy, crowing to Bob Lyons and Percy Muller, "Those Eagles are purring like well-fed British lions!"

A brief discussion ensued about re-topping off the fuel tanks, but it was decided so little petrol had been burned it wasn't necessary. The final preparations then continued on a more prosaic level. As Ted later wrote, "our personal luggage" was hoisted aboard. That term stretched the point—the luggage consisted solely of their toilet kits and food supplies. Ted had chosen to wear his smartly tailored RAF lieutenant's uniform; Jack had selected a rather nondescript, blue serge civilian suit. Both men had donned dress white shirts and dark ties. The heated flying boots and suits; inflatable Grieve waistcoats; fur-lined gloves and flying helmets; and goggles would be worn over their street clothes.

Agnes Dooley had carefully prepared four ham and beef sandwiches, supplemented by several packages of Fry's Milk Chocolate bars, all of which had now been placed aboard the *Vimy*. Agnes had insisted on walking with Alcock out to the Buick Tourer as Jack and Ted prepared to leave the Cochrane for the last time. After the two spoke quietly, she gave him a quick kiss on the cheek, then fled back into the hotel. Ted Brown was quite convinced he'd seen a tear or two in her eye.

In a cockpit corner, Monty Montgomery stowed four bottles of Guinness Stout and two Ferrostat Vacuum Flasks housed in a leather case—one filled with hot coffee; the other nutritious, premixed Horlicks malted beverage. Oxo beef stock cubes in a tin were also available to mix with the Horlicks, if so desired. The fellows had determined that the flight almost surely would not exceed twenty hours and drew the line at including any more food provisions. There was the delicate matter of bodily functions to consider; liquid refreshment was one thing, solid food quite another. Without getting into any detail with the press, Alcock and Brown had quietly devised a system that would allow them to urinate in a glass jar, with the contents dumped overboard after each use.

The all-important gray mailbag was stenciled in black letters
ST. JOHN'S
NFLD
N.P.O.
and had been stowed in the *Vimy* the day before. The St. John's postal authorities embossed 197 private letters with a special "$1.00 Trans-Atlantic Air-Post 1919" inked handstamp overlayed on a regular fifteen-cent postage stamp in recognition of the first airmail to cross the ocean. If the flight were successful, all 197 letters were sure to become collector's items. One of them was from Alcock to his younger sister, who had faithfully written and sent food parcels while he was a Turkish prisoner:

> *My dear Elsie,*
>   *Just a hurried line before we start. This letter will travel with me in the official mailbag, the first mail to be carried over the Atlantic. Love to all.*
>   *Your loving brother,*
>   *Jack*

Ted Brown enclosed a letter to Kay, which he never revealed, and another to an old friend that he later made public:

> *S. Blackley, Room 608*
> *Imperial House, Kingsway, London*
> *10-6-19*
> *Dear Blackley,*
>   *Just a note by aerial post to thank you for your cable, and to thank you for the letter you wrote to New Zealand. I hope to be back in London soon, and to see you before you get this.*
>   *Yours, A. W. Brown*

At 6:00 A.M., Lieutenant Clements affixed the official Royal Aero Club seals near the trailing edge of the lower right wing, close to the fuselage.

Lieutenant Clements (right) affixes the official Royal Aero Club seals. (The Rooms Provincial Archives, St. John's Newfoundland)

By 9:00 A.M., much to everyone's dismay, the winds had still not died down. But by that time, Alcock and Brown had openly resolved to leave this day, *no matter what.* The very idea of the Handley Page getting away first, with the *Vimy* ready to go, had become unthinkable for the two men. So much so, they bluntly refused to discuss it further. In their stubborn resolve, they were allowing outside forces to determine their takeoff parameters rather than the overall suitability of weather, themselves, and the machine. The two flyers had fallen into the same trap that had overcome Raynham and Morgan. At some level, they must have understood this, but with the prize so tantalizingly close, whatever caution they might otherwise have exercised had been figuratively blown away by the gusty winds.

Their dramatic announcement, however, was too much for Percy Muller. He promptly took center stage and resolutely decreed, "Gentlemen, I forbid you to make the attempt! A takeoff under these conditions is tantamount to suicide."

Alcock and Brown were momentarily stunned by the finality of the pronouncement. Seeing his life's dream slipping away, Jack launched into an impassioned rebuttal. For ten minutes, the pilot marshaled every reason he could think of as to why they simply *had* to make the attempt—cajoling, begging, pleading, and even praying for Percy to change his mind. It soon became clear that Alcock's furious onslaught was hitting the mark; the super's resolve began to waver. The turning point came when Muller realized he stood alone; his senior management and the mechanics were with Jack—every one of them wild-eyed, keen to go. It was simply inconceivable that after all the worry, sweat, and treasure already expended, the team should slope away with their tails between their legs. Indeed, for all anyone knew, the Handley Page might already be on its way. *They simply had to try!*

"Very well, Jack," a subdued Muller finally conceded. "I'll take responsibility for the start. If conditions do not worsen further, you may go."

The terrible tension dissolved as quickly as it'd appeared. Attention immediately turned to the most crucial pre-takeoff decision remaining. Which direction should they make the run, easterly or westerly?

Alcock turned to Brown. "What do you think?"

Ted reflexively reached for his pipe. It was Jack's prerogative as ship's captain to make the call, but they were to equally share the danger. After all, this extremely dangerous takeoff would, in all likelihood, be the most hazardous phase of their entire flight. As a matter of fact, for some time, the takeoff *itself* had become the elephant in the room. A Vickers *Vimy* had never before attempted anything near such an over-gross weight takeoff and certainly not with such dangerous crosswinds on a rocky, hilly surface like Lester's Field.

"The book says," Brown began in his usual thoughtful manner, "always make the run head to wind, which for us means a hard pull uphill generally westerly. However, I'm not certain we have enough power to climb it and lift off before running out of field. Taking off to the east would be downhill, but with a 30 to 40 mph wind at our backs, we might have as much or more trouble reaching flying airspeed as in the opposite direction." With a 35-mile wind at their back and a running speed over the ground of 35 mph, their airspeed would be exactly zero. "It's the devil's choice, Jacko."

Alcock grunted. "Anybody else have anything to say?" The group was silent; even a hard glance at Percy Muller failed to get a reaction. On one of their greatest gambles, the Aviation Department of Vickers Ltd. was committing the success of the venture—perhaps even the fate of that arm itself, so great was this throw of the dice—to the sole judgment of Captain John Alcock, the best of their test pilots.

"Let's get the machine up to the west end and ready for an easterly run," Jack said, "see how the wing and tail surfaces react to the wind when in position." He added hopefully, "Perhaps by then it will have died down a bit."

Twenty minutes later, and with the indispensable aid of all thirteen Vickers men and some thirty to forty of Lester's men, reporters, and willing onlookers—all pushing uphill—the nearly seven-ton aeroplane was in position. But ten minutes after that, with momentary gusts registering as high as 45 mph off the tail, the unstable effect on the wing and control surfaces plus the near impossibility of achieving flying speed made it abundantly clear an easterly departure was out of the question.

"I'm very sorry, chaps," Jack yelled over the wind to his equally winded ground crew. "We have no choice; it's got to be a head to wind takeoff." Preparations were made to push the machine the 400-plus yards to the opposite end of Lester's Field.

At least it was downhill to the east end, though the ground had not yet been cleared of banana bunches. Percy Muller was the first to spot trouble. "Look out for that drag rope!" A violent gust had wrapped a loose rope round the undercarriage, and before anyone could say Jack Robinson, the unstoppable, heavy machine rolled through it, tightening one of the wheels against a petrol supply pipe and crushing it. Alcock was too numb to curse at yet another piece of rotten luck. Surprisingly, there was little griping—it had now become, for the grimly determined group of Vickers men and their ground volunteers, an almost do or die situation. After the *Vimy* was chocked into its into-the-wind takeoff position, the mechanics got to work on replacing the pipe.

"That's it, lads," Jack said an hour later. "Peg her down tight. All we can do now is wait out the winds."

A few minutes before noon, Brown and Lieutenant Clements huddled. Using his precisely accurate official timepiece, Clements gave Ted a countdown to an exact "time-tick" on Brown's second-setting Military Pocket Watch. When Clements said, "Now!" Brown started the Mark V. Even an error of ten seconds could result in a celestial fix error of five or more miles.

Shortly thereafter, Percy, Monty, Pitman, Dicker, and Lyons, along with the seven Vickers carpenters, mechanics, and fitters, sat down in the pasture grass around Alcock and Brown. Mingled in among them were perhaps a dozen reporters from America, Canada, and Europe, busily jotting notes about the proceedings, not all of which were being faithfully recorded; the impulse to embellish stories sometimes became irresistible. The mood was convivial, the bantering light, for nothing more could be done to get the flying machine ready. Radiator specialist Davis and general handyman Westcott took it upon themselves to distribute the large picnic lunch of beef tongue, cheese, bread, potted meats, and coffee. Several local boys, anxious to be a part of the proceedings, busied themselves retrieving caps and other odds and ends regularly blown away by the wind. Spellbound, the lads could not have been shooed away from the unfolding drama for anything in the world.

Beyond the roped-off area, erected and policed by St. John's officials, were no more than a couple of hundred onlookers, but a fraction of the crowd on Friday. The strong winds and miserable conditions had convinced most there couldn't possibly be a takeoff today. The truly fanatical had shown up, of course, voicing their usual shouts of encouragement, along with the occasional, mean-spirited catcall. An English reporter later wrote: "A few very vocal Jonahs were shouting gloomy prophecies of the two men's fate."

With the Vickers men and reporters down to their post-lunch tea and coffee, and the parties increasingly mixed together, the individual conversation ranging from the weighty to the mundane. A couple of New York newspapermen plopped down on the grass next to Brown, who they would report to their readers "was in high spirits."

"With this wind," Ted was saying with an air of bonhomie while biting into a hard-boiled egg, "if it continues all the way, we shall be in

Alcock loading the last of the provisions. (Wikimedia Commons)

Ireland in twelve hours. I'll be steering a straight line for Galway Bay and, although I shall do my best, I do not expect to strike it off exactly."

Nearby, Alcock was breezily chatting away with another clutch of newspapermen. "This wind today amuses me," he said with more bravado than he likely felt. "In the very early days, long before the war taught us what flying really is, we used to scatter pieces of paper, and if they blew away, we would not dream of taking a bus out."

Several of the scribblers looked at each other, faces telegraphing their thoughts. This gale was strong enough to blow his entire flying machine away. Perhaps those Jonahs in the crowd weren't such alarmists after all. Several reporters silently congratulated themselves for already completing their "flying fools" obituaries. In the event, there would be a terrific scramble for Mount Pearl, and he who first arrived with his copy ready for transmission would get the scoop.

At noon, Ted Brown sauntered over to Jack's side and said *sotto voce*, "I'm making a trip to the bog." The carpenters had built a discrete sanitary facility adjacent to the storage tent, appearing from the outside to be a tool shed.

"I'll be right behind you," Jack responded.

When they were finished, several of the mechanics helped Alcock and Brown wiggle into their heated flying suits, put on the Grieve inflatable belts, and don heated, fur-lined boots, which, like leggings, protected everything up to their knees. Ted ensured all the electrical connections for both suits were in proper order and ready to be plugged in once they were both seated at their stations. The specially fitted earpieces and "microphone" transmitters, a new innovation that would allow them to communicate by "telephone," were also connected. Alcock sent Westcott to confirm both sets of fur-lined caps and gloves, along with goggles, were waiting on the cockpit seating bench.

At 12:45 P.M., Captain Alcock abruptly stood up and gazed skyward, as if he were a bloodhound who'd just stumbled across a fresh scent. Lieutenant Clements, seemingly on cue, was walking toward him. Jack waited for the weatherman's official forecasts to confirm what he'd been thinking. "Surface winds rapidly diminishing to 20-25 miles per hour, with occasional gusts up to 30," Clements reported. "I can't say they'll lay off much more, but it is a definite improvement." The lieutenant smiled. "The latest reports indicate conditions are also improving over the North Atlantic." The weatherman's expression grew serious when he glanced at the direction the *Vimy* was pointing—the takeoff heading. "You are still going to have a wicked quartering crosswind from the south."

Alcock agreed, his experienced eye having been carefully reassessing the field ever since he sensed the winds were dying down. "Monty!" he suddenly yelled.

Montgomery came jogging over to the clutch of key players gathered around Alcock and Brown. "Yes, Jack?"

"What would you say we pivot the machine about five or ten degrees more to the left, just a bit more southerly? See if we can't cut down on this bleedin' crosswind component?" Alcock's mind was racing. "I want to run as close to the ditch edge as possible." The senior Vickers team had planned for the aeroplane to roll across the middle of a 100-foot filled-in section of Lester's drainage ditch. Jack wanted to get the nose more directly into the wind, but he knew that by getting closer to the ditch the slightest misjudgment of ground-roll path could lead to disaster.

"Percy and I can run down there for a quick look," Montgomery said.

"Take the Buick. Check how firm the soil is close to the drop-off," Jack instructed. He raised his voice for all to hear. "Attention, everybody. Prepare for takeoff! Reporters, return to the civilian side of the ropes immediately!"

The Vickers ground crew sprang into action while a rising ground-swell of excitement rose from the small band of hardy onlookers, those few who had not assumed wind conditions this Saturday would make an attempt impossible. Newspapermen were scribbling ever more hurriedly in their notebooks as the climactic moment drew closer. Everyone present fell silent, understanding they were standing witness to a world-historic moment. It would be something to pass on to one's children, grandchildren, and beyond.

At that moment, Brown discovered his handheld battery light had failed, likely from dead cells. He shouted across the rope line, "Has anyone an electric torch?" When he noticed a wide array of blank expressions, it dawned on him. "A flashlight!" A Mr. Klamber from one of the New York papers raised a hand, shouting back, "I have one!" A grateful Brown grasped the light with one hand and shook the fellow's hand with the other. "Thanks very much," he said with a wide smile. "Shouldn't want to start out without one of these."

Montgomery and Percy Muller came rattling back to the *Vimy*. Alcock and Brown were standing next to the fuselage of the machine. "Jack," said an out-of-breath Percy. "The soil appears firm nearly to the edge, but of course, there can be no guarantees." He paused. "Monty and I agree we can let you have five more degrees to the left, but absolutely no more." He looked very worried.

Alcock flashed his signature smile. "I'll take the five and be grateful for it!" The pilot turned to Monty's men. "We are going to reposition the machine five degrees left. Left tenant Brown will supervise." The almost imperceptible adjustment was quickly completed.

Jack took a very deep breath. "Teddie," he murmured, "if we don't go right now, we probably never will."

Brown said enthusiastically, "Next stop, Ireland!"

Without further ado, Alcock and Brown solemnly shook hands with Lieutenant Clements, Bob Lyons, and all the Vickers executives gathered round. Fred Raynham, who would not have missed this moment for the world, was hanging back, as if not to intrude. Alcock and Brown were having none of that as they stepped over to their treasured friend.

"Thanks for everything, Freddie," Jack said, a catch in his voice. Ted clasped Fred's paw firmly, smiling warmly.

Putting on a brave front, a deeply disappointed Raynham replied, "Good luck."

Alcock said quietly, "See you in London, old fellow. Dinner's on me."

With that, the two flyers clambered aboard their trans-Atlantic aeroplane. It was 1:10 P.M. local.

Alcock crawled into the cockpit first, scuttling across the bench to the starboard side, with Brown following. Ted sat down on Jack's immediate left, their shoulders rubbing as they settled in. Bob Dicker, Alcock's trusted prewar friend, had earlier carefully pre-checked the controls and instrumentation, as well as tidied up the cockpit. He'd also ensured all of Ted's navigation equipment was either in the bench storage compartment or set in its proper place.

Unlike the coldly minimalist, gray/black cockpits that were to come, the *Vimy*'s more resembled the warm décor of a British gentleman's drawing room. The various dials, meters, switches, levers, fuel valves, and knobs making up the dashboard were all mounted on a wood fascia varnished to a golden brown. The floor, or more properly the deck, was also wood paneled but with hardier materials and given several more coats than the dashboard on account of heavier foot traffic. The padded leather bench was finished in yet two more tones of brown—all of it exuding a richness that belied the cockpit's prosaic function. Knobs and switches were made of brass; the four-spoked, black-ribbed, auto-style control wheel appeared more likely in the cockpit of a racing motorcar. Ted had become accustomed to the bare-bones aeroplane control stations of the B.E. 2c "Quirk" variety, and when he climbed into the *Vimy* for the first time, he found himself stepping gingerly, as if afraid to scuff the deck with a shoe or plant a fingerprint on a shiny panel.

After seating themselves, Alcock and Brown made final arrangements to their equipment and navigation aids, then plugged the heated flying suits' electrical leads into the battery beneath their bench. They pulled on their tight-fitting leather caps, complete with fitted telephone earpieces, and strapped on their speaking transmitters. Last came the potentially lifesaving lap belts—Brown silently marveled to himself how just a few short years ago such a sensible precaution had been so universally scorned.

Lester's Field was judged 630 feet above sea level, and Jack set that number in the aneroid altimeter—the local barometric reading was not needed if one knew the field's elevation. At least initially, the instrument would yield reliable en route altitudes. Satisfied all was in order, the wheels chocked, and men holding onto both lower wings, Alcock signaled he was ready to start the engines.

In 1919, there were only two methods of starting a flying machine: twirling or "hand propping" the propeller, thereby energizing the magnetos—used on smaller, single-engine machines—and inertia starting. It was physically impossible to "prop" big ship engines like the *Vimy*'s Eagles because of their size and height off the ground, so the only option was inertia starting.

After approaching the machine from behind, mechanic Potter had scaled a ladder to the lower port wing and took up his position between the port engine nacelle and the fuselage with starting crank in hand. Mechanic Crouch had done the same next to the starboard engine. Bob Dicker, acting as the orchestra director, was standing in front of the *Vimy*'s nose, where he could see and be seen.

Dicker called out to Alcock, "Petrol on, switches off!"

After ensuring fuel was available to the Eagle, the throttle closed and magneto switches flipped down into the "Retard" position, Alcock responded, "Petrol on, switches off!"

The sturdy Potter, accustomed as he was with routine starting procedures, was nevertheless deliberate in his movements. Not only did he have to crank the engine over with sufficient authority, but it was also critical he be sure of his footing so as not to topple into the windmill-like, whirling propeller, which could reduce a man to an unrecognizable bloody pulp in a split second.

Potter nodded at Dicker that he was ready. Dicker acknowledged, then directed his gaze at Alcock while pointing at the port engine with his left hand and twirling his right forefinger above his head. Simultaneously, Dicker shouted up to Jack, "Contact!"

Alcock switched both port engine All-British Watford magnetos to "Advance," using magnets that served as electrical spark generators. The duplicate set offered backup spark to the engine plugs should one of the magnetos fail. Jack responded in kind, "Contact!" Potter inserted the crank through the inertia starting slot on the side of Eagle's left nacelle, in the manner of starting an American Ford Model T.

The mechanic began cranking, slowly at first, then faster and faster as the heavy flywheel built up momentum. After about a dozen turns, or about when the whining wheel sounded like it had reached full speed, Potter pulled a cable that released the flywheel. At that instant, the propeller made three or four induced revolutions, sending propeller and pistons in motion and sparking magnetos. Simultaneously, Alcock adroitly maneuvered mixture and throttle while waiting for the engine to come to life. A few puffs of smoke huffed from the exhaust stack, but then it was quiet.

Not catching on either the first or even second attempt was not an uncommon occurrence—sometimes the engine oil needed loosening or there was a vapor lock. A perspiring Potter wound up the flywheel again, repeating the process. This time the port Eagle roared to life, belching clouds of temporarily oil-rich white smoke.

Alcock opened the throttle for a few moments until it was running smoothly, then brought the engine back to idle—between 500 and 600 revolutions. The starting procedure was repeated on the starboard Eagle, though because of the noise from the port engine, Alcock, Dicker, and the other mechanic, Couch, had a good deal more difficulty hearing one another. Once Jack had the two engines running smoothly, he performed his run-up checks. Turning first to the port Eagle, he switched its left magneto to "Retard," and Brown read the revolution count off the dial on the engine nacelle to make sure the remaining magneto reported something less than a 100-revolution drop. Alcock then went to "Advance" on the left/port magneto and retarded the right/port, again looking for less than a 100-revolution drop. With the two port engine mags looking good, he switched both back to "Advance," ensuring continued redundancy. The same magneto check was repeated on the starboard Eagle. Brown later wrote that with those checks satisfactory and both engines running smoothly, Jack "disconnected the starting magnetos and engine switches to avoid stoppage due to possible short circuits [during the flight]." To say it more clearly, Alcock disconnected the inertia starter circuits, confident the engines themselves would provide the necessary power to the spark plugs. Even with a complete electrical power failure, the engines would continue to provide their own spark. Alcock's precaution was probably wise; there had been enough problems with electrical wire insulation— the wireless being the prime example.

With the Eagles purring contentedly but a few feet away, Alcock and Brown turned their attention to the oil pressure and revolution gauges on each engine nacelle, confirming both Eagles were running normally. Jack gripped his automobile-like control wheel and twisted it hard left and right while watching the ailerons on each side of the wing's trailing edges offer full and easy travel. He next pushed/pulled the wheel column fore and aft while craning his neck to the rear to observe the elevators flap up and down, then kicked the rudder bar hard with left and right foot, wagging the *Vimy*'s twin rudders to ensure full left/right deflection. After a quick scan of the dashboard to make sure all instruments were in order and a quick glance at Ted—Brown gave an enthusiastic thumbs up—Alcock twirled his right forefinger, a signal to his ground crew that prior to this very hazardous takeoff, he was going to conduct a runup of the engines.

With the chocks still in place and several men continuing to hold both lower wings fast, Jack slowly advanced the throttle to 1,900 revolutions, just short of maximum—as high as he dared go sitting in place. Both Alcock and Brown had several times told Percy Muller that the day must come when, like motorcars, flying machines must have some kind of wheel brake. With the howling aeroplane shaking violently, Alcock held the power up for a full five seconds. Brown carefully monitored the port engine gauges, Jack the starboard. Satisfied all was well, the pilot pulled the throttle back to idle.

By unspoken agreement, the airmen pulled goggles down over their eyes. Alcock gave the hitchhiker-thumb signal to Humm and Wand, two of the rigger/carpenters, to pull the chocks clear. With men still holding fast each lower wing, Jack advanced the throttles to all out—2,000-plus propeller revolutions per minute. Alcock's eyes darted left and right to each engine nacelle, instantly taking in their revolution counts. As they approached maximum, Alcock slowly raised and then sharply dropped his right hand. One of the men later said, "We all sat down, and the plane shot forward."

The *Vimy* stormed uphill into the variable west by southwesterly wind, the bumpy terrain being felt immediately. Throughout the run, the aeroplane was battered by sudden gusts, making it even that much harder to control. Ted Brown would remember, "What I feared in particular was that a sudden eddy might lift the plane's [wings] on one side and cause the machine to heel over." The *Vimy* shook and bounced across Lester's pasture, slowly building forward momentum. Alcock kept feeding in left aileron as necessary to counteract the dangerous gusting crosswinds. All the while his right hand stayed pressed against the engine throttle; there could be no recovery in the event of an inadvertent retarding. Jack's eyes stayed focused on the spot where he intended to pass by the ditch edge.

Another sudden gust struck from off the left forward quarter, worse than any previous. Alcock immediately threw the control wheel to full left, which dropped the left aileron aerofoil down against the wind as far as it would go, all the while mitigating right wing upward lift effect by simultaneously applying right rudder. He could only hope these actions would prevent the still-earthbound aeroplane from skittering out of control. Jack was walking an extremely precarious tightrope; he had to have remembered Freddie Raynham's account of the *Raymor* running out of aileron and crashing his machine into bits. Now he, too, had used up all his aileron. The next few seconds would determine whether it was enough.

A nervous Ted watched as the left wheels barely skirted the ditch edge. The machine was still holding reasonably straight-ahead, though only barely. The vibration had become so intense that Brown's dashboard view became a blur. Alcock, he had decided, was now operating on pure pilot instinct. The navigator estimated about 350 yards had already been used and that they were almost at the end of their ground-tether. Although the airspeed indicator continued to build speed, Ted thought it was coming with agonizing slowness.

At last, the wings began generating lift, easing the load the wheels had been bearing and allowing airspeed to build faster. Yet the crosswinds were still having their way; the aeroplane skittering more and more to the right. Owing to a line of hills surrounding the field, the machine was now also encountering a "very bumpy atmosphere," complicating matters even more. As if all that was not enough, the *Vimy* had moved far enough off to the right that it was now headed for a low stone fence, which Mr. Lester's workmen had not removed because it was thought well out of the way. Brown glanced at Alcock and "noticed that the perspiration of acute anxiety was running down his face." Just short of 400 yards, the machine bounced a few feet into the air, then settled back on the ground, hit another rough spot, and again bounced into the air. A wide-eyed Brown looked down to watch the *Vimy*'s left undercarriage skim over the stone fence, clearing it by no more than a yard or two. Alcock "weathervaned" the machine to the left, which is to say he allowed it to naturally settle directly into the southwesterly wind. That helped to relieve the rudder/aileron cross-controlling and added a few precious miles per hour indicated air speed.

Stunningly, after the *Vimy* had clawed its way to perhaps a hundred feet of altitude and seemingly on its way, the formerly vicious/now friendly headwind abruptly died off to practically nothing. It was if those always Capricious Gods of Flight were piqued they had not killed the two "flying fools" on the treacherous takeoff and were turning to a last resort. There was an immediate loss of air speed, which caused the machine to lose lift, forcing Alcock to lower the nose so the aeroplane would not stall. Once again, the not-quite-yet flying machine plunged toward earth.

* * *

From the moment Alcock started his takeoff roll, all eyes stayed transfixed on the Vickers *Vimy*. The awed spectators had been stunned by the fearful thundering of the full-throttled Eagle engines reverberating off the surrounding hills and the appalling flexing of the *Vimy*'s double-decker wings as it rumbled and rocked across Lester's Field. Not a few were convinced the machine would shake itself apart. Freddie Raynham would later remember that he'd got a sinking feeling when the aeroplane passed the edge of the drainage ditch, "showing not the least desire to rise." Just at the moment when all seemed lost, it rose a few feet into the air, settled back down on the ground, and then bounced back into the air. The crowd was on the verge of a cheer when suddenly, from about 100 feet up, the *Vimy* dropped again, sinking from sight behind a hill.

The gasping onlookers, certain the machine had crashed, began rushing toward the spot. A medical doctor volunteer, who had come accompanied by a city blood wagon, began brusquely pushing people aside while shouting, "Make way, they'll be needing me!" Miraculously, at that moment and to wide-eyed cries of joy, the *Vimy* reappeared beyond the hill, rising like a phoenix. The heavily-ladened flying machine was still heading directly into the southwesterly wind, scratching desperately for life-giving altitude.

Takeoff! 1:45 p.m. local, Saturday, June 14, 1919. (The Rooms Provincial Archives, St. John's, Newfoundland)

* * *

Alcock's gloved left hand held grimly to the wheel and his right still pushed against the still wide-open throttle, with the *Vimy* still heading directly into the wind. The revolution counters were holding at the maximum 2,000 and the Eagles were howling for all they were worth—Jack began to worry about the five-minute maximum power limit. Brown was leaning out over the fuselage side and holding his breath, "fearing our undercarriage would hit a roof or a treetop." Ted would always remember those desperate moments. "I am convinced that only Alcock's clever piloting saved us from an early disaster."

After several minutes of an agonizingly slow ascent, the *Vimy* leveled off at a relatively safe 800 feet. Alcock began a very shallow turn to the left. With the machine only a precarious two or three mph above stalling speed, he kept his eyes glued on the indicated airspeed meter; Jack dared not lose any of that critical velocity. If it happened, with insufficient altitude to lower the nose and regain flying speed, the *Vimy* would go into a spin and crash. The pilot continued the turn for nearly 180 degrees until they were heading easterly toward the North Atlantic.

After building a comfortable cushion of flying speed, Jack throttled back to an engine-easing 1,700 revolutions, after which both men heaved an enormous sigh of relief. *They were off!* Within minutes they had passed back over Lester's aerodrome. Brown leaned over the side and waved an enthusiastic farewell to their small but loyal band of well-wishers. He had to make haste; with their now tailwind they were doing well over 100 mph groundspeed! After racing over the field, Alcock started a slow climb to 1,200 feet, their planned "coast-out" altitude. Brown made his first navigation log entry:

1613 GMT, A & B away St. John's, W/V 240/35

Takeoff occurred at 1:45 P.M. local or 1613 (4:13 P.M.) Greenwich Mean Time. For the rest of the flight, due to Brown's celestial navigation requirements, ship's time would be recorded in GMT. Winds at takeoff averaged out of the southwest from 240 degrees with a velocity of 35 mph. Ted Brown thought about the difference in the flight's en route "local" time and GMT and how it would gradually shrink the closer the

Vimy came to the British Isles until, finally, the two times would be very nearly the same.

* * *

At first, Ralphie Moyst thought it was the low rumble of an approaching thunderstorm, but as the sound drew closer and intensified, he realized with a sinking feeling it was the motors of a flying machine—what could only be the *Vimy*! Everyone had said the bad winds would cause the flyers not to make an attempt, and he'd gone ahead and taken a rare opportunity to earn a little hard money. Now he had missed the takeoff! Ralphie craned his head skyward, looking from side to side, trying to locate the flying machine.

It was Saturday—no school—and the boy was delivering milk for a local farmer, Mr. Guzzwell. It was Ralphie's older brother's route, but Bill had skipped out to join his friends buzzing about the doings at Mr. Lester's pasture. Ralphie had wanted to join them, but with no real prospect of Left-tenant Brown's leaving and the opportunity to make a whole shilling, the boy had succumbed to Mr. Guzzwell's desperate pleas. He had been terribly torn—he had not yet missed an afternoon visiting the field—but this rare chance for a crippled boy like him to assume an important responsibility had been too much.

It had been when Ralphie arrived at Le Marchant Road that he finally located the silver colored *Vimy*, then directly overhead. When he saw Lieutenant Brown waving at the city below, he felt both elated and sad, glad they were safely off but sorry he hadn't had a chance to say goodbye to his friend and wish him luck on the great adventure. But moments later, after having found himself caught up in the excitement like all the rest, those unhappy feelings faded. The entire city seemed to have filled the streets, parks, and private pasturages, cheering and waving hats and scarves. Ralphie joined in, jubilantly wig-wagging his own cap and cane; for a moment he lost his balance and nearly fell down. Ralphie wouldn't even have cared, his joy in the moment complete. All too soon, the flying machine could no longer be seen, the sound of its motors gradually fading away.

"I'll remember Left-tenant Brown," the boy said aloud, repeating what had become a vow, the tears streaming down his face and his gaze fixed on where the flying machine had disappeared. "I can do almost anything I want!"

* * *

Brown noted a time of 1628 GMT as the *Vimy* passed over the Newfoundland east coast. The air had been rough above land due to the very hilly countryside surrounding St. John's—the machine "lurched, swayed, and did its best to deviate"—though the turbulence calmed once they were over the ocean. From long experience on the Western Front, Brown had learned much about changing winds near coasts. He was now estimating it as coming directly out of the west at a fairly steady 35 mph. Applying the wind to his premeasured true course of 078 degrees on the Appleyard course and distance calculator, Brown learned he had a drift component of effectively zero and a calculated true air speed of 70 mph. With true course and true heading essentially the same, he added 30 degrees of west variation ("Variation West, Compass Best") and discovered his magnetic, or compass, heading.

Brown spoke into his telephone transmitter and told Alcock, "Ground speed about 100 mph. Use compass heading 108." Jack nodded and turned accordingly.

Brown cranked down the lead ball on the end of his sturdy wireless antenna wire to about fifteen feet below the machine, engaged the transmitter key, and tapped a message out to Mount Pearl, beginning with the station's call sign:

To BZM all well and started.

* * *

As the *Vimy*'s engine noise faded to nothing, the spectators began drifting away, and the Vickers ground crew waded into the massive cleanup. For Muller, Montgomery, Dicker, and all the rest, an enormously empty feeling swept over them. For several months, nearly every man-jack of the Vickers Aviation Department had been utterly devoted to getting the *Vimy* away. And now that it was done, they found themselves empty of purpose and confronted with anticlimax. Like all the rest of the world, they could only wait out the better part of a day to learn whether their efforts had brought success . . . or all had been in vain.

Mr. Charles Lester's men immediately began restoring the Mundy Pond grounds to dray horse pasturage, never mind his earlier stated intention of making the field a North American International Aerodrome. The Percheron/Belgian mixes in the nearby enclosure happily nickered, understanding they would soon be able to walk away from their brown-dry prison rations and feast on the summer's succulent green brome and timothy grasses.

1700 GMT
June 14
Coasting out into the North Atlantic

From the beginning, Alcock had planned to run the Eagles easy, which is to say, rather than cruise at an upper end 1,750 to 1,800 revolutions, he would maintain about 1,600. This not only spared the engines from punishing hard labor, it also reduced petrol consumption and substantially extended the *Vimy*'s range, though the tradeoff was a slower airspeed. By every indication, however, chances were good they could expect favorable tail winds all the way across, with a corresponding increase in ground speed. In the disagreeable event the winds *should* shift from tail to nose, those fuel economies were even more important; stretching every drop of petrol would be critical to reaching safe harbor on Ireland's west coast.

The two flyers were still getting accommodated to their tiny cockpit. They had learned as early as the first test flight that great care had to be taken to avoid getting their feet entangled in the exposed rudder pulley cables. The stiff wires mechanically connected the rudder bar to the twin rudders which had to be kept clear of obstruction. Jack sat between them, with Ted's right boot brushing against the left cable.

Due to scattered scud and Brown's request for a sextant observation on the sun, Alcock had brought the ship up to 1,600 feet elevation above sea level on the aneroid altimeter. Earlier, Ted had precomputed an observation for 1700 GMT. With the body directly on their tail, this "sun line" shot would yield a LOP, or line of position, perpendicular to their course, offering an excellent opportunity to check their ground speed. However, when the time came, the sun was completely obscured by the upper starboard wing.

Truth be told, Brown was a little nervous about the celestial work. While he'd never quite been able to admit it to anyone but Kay, these observations would be *the first he'd ever made aloft*. Yes, though he understood the mathematics intimately, knew the locations of the stars, and had taken hundreds of observations on the ground, plus a score or more on the *Mauretania*, he was nonetheless experienced enough to understand there was no substitute for the real thing. He would have to be, he decided, utterly resolved to accept nothing less than his best effort.

Visibility had been good for this first hour of the flight, which reinforced their already positive feelings regarding eventual success. For reasons Ted could never put his finger on, "I felt a queer but quite definite confidence in our safe arrival over the Irish coast." He had developed an indefinable yet certain faith in himself, the *Vimy*, the Eagles, and especially Alcock—a pilot he thought was "all first-class."

Sixteen hundred feet below stretched a never-ending blue-gray sea, with golden rods of sunlight streaking past a patchwork of puffy cumulous clouds. This in dramatic contrast to the comforting "square-patterned roof mosaic of St. John's" of but a half hour earlier. Now, they beheld a majestic visual panorama that neither of the men had witnessed before. Intermittent sober thoughts interrupted the reverie; out in this vast North Atlantic, and for yet another 1,800 miles, there would be no place to set the machine down should trouble arise. Scattered hither-thither on the horizon were gigantic white icebergs, floating placidly atop the great North Atlantic cocktail. Ted could not help but shudder at the thought of a forced let-down and dunking into bitterly cold water and how, after only a few minutes, fatal hypothermia would overtake them. It would at least be quick; no lingering for days without food and water, chained down all that time by the bitter knowledge that there was no hope of rescue. Brown had all along held little faith in the event of an emergency that they somehow would be able to disengage the petrol tank emergency buoyancy raft—assuming it was empty!—and retrieve the supplies from the tail cupboard. Bitter experience during the war had taught him Providence rarely offered the necessary time and circumstance for such a thing to play out favorably.

Ted glanced at a still adrenaline-charged Alcock, he who was fiercely clutching the wheel with both hands, his eyes dancing furtively from the dashboard to out past the windscreen and then back again to the instruments. It would be several more minutes before heavy fatigue inevitably set in, and Jack realized he was pressing too hard. He forced himself to relax pressure on the controls, though he understood too much of that would allow the machine to get away from him. The pilot had also become frustrated with the steam from his own breath fogging the goggle lenses, to say nothing of the telephone earpieces hurting his ears. At length, it became too much. Alcock angrily pushed the goggles onto his forehead and yanked loose the earpieces and transmitter. Despite the risk of something striking him in the eyes, the goggles stayed off for the rest of the flight. At the air speeds they were traveling, a foreign object impact could be catastrophic, though the six-inch-high transparent windscreen atop the dashboard deflected the lion's share of the slipstream. As long as Jack kept his head down, he would be all right.

Ted wisely chose to say nothing of the pilot's dismantling of their cockpit communication system, waiting a minute or two before gently unplugging Jack's earpieces and transmitter from the wireless and untangling the cords from around the pilot's neck. Alcock was under a tremendous strain, and if getting rid of the telephone settled him down, that was fine by Brown. While they could still communicate by loud shouts—Ted would soon decide that wasn't practical—hand signals and written notes were the best alternative. The navigator would, of course, keep his own earpieces in; he still had to mind their ground communications. However, he too would soon dispense with fogged over goggles.

Despite the turbulence—fairly constant during the entire voyage—Brown stayed hard at his figures, the Appleyard calculator in his left hand and the Baker navigation machine on his lap. It'd been important for his dead reckoning to get the *Vimy* off to a good start; a solid anchor departure fix had accomplished that. During this first hour, he stayed especially alert to see if the winds would change over the ocean. Peering over the left side of the fuselage and observing the waves below, Brown recalled what Captain Rostrom of the *Mauretania* had taught him about reading wind speed and direction. The *Vimy* had dropped down to 1,500 feet—Jack was looking for a less bumpy air seam—which had the added benefit of increasing chances the wind conditions on the water's surface would match those at their altitude. The wind direction, Rostrom had explained, is always perpendicular to the line of white caps. If they are regular in size, the wind velocity is 10 to 12 mph. If the white caps are breaking and foaming, velocity is at least 20 mph. The nature of what Ted was observing led him to estimate wind speed at 20 mph plus, with the direction appearing to have shifted more southwesterly.

Brown decided to cross-check that value with his "Wind Gauge Bearing Plate." He had attached the base portion to the cockpit rim and could adjust the rotatable plate while facing aft for unobstructed observations and with his back to the slipstream. Ted waited a few seconds for a white cap to hold steady during the several seconds needed for an accurate reading. After lining it up on the plate's rotatable vertical cursor—the one perpendicular to the wave—he turned the plate until the drift was killed, *i.e.*, the cursor no longer drifted off the white cap. The drift reading showed 12 degrees left, requiring a 12-degree right heading correction to compensate. The next step was to time how long in seconds the white cap took to travel between two horizontal cursors on the plate. He spun the data collected on his Appleyard calculator to determine his ground speed, then compared that with time elapsed from his departure fix. With that track and ground speed data in hand, he calculated their current dead reckoning position using the Bigsworth plotter and Royal Navy dividers, then marked the point on his chart. In order to "stay ahead of the aeroplane" Brown "threw out" a future DR position, *i.e.*, where he thought the plane would be in an hour based on the same ground speed and drift, roughly another hundred miles down the road.

As a backup, Ted also carried Royal Navy Traverse Tables, which could also be utilized to establish dead reckoning positions. Long employed by mariners, these precomputed tables used trigonometric calculations to solve the same problems as the Appleyard-type calculators carried by airmen. More cumbersome and only accurate up to a distance of not more than 600 miles, Ted would find the Tables increasingly ineffective for a fast-moving flying machine and soon set them aside.

Satisfied he had derived their position as best he could from the information available, Brown logged the data:

1720 GMT

Estimated at 47 degrees, 52 minutes North Latitude, 47-00 West
    Longitude

Est. track 082 degrees, Est. W/V 220/30

Drift 12 degrees left, west variation 30 degrees,

New compass heading 124 degrees

Indicated airspeed 70 mph, Est. ground speed 94 mph

Altitude 1,500 feet, distance flown 104 miles

Ted wrote the new compass heading on a piece of paper and showed it to Alcock, who obediently turned right to 124 degrees. At this point, it must have become clear to Brown that he would have trouble maintaining a comprehensible in-flight log. The rough air and lack of a desk alone were almost too much; he couldn't imagine legibly writing in darkness or rain as well. Later, he would reconstruct his hasty scribblings into something more readable, though in the process, he would inadvertently introduce conflicting data, most often with regard to which type of air speed he was recording. In all fairness, to that date, no one had developed a formal flight log format for both pre-flight planning of speeds, distances, courses, and altitudes alongside a running comparison of actual conditions encountered aloft, never mind an environment that even made possible logging the information.

In addition to the knots/mph confusion in his notes, Brown did not always specify whether he was recording indicated air speed (IAS) or true air speed (TAS). TAS is determined by applying the outside air temperature and altitude (higher altitudes mean lower temperatures and atmospheric pressure) against the IAS as shown on the airspeed meter. At 1,000 feet altitude, for example, IAS and TAS are virtually identical. At say 5,000 feet, however, on the Appleyard, a 70-mph IAS yielded a TAS something on the order of 75-80 mph. It is from TAS that ground speed is calculated; the higher and faster one flies, the greater the error induced by not taking this factor into account.

Alcock was having more trouble holding the assigned headings than even he had anticipated. The *Vimy* had never been operated over so hostile an environment like the North Atlantic, and the machine's control surfaces were in continual danger of being overwhelmed. What's more, the aeroplane had a built-in tendency to yaw—its pivoting motion left or right about a vertical axis—making the ailerons of the Vickers machine seem to work backward. Once, in discussions with engineers about the problem, Alcock commented only half-facetiously that you didn't really control the heavy-handed *Vimy*, you gave it suggestions.

Quite abruptly, all traces of blue sky and sunlight disappeared, along with any hopes of a sun shot. The two men looked around to find themselves sandwiched in a two-thousand-foot clear layer between fog below and dense gray cloud above. It was disorienting, as if they were suspended in some ephemeral world, where up and down and left and right no longer existed. Although Jack could still see well enough not to experience difficulties controlling the machine, Ted had no navigation references from either the heavens or the sea. The only option remaining was to continue advancing his last known position, the departure fix leaving Newfoundland, using only heading, wind/drift and ground speed readings from the drift bearing plate, and time elapsed.

Brown had been so caught up in his navigation, he'd forgotten to tap out a scheduled position update to Mount Pearl. He lowered the weighted antenna, keyed the wireless transmitter, and ditty-dotted out a message. At once, he sensed something was wrong. He tapped the message out again. Nothing. Brown checked the electrical connections; everything appeared in order. After getting clear of his navigation equipment and opening his lap belt, he struggled halfway to his feet—the pain in his left leg was excruciating—and braced himself against the slipstream, peering over Jack's head at the wireless wind generator screw under the starboard engine. The tiny 12-inch-wide propeller was gone, snapped off and blown away. Ted collapsed in his seat, astonished. After all that bloody thing had put Jack and him through! Worse, they were now cut off from the world, no less alone than if they had embarked on a voyage to the moon. The cause of the wind screw failure would never be known.

A subdued Ted wrote Jack another note. *Wireless generator smashed. The propeller has gone.*

Alcock gave his navigator a devastating look, then slowly shook his head. Brown could only bury himself in his work, grateful the telephone was disabled, and he would at least be spared the tongue-lashing he undoubtedly deserved.

1920 GMT
Altitude: 3,000 feet
West Variation: 31 degrees
Compass Heading: 120 degrees
Estimated Ground Speed: 100 mph
Estimated Distance Flown: 324 miles
Remarks: "No chance of sights"

For the preceding two hours, Alcock had been trying different altitudes in an effort to get out of the scud long enough for Brown to get either another drift reading or a sun line. Even if they were in the clear, there would be only the sun available for a celestial observation, not enough for a solid "fix," though it would offer a firm speed line—a line of position perpendicular to their course. Sunset was still over four hours away, which meant none of Ted's other five celestial bodies were yet available to him. He passed a note to the pilot: *I can't get an obs. in this fog. Will estimate the same wind holds and continue working by dead reckoning.* When darkness finally came, he would first try for Polaris, the Pole Star, followed by either Venus or Vega. A Polaris observation had long been a navigator's most favored night celestial body because, like the noon sun, its observed altitude above the horizon could be easily converted to the observer's latitude under most conditions. Even better from Ted's standpoint, a Pole Star shot would give him a solid *course* LOP, which, at the moment, was of more concern than how fast he was going. Brown passed another note to Alcock, emphasizing his concern about that course and the pilot's ability to hold the desired compass heading: *Keep her nearer 120 degrees than 140.* The *Vimy* continued to be difficult to control directionally, its inherent instability and the rough air all that Jack could handle. This instability problem was shared by nearly all the new, giant flying machines; Alcock had long preached to anyone who would listen that it simply had to be brought to heel for successful commercial air transportation.

The issue was being driven home in spades on this, the longest flight Jack had ever attempted. It was taking a great deal out of him to maintain control of the machine—except for very brief periods to take food and drink or stretch a cramp, his hands and feet could never leave the controls. The *Vimy*'s particular difficulty had been anticipated, with the riggers constructing an elastic rubber device that joined the control wheel and the rudder to reduce the workload. Alcock had been dismayed to discover they'd bungled the job. With all the hubbub preceding the takeoff, the cord had been cut too short; the pilot would have to bear the full weight of the controls.

Brown saw by the clock it was time to turn the dashboard fuel selector valve to another of the seven tanks. Each engine was fed from a single fifteen-gallon service tank located in the upper port and starboard wings. Petrol was brought up to each from one of the seven fuselage tanks by a centrifugal pump, powered by the same port side airscrew that serviced the cockpit instruments. The service tank was kept constantly full, with fuel flow down to the engines powered by gravity. In a pre-flight interview with a *Daily Mail* reporter, Alcock had been surprisingly candid about not only properly managing the petrol supply but the implications of an early engine failure: "If any mishap should befall one engine when the journey is half-completed, the other will carry the plane safely to Ireland. But should an accident happen before the fuel load has been reduced by half, the machine would have to come down."

Despite Ted's inability to transmit on the wireless, its residual battery charge enabled him to intercept transmissions. In addition to communications with ground stations, his radio had been designed for emergency communications with other aircraft and ships at sea. Currently, the navigator was picking up a good deal of steamer traffic. He scribbled a note and held it up for Alcock to read: *Wireless busy, no message for us yet.* These communications were both reassuring and dismaying—solace in having human contact from beyond the void but yet unable to call for help if anything *did* happen.

Suddenly, the flyers were rocked by "a loud rhythmic chattering, rather like the noise of a machine gun fired at close quarters." They were momentarily bewildered by this dreadful new racket, looking frantically both inside and outside the cockpit. It was quickly discovered an exhaust pipe on the right engine had burst, allowing its dissipate to blow straight out the cylinders without any so-called "muffling." There had been engine/exhaust noise before, but now it was nothing short of an ear-shattering howling. Not only that, the red-hot exhaust was also blowing uncomfortably close to one of the wing's cross-bracing wires. Nothing could be done about it; Alcock and Brown could only hope the machine would not be subject to any more damage. They would have to live with the incredible din itself, and eventually, either it did settle down or they simply became accustomed to the rat-a-tat-tat.

Paradoxically, for Ted Brown at least, the unrestrained engine clamor became something of a comfort, as if giving voice to a *Vimy* equally angry over fate's insistence on their complete isolation. Without the constant, terrible racket, their journey through the all-enveloping fog while cut off from the rest of humanity would have otherwise been "a very lonely affair."

After two hours of totally blind flying, Brown became increasingly apprehensive about his inability to get a solid position "fix." While there had been no indication of any serious crosswinds—powerful aloft winds from either the north or south posed the only real threat to the *Vimy* going seriously off course—there was always the possibility such conditions had gone undetected. The aerial voyager could rely on dead reckoning for just so long. Brown resolved to remain patient, reluctant to share his anxieties with Alcock just yet.

Thinking they both needed some kind of diversion from the noisome, monotonous, and increasingly uncomfortable crossing, Ted hand-signaled a question at Jack. Would he like something to eat? Alcock nodded; Brown reached into the little cupboard behind him and withdrew one of Agnes Dooley's thick roast beef sandwiches. Holding the wheel firmly in his right hand, Jack took the sandwich with his left and dug in. Brown followed that up with a cup of Horlick's malted beverage from one of the vacuum flasks, which, still hot, Alcock slowly sipped. After finishing, Jack motioned for a Guinness, from which he took a long pull, smacking his lips with exaggerated satisfaction.

At 1940 GMT, Brown wrote a note asking Jack to try getting above some of the weather. By 2000 GMT, the *Vimy* was level at 4,500 feet on the aneroid. Of course, by this time, and as Alcock and Brown were well aware, atmospheric pressure conditions would certainly have changed from that over St. John's. This meant that without a new barometric reading from a station directly below, their *absolute* altitude above the sea could actually be as much as several hundred feet above or below what their altimeter was now indicating.

A short time later, the *Vimy* passed into a large gap in the clouds, and at long last, the sun burst suddenly through. Brown wasted no time getting in his shots, making several observations over ten minutes and reconciling them to a single time of 2031 GMT. He had kneeled on his seat, facing backward, and shot the sun through a gap in the two port

Artist's visualization of the Vimy *over the North Atlantic. (Alamy Stock Photo)*

wings. Due to cloud below, the horizon was not visible, so he was obliged to bring his spirit level into play. After plotting his speed line LOP and running the numbers through his Appleyard course and distance calculator, Ted smiled.

We must be much farther east, he noted to Alcock, *than my earlier dead reckoning calculations had indicated. Ground speed works out to 143 mph.*

The recent advent of the Appleyard-type circular slide rule course and distance calculators had been a major breakthrough in air navigation. They represented the prototype for all the air navigation handheld calculators that preceded the digital/satellite GPS age. For the Americans, the Appleyard foreshadowed the World War Two-era "whiz wheel," more formally known as the "Type E6-B Flight computer." British Commonwealth navigators referred to the same device as the "Dalton Dead Reckoning Computer," after its inventor, US Navy Reserve pilot Philip Dalton. A well-known Allied navigator ditty ran:

> *His computer is the instrument on which he stakes his life,*
> *Don't ask for his computer, for he'd sooner lend his wife.*

During the Vietnam era, US navigators inherited the E-6B's direct descendent, the "Air Navigation, Dead Reckoning, Type MB-4."

Alcock mouthed a question about their compass heading. Without any new course information to go on, Brown indicated he maintain 120 degrees. Ted entered the position information and other remarks on his log. They had traveled 680 miles, about one-third of the way across.

The undercast below suddenly broke at 2115 GMT, exposing a pitching, gray North Atlantic. Brown snatched the chance to cross-check the accuracy of his sun line observations. He'd had some trouble getting the sextant's spirit level properly aligned and was a little concerned that might have induced some error in the sun's observed altitude. A confirmation of the LOP's accuracy could come by performing a "double drift" procedure off an object on the earth's surface.

A double drift was a technique new to aerial navigators, with only a few men having actually used it over water. Indeed, while Brown thoroughly understood the maneuver and how to perform it, this would be his first attempt. Anticipating its use, Ted had talked Alcock through the procedure during one of their planning sessions at the Cochrane Hotel. Brown jotted *double-drift* on a note and showed it to Alcock. On the navigator's signal, the pilot made a 45-degree turn to the right. Looking backwards through the drift bearing plate, Ted took a drift reading off a convenient iceberg and jotted the number down. After precisely ninety seconds had elapsed on the dashboard clock, Brown signaled for a 90-degree turn to the left. The navigator took another drift reading off another, smaller iceberg, and at the end of another ninety seconds, signaled Alcock to turn 45 degrees back to the right, rolling out on the original compass heading. A bit later, after manipulating the Appleyard, a relieved Ted showed Jack the results. *DD shows 140 GS.* The sun speed line was confirmed.

Shortly after that, the hole below abruptly closed, and they were back to blind flying. At 2130 GMT, the light began to fade. Within thirty minutes, they were enveloped in darkness, the glowing red noxious vapor still blasting out the ruptured starboard engine exhaust pipe and flood-lighting their now yellow-opaque, goldfish-bowl world. Although by flying toward the sunrise the night would only last for six and a half hours, it nevertheless promised to be a long and lonely passage. Despite their heavy, fur-lined suits and boots, both men felt a distinct chill—and not just from the increasingly colder slipstream—as they continued to plunge into the dark void. For *fear* had all at once begun to stalk them, in the manner of a seemingly innocent though somehow discomfiting morning snow shower that mutated into a deadly afternoon blizzard.

As if on cue, Alcock suddenly noticed there was a frost/ice buildup on the cockpit windscreen. While at the time it was not fully understood why ice abruptly appeared and accumulated on wings, sometimes at rather astonishing rates, it was known to occur most often when the outside air temperature hovered at the freezing point while in heavy cloud—the conditions they were experiencing at that very moment. Alcock pointed at it, prompting Ted to flick on his torch and begin a rigorous, methodical scan of the lower wings. After studying the same spot on the left wing for several minutes, Brown concluded the traces were not growing. Both men understood any significant ice buildup would disrupt the air flow over the wings, to say nothing of the additional dead weight, which if it went too far would result in a loss of lift and a subsequent fatal wing stall. As with the red-orange starboard engine exhaust still blasting near the wing cross-bracing wires, the two men could only leave their fate to Providence.

Without calling it by that yet unknown phrase "flying on instruments," Alcock was operating the machine with little benefit from his visual senses, having only the inclinometer, aneroid altimeter, and airspeed indicator for guidance. Very soon, Jack would discover how wholly inadequate those pitifully few aids were and, even more profoundly, how dreadfully misguided his theories were on inborn abilities to successfully blind-fly.

Fifty minutes later, at 2220 GMT, the *Vimy* still suspended in the forbidding blackness, Brown made a belated log entry: *No observations. Could not get above clouds for sunset. Will wait check by stars.*

Missing the sunset had been another disappointment for navigator Brown. By having Jack point the *Vimy*'s nose directly at the sun and recording the exact moment it dipped below the horizon, Ted could have taken a simultaneous bearing with his handheld prismatic compass and, with a few Appleyard slide rule calculations, verified the accuracy of the primary aperiodic compass. In that time of still relatively crude instrumentation, when even previously reliable compasses might inexplicably fail, any heading cross-check was invaluable. Fortunately, the results of the earlier sun line observation and double-drift procedure would have almost certainly revealed any systemic issues. Overall, Brown was satisfied he and the flying machine's navigation aids were functioning properly.

It had remained castle-dungeon dark below the *Vimy*, though above, Brown could catch the faint glimmer of stars from time to time. That was a hopeful sign; they had flown at least 900 miles without a single true fix, and Ted's apprehension had grown. Although Alcock had not expressed concern, Brown was certain his pilot understood how crucial it was that they establish a fixed position. Only aviators who have found themselves flying blind for nearly seven hours without knowing where they'd been or were now can fully appreciate the clammy-hands fear that condition creates.

All the same, ongoing flight routines had still to be regularly observed. When night fell, the cockpit setup had to be readjusted. Ted turned on a small electric lamp and pointed it at his Baker navigation machine/Mercator rolling chart. He leaned across Jack's left knee and switched on a tiny bulb that illuminated the aperiodic compass face. With their radium etchings, the balance of the dashboard instruments were self-luminous. Brown used his electric torch for regular engine inspections and reading the temperature and engine revolution gauges. Thankfully, both Eagles were performing flawlessly. After yet another petrol tank switch, Ted had made ready for a star fix. He did not want to waste a second once the opportunity arose.

Shortly after 0001 GMT, June 15, it finally did. Although the solid scud below remained unchanged, the *Vimy* had at last broken into partly clear above. In a gap between clouds to his northeast, Brown identified

Vega. To the direct north, the Pole Star was also visible. Thanks to the moonlight, a horizontal low-cloud horizon could also be seen, enabling Ted to dispense with the clumsy spirit level. With Alcock's determinedly steady flying, the shots went smoothly. After reconciling the observations to a common time of 0025 GMT, Brown plotted the two LOPs and ran the raw data through the Appleyard. *We are but 10 miles south of course,* an exultant Ted scribbled to Jack, *980 miles from St. John's.* They were halfway across! *Average ground speed since leaving St. John's 122 mph.* Brown went on to log their position as 50-07 North and 31-00 West with 27 degrees West variation. With that deeply comforting knowledge in hand, neither man was terribly upset when cloud above again covered the stars.

The navigator judged that Alcock's compass heading over the latest leg had averaged 115 degrees—only five degrees from the ideal Ted had been looking for, which was in itself remarkable considering the instability of the machine and the rough air the pilot was encountering. Ironically, that five-degree "error" had worked to their advantage; a 120-degree course would have put them even farther south. With that in mind, Brown ordered a new compass heading of 110 degrees. A five-degree turn to the left, or north, offered a convergence heading that would bring them back to their desired track.

Up to this point, John Alcock had been holding about 1,600 revolutions on the Eagles. With the knowledge they were enjoying a tremendous tailwind and its correspondingly favorable ground speed, the pilot decided to ease engine stress even more. He throttled back to 1,450 revolutions, which yielded a 65-mph indicated air speed on the meter, both men understanding now that with a solid fix under their belt, the pressure to stay above the scud was, at least temporarily, eased. The new power setting would, however, cause the *Vimy* to very slowly settle toward the sea. Alcock had been sorely tempted to keep the throttles up and maintain altitude, but the core fears of engine failure and petrol exhaustion had trumped all. The lower revolution setting also reduced fuel consumption. By 0120 GMT, the flying machine was at 4,000 feet; an hour later at 3,600 feet.

Both Alcock and Brown found themselves hungry again; the passing of the halfway point so soon and their position newly fixed had whetted appetites. Jack was still wearing a self-satisfied smile when Ted reached for the lunch pantry door. Brown understood why; should even one of Alcock's beloved Eagles decide to pack it in, they still stood an excellent chance of making it to Ireland. No matter the lonely *Vimy* was still plunging through a black void, with the two men seeing nothing and hearing only "the changeless drone, drone, drone of the engines," they nevertheless bit happily into their sandwiches. Not even the belching starboard exhaust pipe could disturb them. Jack finished up with two Fry's chocolate bars for dessert and washed everything down with hot coffee.

At 0200 GMT, and for the third time since they'd entered the thick soup, Alcock gestured at the Petrol Overflow Gauge located three feet above Brown's head. Once again, the meter face had been obscured by a hardening heavy sleet and could no longer be read by the sitting crew in the cockpit. Once again, Brown braced himself to scrape the glass face clear. While the petrol supply to the engines had so far been pumping normally, it was critical to continue monitoring the flow. Too little fuel and the Eagles would quit; too much and the carburetors would flood.

After tightening his leather cap and fully buttoning the front of his flying coveralls, Brown rose up and painfully turned himself toward the tail. With the slipstream pummeling his back and head, Ted steadied his feet on the cockpit deck, grabbed a vertical strut, and straightened to a standing position. The near 100-mph gale slammed into him with jackhammer force, and it was all he could do to keep from being swept out of the cockpit.

Ted had led with his good right leg, knowing he would need all his strength to raise the weaker left leg into position. However, unlike the two previous risings, this one had sent a lightning-like bolt of pain shooting from hip to ankle, as if the leg had been set afire. Brown had screamed, he was sure of that; he could only hope the engine, exhaust, and slipstream noises had masked the sound. Overriding even the unspeakable pain was an utter determination to shield his agony from Jack. Brown was utterly determined to disabuse Alcock of any notion he couldn't perform his duties.

Breathing in short heavy gasps, and through sheer force of will, Ted wrapped his left arm around the strut for an anchor, withdrew his knife, and chipped the sleet/ice off the gauge face until he could read the dial.

Satisfied it was still within limits, Brown slumped back into the cockpit, sending another series of lightning bolts through the left leg. Bizarrely, as these things sometimes happen, for just an instant, he'd glanced at a forlorn-looking Lucky Jim, coated with frozen sleet from kitty nose to paw. The near-delusional navigator imagined the doll a lonely sentry, guarding the Petrol Overflow Gauge—good soldier, he! Ted slipped below the windscreen, and the terrible freezing gale instantly disappeared, like a light switching off.

Alcock, watching out of the corner of an eye, resisted a strong impulse to reach out and help his comrade. Ted laboriously twisted himself back into his seat, unavoidably bumping against the pilot in the cramped cockpit. After finally getting his lap belt secured, though still breathing heavily, Brown faced Jack and nodded, the prearranged signal petrol was flowing normally. Much to Ted's horror, had he known, Alcock's keen sense of observation had taken in the full drama. The pilot's thoughts went back to that day at Brooklands when they'd first met. "I'm quite certain the fellow has the guts and know-how for the flight," he'd remarked to Superintendent Percy Muller. "The question is, does he have the stamina?" Jack now had his answer, in spades.

Careful not to reveal even a trace of pity, Alcock caught his mate's eye and gave him a thumbs-up. Brown smiled back weakly. After a few more minutes of collecting himself, the navigator retrieved his Baker navigation machine and began throwing out another dead reckoning position, something he did religiously at least every hour. Although hating the discomfort the effort caused, Brown detested to an even greater degree being "behind the aeroplane," and he was already past due for the position update.

The Eagles droned on; each man lost in his own work. Alcock began to feel the physical fatigue on another level, something deeper than he had ever experienced before. His hands had become numb from gripping the wheel despite constantly switching them, and his legs kept falling asleep. His entire upper body ached throughout, while his backside had gone completely numb. Ted administered another Guinness. It was a delicate balance; Alcock mustn't have too much at too frequent intervals—with his fatigue levels so high, too much alcohol could backfire disastrously.

The pilot perked up some—perhaps from nothing more than a placebo effect—and Brown hoped the crisis had passed. Jack would tell Ted later that he'd had a sudden inspiration; by balancing the rudder bar behind his ankles and pressing the bottom of his feet against the forward bulkhead, he was able to straighten his knees and lift his rump off the seat for a few seconds of blessed relief.

Another half-hour passed wordlessly. Both men began thinking of the sunrise, that longed-for moment when they could throw off the black night's chains and behold the light of a new day. A glance at the dashboard clock told them dawn would arrive in less than an hour. Oddly enough, neither felt sleepy. Ted would later ponder this with some wonder, ultimately deciding the reason for his and Alcock's continued alertness was because they hadn't reached their objective—the adrenaline still flowed. During the war it had been different. After a bombing sortie, the mission having been accomplished, that special alertness required in combat was no longer necessary, replaced instead by a dreadfully monotonous flight of several hours back to the home field.

With the successful passing of each hour and the prospect of sunrise growing closer, Alcock and Brown found themselves becoming increasingly optimistic about their chances of success. They'd been in the air for over ten hours, the engines were running splendidly, and petrol was abundant. Even more astounding, the machine was fairly rocketing across the North Atlantic; surely it could take no more than another eight hours to reach Ireland, even if the favorable tail winds fell away. With the *Vimy* performing so superbly and the crew's spirits improving by the minute, Ted concluded that only some dramatic, unforeseen event could now stand in their way.

At 0310 GMT and 1,150 miles into the flight, a moment nearly coinciding with that longed-for sunrise, that unforeseen event occurred. Alcock had the flying machine at 3,500 feet on the altimeter, though both he and Brown were quite certain the differences in atmospheric pressure and temperature from their departure point put much doubt in the reliability of the reading—they could not know with any certainty their *absolute altitude* above sea level. Alcock had therefore decided to err on the side of caution; he would not allow the *Vimy* to dip below a 500-foot aneroid reading. Minutes earlier, they had entered the densest bank of cloud yet encountered, "which even cut off from our range of vision the machine's wing-tips and the fore-end of the fuselage" only a few feet away.

John Alcock had never before been caught in such difficult blind flying conditions, to say nothing of how much this new burden was adding to his already profound fatigue. With no external references available to maintain visual flight, the pilot had only the meager cockpit resources of the inclinometer, indicated air speed, and altimeter to assist him. Unfortunately, that was not nearly enough. As Brown later put it, "we [suddenly] lost our balance. The machine, left to its own devices, swung, flew amok, and began to perform circus tricks." That circus performance ended when the *Vimy* heeled over into an out-of-control, tumbling spin.

As it happened, the British aircraft industry had still not fully grasped the importance of the German Imperial Air Service's unique blind-flight instrument. The Drexler Aircraft Steering Gauge contained an inclinometer with a visually depicted aeroplane and its orientation relative to Earth. The instrument became the first gyroscopic attitude instrument, the gauge's air-driven gyro providing a horizon in roll (wing up or down), though not in pitch (nose up or down). It was far ahead of its time; Sperry would not invent the first truly functional *artificial horizon* until 1929, the same year the American Jimmy Doolittle demonstrated the world's first takeoff to landing blind flight. For certain, there was nothing in the *Vimy*'s cockpit even close to the Drexler aid.

What John Alcock experienced at 0310 GMT would not be fully understood until years later. The top pilots of his era believed in their inherent ability to "fly by the seat of their pants." Which is to say they were convinced they possessed an inborn natural balance that allowed them to retain their equilibrium even in zero-zero weather. These flyers pooh-poohed the scientific long-hairs and their attempts to perfect blind flying gadgets. Such thinking had become so ingrained that, nearly a decade later, many of the world's top pilots were still resisting the very idea of "flying on instruments."

One classic example: In June 1927, only a month after Charles Lindbergh's New York to Paris flight, US Navy then-Commander Richard E. Byrd—the same man who had offered Brown his newly-developed bubble sextant—and his crew of three took off from New York in a Fokker Trimotor in an attempt to duplicate, perhaps even top, Lindbergh's epic flight. The chief pilot was Bert Acosta, one of the most accomplished American captains. En route over the North Atlantic, the Trimotor flew into heavy clouds. Shortly thereafter, the plane went into an out-of-control spin, very much in the same way Alcock had. The copilot was a young Norwegian named Bernt Balchen, who fortunately had made himself a skilled instrument pilot. Balchen recovered the plane from the spin and set the Fokker back on course to Paris. Much to Acosta's credit, he sheepishly acknowledged his inability to fly blind and told Balchen that, henceforth, the young man would take command whenever they were in instrument conditions.

All that was in the future, of course. Alcock, in 1919, was a prisoner of his time, naively secure in his ability to handle blind flying—that is, until this very moment. Away went the corkscrewing *Vimy* in ever more violent pitching, turning, and skidding, the centrifugal force pinning the crew to one side of the cockpit and then the other. It had all broken so fast Alcock either did not notice or was unable to react when just prior to the violent stall that started it all his indicated air speed had bled off to virtually nothing, a sure sign his nose was much too high. Further, the compass needle was rotating rapidly, though Alcock, who may or may not in all the confusion have been able to read the aperiodic, didn't sense he was in a turn. Neither did he apparently consult his inclinometer, which would have informed him his wings were dangerously out of level. Perhaps, in the dark and with the machine performing such "circus tricks," he simply could not focus on anything other than his physical senses, which the more one ponders, the more one suspects. In moments of extreme peril, the human pilot is at the full mercy of his training and instincts. In the final analysis, one can only conclude John Alcock had inadvertently put the aeroplane in a steep climb from which the machine assumed an unusual attitude. When one of the wings lost sufficient lift, the *Vimy* went completely out of control.

Brown would later write that he and Alcock believed the incident was largely caused by the "air speed meter [becoming] jammed." This seems unlikely in that there was no evidence of pitot tube icing—the easily-viewed tube was secured on a strut just a few feet above their heads—and that was the only occasion they complained about the air speed indicator. What surely must have happened is what still occurs today to pilots inexperienced in instrument flying conditions. Alcock (as did Bert Acosta eight years later) became "spatially disoriented," a modern aviation term (sometimes called vertigo) that refers to the pilot's inability to determine his position, location, and motion relative to his environment. The root cause is a tumbling of the inner ear's "gyros," the organs of the vestibular nerve. The condition causes false signals to the brain, deceiving the pilot as to what is actually happening to him. Without instrument instruction and the firm discipline to ignore what the senses are telling him, *any pilot untrained in blind flying conditions* who experiences spatial disorientation will almost certainly lose control of his aeroplane (think John F. Kennedy, Jr.).

Still tumbling through space, Alcock felt the machine vibrate with increasing intensity and, even without having the instruments at his command, grasped he was plunging downward. Jack correctly pulled the throttle back to idle, almost instantly stopping the vibration. But he still did not know whether the machine was in "either a spinning nosedive or a very deep spiral." As a consequence, he was uncertain what control inputs to give the rudder bar and steering yoke in order to return to straight and level flight. What's more, with the ship corkscrewing so violently, both men feared the *Vimy* might tear itself apart. The altimeter continued to unwind at an alarming rate; perhaps as much as 1,500 feet per minute. Down they went—2,000 feet, 1,500 feet, 1,000 feet.

When the aneroid, still set to the atmospheric pressure above St. John's a half-day earlier, passed 500 feet and with the machine still out of control, Brown was "searching vainly for any kind of external reference, but saw nothing but opaque nebulousness." It was probable, Ted thought, the cloud stretched all the way to the ocean's surface. Preparing for the worst, the navigator loosened his safety belt and stuffed the precious navigation log inside his flying suit. It was all, of course, pointless. Clearly, the machine would hit the sea at a high angle and almost certainly smash itself to bits. In the impossibly small chance the two men survived the impact and managed to avoid drowning, there was still the matter of disengaging the emergency fuel tank lifeboat—assuming it was also intact—then somehow extracting the emergency supplies from the tail cupboard. And even if this series of saint-qualifying miracles occurred, they *still* were at least 100 or more miles north of the shipping lanes. The mathematician in Arthur Whitten Brown would have calculated their chances of survival at only infinitesimally above zero.

Somewhere between 200 and 300 feet on the altimeter—Alcock and Brown would never know for certain—the machine tumbled out of the murk and into the clear. Alcock glanced below the fuselage and saw—nothing. Bewildered, the pilot's gaze shifted upward. No more than a wingspan away, it seemed, were whipping white caps and the cold, forbidding gray waters of the North Atlantic. He was past perpendicular to the sea, the machine very nearly inverted.

Instinct took over; Alcock's catlike reflexes engaged the rudder bar and joy-stick wheel. Although the aeroplane was inherently unstable, its large control surfaces—elevator, ailerons, and rudder—allowed almost instant responses. The *Vimy* snapped upright in a manner comparable to Jack's nimble wartime Sopwith Camel. Simultaneously, the pilot shoved the throttle forward to maximum power and raised the nose ever so slightly. The machine hung level for a long moment *just* at flying speed, as if catching its breath, then finally roared ahead in a very slight climb. Brown estimated their lowest point was about fifty feet above the waves, amazed at having felt the salt spray on his face. Ted later wrote at that instant, before Jack advanced the throttle and the engines roared, the two men fancied "we could actually hear the voice of the cheated ocean as its waves swelled, broke, and swelled again."

After momentarily climbing back into solid cloud, Alcock realized he wanted no more blind flying and dipped down to just below the murk, leveling off at 150 feet above the waves. His quick-thinking navigator, utilizing a Mark One Eyeball, reset their aneroid altimeter by sight, providing a solid altitude foundation for the balance of the flight. Jack instinctively turned the aeroplane around to a general heading of East—090 degrees. After Ted had a chance to get his bearings, he passed a note to Alcock refining that compass heading to 100 degrees. For now, the Vickers *Vimy* would be content to remain at 150 feet altitude and safely out of cloud.

0357 GMT, Sunrise
Altitude: 6,200 feet
West Variation: 24 degrees
Compass Heading: 100 degrees

The appearance of the sun was only apparent because of a gradual lightening of the broken cloud they were flying through. The solid overcast had finally given way, allowing Jack to pick his way skyward in an attempt to get above the scud and give Brown a chance to get a celestial observation. The stall-spin had thoroughly shaken Alcock—to say nothing of the hair-raising recovery—and it was taking some time to shake it off. He could not understand what had happened to his physical senses; never before had they failed him so profoundly.

Determined to blot out the chilling experience, Alcock and Brown got back to the business at hand. The most urgent item on their agenda was navigation. They had been running on straight dead reckoning for three and a half hours—much too long. The arrival of daytime precluded the most accurate of positioning methods, a two- or three-star fix. From now on, it would have to be dead reckoning, supplemented by sun lines, drift bearing plate readings, and double-drift procedures. With the cloud likely extending all the way to Ireland, their only serious option was to try to get above the weather, which was why they had made the earlier climb to 6,200 feet. Unfortunately, visibility was no better there than at the lower levels.

As with the previous night's sunset, cloud stymied any attempt to observe the exact moment the sun rose. Ted had scribbled a note to Jack, *"Immediately you see rising, point machine straight towards it and I will get a compass bearing with the prismatic."* Once again, Ted had precomputed tables of the sun's hour angles to use as another crosscheck of their aperiodic compass—should their primary directional aid be giving undetected and seriously false readings, the result could be catastrophic. Fortunately, there still hadn't been anything to indicate a malfunction. They would simply have to put their trust in the compass.

At approximately 0430 GMT, with the *Vimy* twelve hours and seventeen minutes out of St. John's, heavy rain began falling. Coming horizontally due mostly to the *Vimy's* relatively high speed through the air, the rain shortly turned to sleet, and then came hail mixed with snow. Brown stowed his Baker navigation machine and sextant under his seat to ensure they stayed dry, though very little moisture was coming into the cockpit owing to the dashboard windshield diverting the flow over their heads. The two men stayed hunkered down, getting only occasional splashes of moisture.

After a brief exchange of notes and gestures, it was decided to maintain the current magnetic heading of 100 degrees but start another climb in an attempt to get above the weather. As the machine passed through 6,500 feet, the indicated airspeed read 70 mph. Brown calculated their true air speed at 80 mph, which yielded an estimated ground speed of 100 mph, Ted having judged the winds had somewhat diminished since they transited the halfway point. Alcock reluctantly moved the power up to 1,800 revolutions in order to make any climbing headway at all—the pilot was no longer worried about fuel consumption rates, but neither did he wish to subject the Eagles to more stress than was necessary.

With the increasing altitude, the temperature grew colder. Both men were grateful for their heated Burberry flying suits, though they had to be used sparingly in that the suits shared the same battery as the wireless, which of course could no longer be recharged due to the loss of the wing-mounted propeller screw. There were three variable settings—"hands, feet, body." As the flyers' toes and fingers were the most vulnerable, and the power drain too much if all three were used together over an extended period, the flyers decided their bulky flying suits alone would keep their torsos reasonably warm and dispensed with the "body" setting.

The crew settled into another long period of silence, each man lost in his own thoughts. Brown could only marvel at Alcock's enormous fortitude at the helm, the *Vimy* not giving him even a moment's respite in its continual demands. The situation was particularly awkward when the time came for Alcock to relieve himself. Indeed, at least once, he had to pass fluid into his flying coveralls, hoping it would not short out the heating elements. Ted was concerned Jack was allowing himself to become dehydrated to alleviate the stressful circumstance but said nothing.

After passing through 8,800 feet and upon completing another round of engine instrument checks and fuel tank switching, Ted noticed the glass face of the Petrol Overflow Gauge had again become clotted by sleet and snow. Once more—this the sixth check—he performed the inspection ritual, ignoring the terrible pain in his leg as much as possible. This time, however, as he straightened up next to the gauge a sudden side gust of wind hit the machine. For a terrible moment, Brown feared he'd be pitched out of the *Vimy*. An alert Alcock immediately grabbed a fistful of Ted's baggy flight suit and held on for all he was worth. Still clutching the strut with his left hand and arm, Brown managed to scrape off and read the gauge, before sinking gratefully down into his seat. Alcock did not let go until Ted had slipped below the windscreen.

As Brown caught his breath and refastened the lap belt, he glanced at Alcock, who was wearing a grave, pained expression—one Ted had never before witnessed, not even during the awful stall-spin. Clearly the man had been terrified he'd almost lost his navigator. Quite out of the blue, Brown was seized with the ludicrousness of the moment and, despite his enormous leg discomfort, burst out laughing. Here they were on this incredibly dangerous adventure, with one near catastrophe after another, and his brave pilot appeared in danger of becoming unglued over a meter reading mishap! Brown's reaction startled an uncomprehending Alcock. Ted saw he'd better give an impromptu explanation now and explain it fully later. He scribbled, *On reflection not cut out to be a high-dive artist!* Their joint and very much relieved headshaking lasted a full minute.

The faithful *Vimy* rumbled on, the reassuring, steady purring of those wonderful Eagles marred only by the racket from the right engine's broken exhaust pipe. With nothing urgent at hand and while massaging his bad leg, Ted listened in on the ditty-dotting coming over the wireless receiver and shared the reports with Jack. Both men had been secretly hoping for a cheering message of encouragement; if nothing else, a broadcast in the clear saying "trust all is well and wishing you Godspeed." Anything of the kind would have been most welcome; never had either of the fellows felt so alone and out of touch with the rest of the world. The lack of mention of them or their flight brought both to one of their lowest moments, as if "nobody cared a darn about us."

At 0620 GMT, Brown wrote in his log they had reached 9,400 feet and remained in thick cloud with sleet and snow still falling. Moments later, Brown was startled when Alcock's head went on a swivel, as if the man had suddenly gone on lookout for a Fokker or Halberstadt fighter. It was immediately apparent, however, that it was the machine's lower wing surfaces that had his attention, where a hard, white crust was rapidly accumulating. Although it couldn't be seen, it was a certainty there was similar activity on the top wing. *Ice!*

This most unwelcome development had reared its menacing head seemingly in a matter of seconds. Again, wing ice was only known to occur when encountering a certain combination of moisture and temperature, always around 32 degrees Fahrenheit. Ice on an airfoil surface not only added dead weight to the machine, it also seriously disrupted the airflow over the wings and broke up lift. Already, the buildup was affecting the flight controls. An increasingly alarmed Alcock vigorously cycled the ailerons and rudders in hopes of keeping them free. The larger rudder mechanisms remained responsive, but the smaller aileron hinges quickly gave up the ghost. Which meant the control wheel was frozen laterally. Jack could also push the wheel forward and aft, which meant the elevators were operating as well, but there would be no left or right coordinated turning. This was not good. Nevertheless, and while he had to cope with a good deal of skidding, Alcock could crudely steer the ship with the still-usable rudder, roughly maintaining his compass heading.

It was decided to keep climbing in an attempt to get above the dangerous weather. Because of the growing weight of the ice and loss of wing lift, Alcock was forced to increase his power settings to 1,900 revolutions in order to make any headway at all. It helped tremendously that the machine had burned off over two tons of dead weight petrol—if the ice had come six to eight hours earlier, they would already have been in the drink. But the power setting was still asking a lot of the engines. The only thing to do was to press on and hope the Eagles could take it.

While Alcock continued to struggle skyward, Brown made ready his sextant and Baker navigation machine, along with the Sumner transparent overlays for the sun. He wanted to be prepared should it peek through the overcast. With no visibility below, the earth's star represented the sole means to secure at least a partially known position; that is, an observed sun speed line that could be combined with an estimated dead reckoning course line.

The ice had made the *Vimy* difficult to control. Due to the additional weight and airfoil distortions, it was also barely climbing—Jack thought it could be as little as 20 to 30 feet per minute. And with no aileron control, he had to be extremely careful inducing any attitude changes— another stall-spin under these conditions would almost certainly be fatal. Fortunately, at their higher, dryer altitude, the ice appeared to have stopped building, perhaps even eroding a bit. As a bomber, the *Vimy*'s published service ceiling was 10,500 feet. Alcock had only been able to coax it this high because of the several fuselage streamlining modifications and with most of the petrol expended.

As the *Vimy* grappled toward 11,000 feet, the Gods at last smiled. Brown caught a glimpse of the sun, "just a pin-point glimmer through a cloud-gap." Wasting not a moment, and with the necessary assistance of the Abney spirit level—Ted could not see the horizon—he got several solid observations, resolving the speed line of position to a time of 0720 GMT. He passed an exultant note to Alcock: *Less than 100 miles to Ireland!* A few minutes later, after spinning the circular Appleyard course and distance calculator a few more times, he added: *Believe we are north of course. New compass heading right ten degrees to 110.*

After glancing at the aperiodic to be sure Alcock had steadied up on the new heading, Brown stowed his sextant, Baker, and Appleyard and thought to write still another note: *We had better go lower down, air is warmer, and we might pick up a steamer.* With the Irish coast so close, they could afford to give up some altitude. To say nothing of adding a few miles per hour to the air speed and better controllability going downhill. Further, both men had a sense the temperature lower down would be considerably warmer than earlier, well above freezing, which would greatly facilitate melting the ice.

Alcock nodded agreement and was about to begin a descent when the starboard engine burst into a terrific backfiring fit. This, of course, was the same engine that lost part of its exhaust pipe and had already been such an awful nuisance for the past twelve hours. An alarmed Jack adjusted the knob on the throttle and brought the right engine back to idle; the "pops" promptly stopped. Alcock could only conclude the ice buildup was somehow fouling the engine. As the *Vimy* began settling toward the sea, both men shook their heads at this latest spanner in the works. What more could the old bus throw at them? To avoid asymmetrical thrust, Alcock reduced the revolutions on the port engine as well before deciding to run them together at a count somewhere between idle and renewed backfiring. This procedure also considerably lessened the chances the ice-encrusted radiators would cause engine overheating and to accommodate a fairly rapid descent without building excessive airspeed. By 0745 GMT, the *Vimy* was down to 1,000 feet. Jack leveled off and eased the power forward to 1,600 revolutions in order to arrest the descent. To their immense relief, the backfiring did not return, though their machine was still surrounded by "cloudy vapor." Happily, the air was much warmer, perhaps in the high-40s, and the dreaded ice was at last melting. Within minutes, a smiling Alcock elbowed Brown, drawing his attention to the control wheel. The ailerons were working again!

After a time and frustrated with still being in the soup after so many hours, the pilot decided to inch his way downward in an attempt to break into the clear. The obvious danger, of course, was that cloud might

188 ROBERT O. HARDER

extend all the way to the sea, but it was a chance he felt he had to take. Without being conscious of it, Alcock was getting the hang of real blind flying. He was paying much closer attention to the inclinometer, which would tell him if his wings fell out of level. If the air speed indicator did not fluctuate up or down with a steady power setting, he could be assured he was not climbing or descending. This could also be confirmed by the altimeter maintaining its altitude. Jack was holding a reasonably proper blind flying attitude—granted, in a rudimentary manner—by what a later generation would call "scanning the instruments."

Still, this more precise work was almost beyond endurance; after so many hours flying without the slightest break from the controls, Alcock's body was screaming for relief. The man was desperate for a return to visual conditions. To make matters worse, they were again faced with the uncertain accuracy of their altimeter, it being many hours and hundreds of miles since Brown eyeballed a new setting following the near-fatal stall-spin.

Jack decided to level off at a 900-foot reading, assess conditions, then creep down to 800 feet. In this manner, he could step the machine down in very careful 100-foot increments. One can only imagine the tension in the cockpit as they descended through the murk, knowing that at any moment, the *Vimy* might smash into the sea. Alcock let down through 700, then 600, and then, with great trepidation, gingerly lowered to 500 feet on the aneroid. Nothing. The two men looked at each other in a silent consultation before Brown nodded. They would try for one last step-down before giving it up—the risks were simply becoming too great.

One can only imagine the relief when, at 450 feet on the altimeter, the *Vimy* broke into the clear. The greatest of tree-spectacled, lush-green mountain vistas could not have looked more beautiful than the angry, dull-gray, wind-chopped North Atlantic below! In a rare display of emotion, Brown slapped the dashboard in joy. Jack leveled off just below the cloud ceiling, and Brown reset the altimeter to what he judged to be 300 feet above the waves. Remarkably, the pressure altimeter had been off by very little, yet another indication their route's weather conditions—despite the heavy cloud—had been surprisingly benign.

Navigator Brown jumped at this chance for a wind calculation, lining up the drift bearing plate and putting in motion another double-drift procedure. After comparing those results with observations from Captain Rostrom's wave-reading formula, Ted estimated the wind was coming from 215 degrees at 35 mph, with their ground speed at the higher altitudes having probably averaged about 125 mph. This meant all those winds coming from out of the southwest had, likely for hours, been stronger than Ted had thought—more like what they had encountered earlier in the flight. And, judging from the generally southern wind direction, surely the *Vimy* had been blown farther north of course than his earlier running dead reckoning position had put it. Which meant a significant alter heading to the south was called for. Brown was very glad they'd had that earlier discussion at the Cochrane Hotel regarding the possibility of an "African Sahara" compass heading. After plotting his presumed position on the Mercator chart, Brown ran the numbers through the Appleyard and calculated a true course to Clifden, Ireland, of 125 degrees, then factored in the drift and variation. At 0800 GMT, Brown passed the word to Alcock: *New compass heading 170 degrees. Don't be afraid of going S. We have too much north already.*

John Alcock gave Arthur Whitten Brown a wry, almost amused look and then complied, remaining between 250 to 300 feet in order to stay clear of cloud. Brown informed Jack they now had to be very close to the Irish coast, somewhere off to their left, between the wings and the nose. Both men found themselves straining to be the first to sight land, in the manner of the crow's nest sailor on Columbus's *Santa María*, who first spotted the New World. They had to resist the temptation to start an early celebration; both flyers understood that the end of a long, exhausting flight—especially the landing—represented a dangerous moment. Any lapses now could have a horrific result.

Despite Brown's rigid adherence to the petrol tank usage schedule, the rear tanks were mostly empty, and the large nose tank in the old forward observer position was still full, which made the *Vimy* unavoidably nose heavy. Alcock had foreseen the problem in discussions with Vickers management, suggesting that a way should be found where all seven tanks could be drawn off a little at a time to maintain the ship's equilibrium, but the metering and engineering problems had been too difficult to overcome. Each tank had to be nearly exhausted before switching to another, inevitably leading to the machine going out of longitudinal balance. As a result, it had now become necessary for Jack to "exert a continuous backward pressure on the joystick." This condition also exacerbated the pilot's ability to make coordinated turns (with ailerons and rudder bar) and climbs and descents (up and down pitch of the tail elevators).

Brown's keen observations of his pilot told him Alcock's energy levels were dangerously low; the pilot had become so fixated on his flying duties he had given little to no thought of his own needs. Ted pointed to his own mouth and gave a bottoms-up gesture with a hand. Would you like something to eat and drink? Alcock smiled weakly and nodded, as if at some level he had been thinking the same thing. Straight away, Jack wolfed down the food and drink, this time sans the Guinness.

Tidying up, Ted was screwing on the lid of the coffee thermos flask and putting the leftovers back in the tiny cupboard behind his seat when suddenly Alcock grabbed his shoulder and spun him around. Jack's lips were moving excitedly, but of course, Ted could hear nothing over the thundering starboard engine exhaust. Brown followed the pilot's forefinger out toward the horizon and saw "barely visible through the mist" two brown/green specks of land. The navigator looked at his watch. The time was 0815 GMT on June 15, 1919.

Without prompting, Alcock turned toward and crossed over the islands—Eeshal and Turbot, they later learned. Visible just ahead was the coast of Ireland, which the *Vimy* crossed at 0825 GMT, still just under the clouds at 250 feet. Jack was all of a sudden aware of an even greater wonder than this landfall. All his pain and discomfort had magically disappeared.

Brown was uncertain exactly where they were and suggested that Alcock find a railway line and follow it south; the navigator still suspected the machine was well north of track. However, within minutes both men were astounded to blunder over none other than the Clifden Marconi Station at the end of Mannin Bay. The two flyers whooped in joy, slapping each other on the knee. Ted could not help but recall Jack's brash pre-takeoff remark about hanging their hats "on the aerials of the Clifden wireless station as we go by." Despite all the wanderings and near-catastrophes and considering that during the entire trip, he'd logged just four celestial observations plus the double drift readings, navigator Brown had hit the destination on its head!

Earlier, just after sighting the Irish coast, Alcock had, mostly with gestures, mused that with their being so "fat" on petrol, it might be possible to continue all the way to London. A heady idea, and indeed Brown promptly did an endurance calculation that showed they could stay aloft for up to eight additional hours—one-third of their petrol still remained in the tanks. If strong tail winds continued, then it was not beyond possibility that the *Vimy* could reach all the way to Paris!

Alas, such an attempt was out of the question. God alone knew how much longer the faithful Rolls-Royce engines could be sustained; Alcock and Brown felt they had already asked too much of them. What's more, the sky ahead was thoroughly obscured by cloud and mist, and the cluster of hills to the east promised unknown dangers to flying machines skirting just above the ground. Finally, with the prime goal of Clifden literally under their feet, a deep fatigue had set in, and rather abruptly, the adrenaline ceased to flow. It'd been over twenty-seven stressful, exhausting hours since either had slept, and then only fitfully, and all of it was catching up at once. Bidding the fleeting Paris chimera goodbye, Alcock swept past the wireless station and headed for the village of Clifden. As they had discussed before the flight, if the *Vimy* arrived in Ireland in good shape, they would land and push on to England the following day.

As the machine circled above the little town, and in an attempt to draw attention, Brown fired two red flares from his Very pistol. Much to both men's surprise, no one seemed to notice—aside from a very few figures who barely looked up, the village appeared deserted, once again reenforcing their fears they'd been forgotten. Later, they would learn that wasn't so; most of the inhabitants were preparing for Sunday morning church services and had their minds on other things.

Not seeing a suitable let-down field near Clifden town and puzzled by the inhabitants' seemingly lack of interest, Alcock brought the *Vimy* back around toward the Marconi station. On this second pass, Brown was startled to discover the wireless aerials were not supported by the expected masts but instead were held in the air by a series of kites! There would be, he knew, men on duty there who could assist them upon their arrival, as well as provide an immediate means to notify the world-at-large of their safe arrival. Both he and Alcock hoped the soldiers had seen the red Very flares. The pilot decided to set the machine down as near as possible to the station. Most of the land below was hilly, with rocky ridges, small ponds, and other unpromising terrain. At length, he spotted a sizable, level patch of green grassland, what he later described as looking "like a lovely field." Elated over their great good fortune having stumbled across what for all the world appeared to be an ideal landing spot, Alcock still dragged the field at fifty feet to ensure there were indeed no obstacles. Satisfied, he lined up the *Vimy* into the wind, heading westerly, and began the let-down.

After picking the spot where he wished to touch wheels, and at just the right moment, Jack brought the engines to idle and settled into a final glide. Both Brown and Alcock could see men from the wireless station waving vigorously at them as they floated in. At last, a hearty greeting for the conquering heroes! A grinning Brown returned the waves with great sweeps of his arm. Jack kept the machine just barely above stall speed as he approached the surface—the slower the approach, the safer. At the correct instant, he raised the nose, timing it so the wings would stall simultaneously with the *Vimy*'s wheels meeting the ground. Brown later wrote, "Alcock [had] flattened out at exactly the right moment." The *Vimy* kissed the earth's surface perfectly, with the crew anticipating a nice, normal roll-out. At that moment, Ted remembered thinking it was a perfect landing ending an almost-perfect flight.

The landing and early roll had been so gentle that at first neither noticed the tail of the *Vimy* rising and the nose sinking. The two were therefore astonished to see and feel the machine plowing up the ground in front of them. And when the aeroplane abruptly came to a full and violent stop after but fifty yards of run, there was "an unpleasant squelch, [the *Vimy*] tipped forward, shook itself, and remained poised on a slant, with its fore end buried in the ground, as if trying to stand on its head." A moment later it was over, and the *Vimy* went silent.

The "lovely field" had instead been a watery bog, the brilliantly green spring marsh grass a charming deceiver beckoning them into the trap. Ted would later recall Homer and his story of Odysseus and the Sirens, who lured countless sailors to shipwreck on the rocky (in this case, swampy) island of Anthemoessa. Later, back in England, Alcock told Bob Dicker the unceremonious end to his epic flight was the biggest disappointment of his life—the dream of a triumphant airborne London arrival smashed to smithereens. "I thought at first it was a damaged axle," he told his old friend, "But then I realized we were in a bog . . . Bob, I could have cried." Alcock would profoundly regret not securing detailed maps of western Ireland, especially after learning there was a perfectly serviceable aerodrome at Oranmore, not ten miles east of nearby Galway town.

On impact, Brown reached out to brace himself against the dashboard. His ill-luck with crashes held; while Alcock was able to brace his legs against the rudder bar and escape injury—the pilot nearly bent the hollow steel straight bar into the shape of a horseshoe, Ted received a severe bang on the bridge of his nose when it went up against the dashboard. It was enough for Brown to see the proverbial stars, causing

The Vimy *succumbs to marshy ground near the Cliveden Marconi Station. (Alamy Stock Photo)*

intermittent headaches for the next several days. He never mentioned the discomfort publicly; the skin had not lacerated, and he'd bled only a trickle. It could have been much worse for both—the half-empty petrol tank in the former nose observer position had collapsed accordion-style, which fortunately absorbed the bulk of the crash's kinetic energy. It was at that moment, still sitting dazed in the cockpit, that it dawned on them the frantic waving from the men on the ground had not been a greeting but instead a warning to stay away.

Miraculously, the crew did not have to endure a fire, the most probable result of such an accident. The ever-alert Alcock had "switched off the current on the magnetos, as soon as he realized a crash was imminent, so the sparks should have no chance of starting a fire." Still, the damage was extensive. The *Vimy's* nose and lower wings had torpedoed deep into the bog, badly denting the machine. Four of the eight propeller blades were also buried, though all would eventually be recovered unbroken. And while the tail empennage had stabilized in place, it was cocked at a forty-five-degree angle from the ground. Much later, there was grumbling back at Vickers that Alcock's insistence on removing the nose skid, for streamlining reasons, had exacerbated the crash damage.

The two men had remained seated, still a bit stunned, when Brown pointed animatedly at a ruptured fuel line, along with gushers of petrol spurting into the cockpit. Although Jack had switched off all his electrical switches, the two men would be incinerated in a flash if even the slightest spark appeared. Hurriedly undoing their lap belts, Brown retrieved the already damaged log and Baker navigation machine with its marked-up Mercator chart and stepped out and over the cockpit rim to solid ground. Alcock clutched the symbolically important mailbag and did the same on his starboard side. In this case, it was fortunate the nose was buried so deeply; a normal landing would have left them ten feet high in the air. As all airmen did and continue to do, they quickly distanced themselves from the still dangerous wreck.

During the final approach glide, and despite there being no reason to be concerned about the landing, yet hardened by bitter experience, Alcock and Brown had reflexively stuffed the flare pistol and other irreplaceable items inside their flying suits. Now, as Ted and Jack caught their breath after a 75- to 100-yard sprint, Ted triggered off two white flares, the signal for help. Before the smoke had cleared, a party of officers and men from the Clifden military detachment could be seen rushing toward them, having spotted the earlier Very discharges.

* * *

Eighteen-year-old Alannah Heather had seen the red fireworks coming out of the flying machine before it turned back and flew over Clifden Castle. Two miles to the south, she and her family were on their way to Sunday morning church. She much later wrote, "the Rector came hurrying up on a motor-bicycle shouting 'No service today. Alcock and Brown are above.'" Although unfamiliar with their names, she grasped they had to be one of the British flying teams attempting to win the big Atlantic crossing prize.

Alannah and her family lived on what was locally known as Errislannan, or Flannan's Peninsula, south of Clifden Bay near the Marconi

Station. A deferential and dutiful young woman, she was nevertheless only going to church because it was expected of her. The Rector's announcement could not have been better news.

The aeroplane motors were getting louder and louder. Alannah, a bright girl who would go on to a long and fruitful life as a highly accomplished landscape and portrait artist, realized the flying machine was headed for the Marconi kites. As the huge apparition—she had only seen one other aeroplane before and it was much smaller—swung over their heads and began circling the aerials, it became clear they intended to land.

"Papa!" she exclaimed. "Let's run over and watch them come down!"

Her father was frowning, having come to a like conclusion the machine was preparing to alight. "Darlin'," he said to his daughter, "just yesterday, you walked that moorland round the station. Is it not a near bog this time of year?"

Alannah nodded, understanding at once what he meant.

"I'll wager a guinea," Papa said, "the pilot does not know that." He looked at his family. "Come all. We may need to render assistance." On the way, the Heather family was joined by others who also were rushing to greet the flyers. They arrived only minutes after the aeroplane landed, or rather crashed, as was plain to see with its nose buried in the muck and its tail skewed higher than a proud rooster's.

Alannah ran on ahead of the others toward the two aeromen standing about 100 yards from the wreck. One of the men shot a white firework into the air, followed by a second. She presumed it was a signal to the soldiers, though they were already rushing toward the machine. Alannah stared at the two bulky looking men. They looked desperately cold and exhausted, she imagining they might just as well be men arrived from Mars!

Already, a score of people were rummaging through the broken machine; Alannah spotted several furtively running away with objects in their hands. Over the moor's rustling wind, she could hear the angry voices of the English flyers scolding the vandals. When several Irishmen lit their smokes, one of the flyers became enraged. "You bloody fools," he screamed. "There's petrol everywhere; you'll blow yourselves to Kingdom Come!"

None of the remonstrating did any good; even Alannah found herself so caught up in the excitement she was compelled to join in the pillaging. "As the wings were broken, we began pulling the plane apart, taking pieces of canvas and wood. Squares of this tough canvas crowned little haycocks for many years to come." Several people noted with wonder the aeroplane had only just missed several large, mostly buried rocks. It was agreed the flyers surely would have been seriously injured had the boulders been struck.

After the soldiers came to take the flyers to the station, the Heather family and many others went home to safeguard their precious souvenirs, then returned to the crash site with cameras. The locals were treated to more excitement when later that afternoon a small aeroplane from Galway carrying a newspaper reporter tried to land and also nosedived into the bog, leaving the two planes standing side-by-side, tails up.

The momentous event made a lasting impression on Alannah Heather. Six decades later, after a lifetime of remarkable, almost unique success as an Irish artist, she recalled the breathless excitement of that special day in her autobiography, *Errislannan: Scenes from a Painter's Life*.

* * *

Brown made a final log entry: *Landed 0840 GMT. Total flying time 16 hours and 27 minutes. Distance flown 1,890 miles. Average ground speed takeoff to landing 114.6 mph.*

It had been the abrupt change of scene and utter silence that was so disorienting. Only minutes earlier, their world had been the tiny, cacophonic *Vimy* cockpit with its otherworldly, groundbreaking technology. Now, Alcock and Brown found themselves literally embraced by a green and warm Mother Earth. After so many hours of the thunderous engines blasting into their ears, both men had become deaf, hopefully only temporarily. They stood on the moor gazing back at their half-buried flying machine, trying to absorb what could only be described as a stupendous and most unlikely success—despite the ignoble and embarrassing landing. They could hardly believe that not only was the flight over, but they had survived!

Brown, who found himself unable to resist giving himself a pat on the back, shouted: "Well, what did you think of that for fancy navigating?"

Alcock smiled and shouted back: "Very good!"

Despite their chapped lips, windburned, ruddy faces, and wobbly "fallen-asleep" limbs, nothing could have held back the back slaps, handshaking, and wide smiles. As the day wore on, their hearing would improve, but the full effect did not disappear for nearly a week. Indeed, while Ted fully recovered, John Alcock suffered permanent ear damage, he being the closest to that infernal starboard engine.

Both became aware of a number of local Irish running toward them from every direction, with a troop of uniformed soldiers from the Marconi station appearing over a rise. The military men were the first to arrive.

"Anybody hurt?" the breathless soldiers asked. Alcock and Brown shook their heads no, having more to lip read than hear actual words spoken. More questions ensued while Alcock led the group back to the machine—he was satisfied any danger from an explosion had passed and was determined to retrieve the balance of their valuables before the fortune-hunting took everything.

"Where did you come from?" asked the officer.

John Alcock barked a laugh. "America!" he exclaimed. *"Yesterday, we were in America!"* Little could Jack have imagined that this memorable phrase would be on the lips of millions over the days and weeks to come.

Several soldiers grinned nervously while the others looked at one another. Perhaps the crash had made the man daft. No such thing was possible.

Ted noted the men's skepticism. "No," he insisted, "it's all quite true." Jack impatiently interjected. "We are the Atlantic flyers Alcock and Brown. We are very tired and need your assistance."

As the two men would later learn, their names meant nothing to these isolated enlisted men. Fortunately, though he was unaware of the details, the officer in charge knew of the *Daily Mail* race. His initial thought, however, was these two fellows were search pilots on the lookout for downed flyers and were perhaps having a bit of sport with him. Alcock, who was becoming increasingly frustrated with this preposterous confusion, had a sudden inspiration.

"Look here," he said, as he held up the mailbag he'd been clutching the entire time, which showed the official St. John's, Newfoundland, stenciled markings.

The Clifden soldiers' eyes lit up. It was true then! The two bedraggled flyers standing before them had indeed achieved the near-impossible by flying non-stop across the North Atlantic! Joyous whoops and cheers, along with even more backslapping, followed. The alert officer, sensing how completely drained the flyers were, gently asked how they were feeling.

The proud Alcock purported to be "not at all tired," but Brown admitted he was "a bit fagged out."

"Right," the officer stated flatly. "Let's be off. You men"—he pointed at two soldiers—"give a hand gathering up their things." After Alcock and

Brown's valuable instruments, charts, logs, and other personal belongings were collected, the combined party set off for the Marconi station proper, several hundred yards away. Two soldiers were left behind with orders to rope off the flying machine and keep the growing crowd of onlookers at bay, what quickly became a hopeless task. Despite the soldiers' admonishments, locals were already combing through the wreckage. A chunk of ice nearly a foot across was immediately discovered buried in the *Vimy*'s upper wing. Onlookers could only shake their heads at what the flyers must have gone through.

The hike to the wireless station became a real slog, "burdened as we were with flying kit and heavy boots." Brown said that "I suddenly discovered an intense sleepiness and could easily have let myself lose consciousness while standing upright." Jack, on the other hand, though just as fatigued, was perfectly content to remain on his feet. As Ted later wrote, "Alcock, who during the whole period had kept his feet on the rudder-bar and [at least one hand on the control yoke], would not confess to anything worse than a desire to stand up for the rest of his life—or at least until he could sit down painlessly." All the while, for both men, their ears would not stop ringing.

After arriving at the station, the dog-tired flyers gratefully shed their bulky flying suits and boots, stripping down to Alcock's blue serge suit and Brown's RAF uniform. After receiving a generous bit of strong refreshment—no pharmacy scrip required!—their first acts were to send a series of all-important telegrams via the convenient worldwide Marconi wireless only steps away. Despite their profound fatigue, Alcock and Brown felt a solemn obligation to immediately notify and thank all who had been instrumental in their success. One of the Clifden radio operators, Mr. Frank H. Teague, put himself exclusively at their disposal.

To the Vickers executives and men still at St. John's, those who had heard not a word since Brown's "all well and started" signal and were, Jack knew, desperate to learn of their fate, Alcock sent: *Your hard work and splendid efforts have been rewarded. We did not let you down. Alcock and Brown.* Percy Muller, Monty Montgomery, Bob Dicker, and the others were fast asleep when the messenger from Mount Pearl arrived. They were, of course, elated but were themselves so exhausted the celebration was muted. Bob Dicker said he managed to enjoy a large scoop of ice cream and hinted that there may have been an early morning rush on fresh "prescriptions" for "tonic water."

To the Royal Aero Club: *Landed Clifden 0840 GMT June 15, Vickers Vimy Atlantic machine, leaving Newfoundland 1613 GMT June 14. Total time in air 16 hours 27 minutes. Captain Alcock, Pilot. Lieutenant Brown, Navigator.* The club responded: *Keep machine intact until observer arrives.*

To Mr. Claude Johnson, Rolls-Royce Managing Director: *Congratulations on the two Eagle Rolls-Royce engines, which propelled the Vickers Vimy safely across the Atlantic.*

With those essential duties discharged, the flyers were anxious to clean up. Shaving was not pleasant; they had heavy beards and both faces were windburned. Brown was relieved his face had not become discolored, though he had to gingerly negotiate his ablutions around a very bruised nose. Following a scrumptious breakfast in the station's officer mess, more wires were sent. Alcock sent word back to his family in Manchester that the prize had been won and he was fine. At 12:55 P.M. local,

The two flyers enjoying a post-flight breakfast at the Marconi Station Officer's Mess. (Theodore Von Karman Papers, California Institute of Technology Archives)

Brown cabled Kathleen Kennedy in London: *Landed Clifden Ireland safely this morning. Will be with you very soon. Teddy.* A few hours later, his extremely relieved fiancée replied, she not knowing the machine had been too badly damaged to continue on to England: *Magnificent—never doubted your success. Wire when leaving for Brooklands. Will meet you there. Micki.*

It was a later postal letter that John Alcock would prize the most, written by the man who did more than any other single individual to bring about transoceanic air travel:

> *My dear Alcock,*
>
>   *A very hearty welcome to the pioneer of direct Atlantic flight. Your journey with your brave companion, Whitten Brown, is a typical exhibition of British courage and organising efficiency . . . I look forward with certainty to the time when London morning newspapers will be selling in New York in the evening . . . Then, too, the American and British peoples will understand each other better as they are brought into closer daily touch.*
>
>   *Illness prevents me from shaking you by the hand and personally presenting the prize. But I can assure you that your welcome will be equal to that of Hawker and his gallant American compere, [the US Navy's NC-4 pilot Lieutenant Commander Albert] Read, whose great accomplishment has given us such valuable data for future Atlantic work . . .*
>
>   *Yours sincerely,*
>   *Northcliffe*

After the telegramming had finished, one of the station's operators tapped out the news directly to the Air Ministry, the *Daily Mail,* and the other London newspapers. Alas, Northcliffe's *Daily Mail,* which richly deserved the "scoop," did not run a Sunday edition, and it was the *Sunday Evening Telegram* in a "Night Extra" that reaped the immediate fruits of the GREAT BRITISH AIR TRIUMPH, as their headline screamed. Below the main story were two related columns. One sub-headline read CON-GRATULATIONS FROM HAWKER, in which Harry heaped praise on

Front page of the New York Sun, *Monday, June 16, 1919. (Library of Congress)*

both men, "a very, very fine performance indeed." The other, accompanied by a photo of Ted Brown, read MISS KENNEDY DELIGHTED. Speaking by telephone to a *Telegram* representative, Kay reported that there was great rejoicing at the Kennedys' Ealing home. "After a night of great anxiety," she said, "we are tremendously relieved and delighted at the success, more especially in view of the fact the navigator has succeeded in reaching the place that he aimed for—namely [Clifden] . . . we have got the whole front of the house decorated." Major Kennedy chimed in, "Miss Kennedy is very delighted—almost overwhelmed."

The *Daily Mail* was able to somewhat recover in its Monday edition when it published an exclusive, lengthy interview by "Captain J. Alcock, DSC." The pilot didn't sugarcoat the hazards they'd faced, beginning his account with, "We had a terrible journey. The wonder is we are here at all." He went on to explain their many vicissitudes.

Neither man was in the least prepared for what would be happening to them over the next several days. At 2 P.M., after ensuring arrangements had been made regarding the arrival of the Royal Aero Club representative to officially certify the *Vimy*, Alcock and Brown prepared to be "motored" to Galway, a coastal city at the end of Galway Bay about fifty miles southeast of Clifden. Because the roads in that part of Ireland were still marginal at best, the wireless station had developed its own narrow-gauge railway using modified open motorcars. Dubbed the "Marconi Express," it provided comfortable and rapid transportation to and from the station to Galway town. As the two men got into the car, they glanced out across the moor at their faithful but injured machine with a certain melancholia. To the flyers, "the *Vimy* looked in the distance like a stranded whale, its tail waving a reproachful farewell," as twenty-first-century writer Brendan Lynch so aptly put it. Arrangements had already been made to disassemble the machine and have it shipped to Brooklands.

Despite the heavy fatigue that was beginning to catch up to him, Brown marveled at the endless knots of people—large and small—that greeted their car as they passed through, the folks seemingly having materialized spontaneously. He could not imagine how word of their journey to Galway had spread so rapidly. As if that was not remarkable enough, when nearing the city, they were stopped by another Express going the other way carrying a Major Mays, or perhaps it was Mayo—Ted's mental fog that day confused a number of things—from the Royal Aero Club. Major Mays/Mayo promised he would certify the *Vimy*'s seals and make sure it was secured. Unfortunately, as Alcock and Brown would later learn, their flying machine had already been vandalized by souvenir hunters, damaging it even more—the soldier guards had not been up to their task. The two Atlantic flyers would always be grateful that, despite their dazed state, they had taken the precaution of removing their most

Riding the Marconi Express *from the wireless station to Galway, Ireland. (Mary Evans Picture Library)*

precious instruments, logs, and personal items. Most especially, they had not forgotten their loyal mascots, Twinkle Toes and a still mostly frigid Lucky Jim.

An elaborate reception and supper had been hastily prepared at the Clifden Railway Hotel by the District Council, but when the Galway city fathers saw how dreadfully exhausted the flyers were, they made it "a short and informal affair." From there, it was off to comfortable rooms in the Great Southern Hotel, where Alcock and Brown flopped into bed for the first time in over forty hours.

* * *

Back at Harbour Grace, Newfoundland, the Handley Page was soon fit to fly, but Admiral Kerr had no stomach for coming in a straggly second. The team instead decided to bring their huge machine to the United States and go on tour. Unfortunately, it crashed in a cornfield near Cleveland, Ohio. The crew survived, but the bomber was destroyed.

7:00 a.m. Local Time, Monday, June 16, 1919
Great Southern Hotel
City of Galway

Alcock and Brown were puzzled why they had to struggle awake after a sound sleep of nine hours, a condition that would lead them to discover a previously unknown phenomenon, something a much later age would call "jet lag." While Alcock and Brown's experience was relatively mild in its effects, it was nevertheless apparent. Brown later noted they had "overtaken time" flying west to east; that is, the two men had flown against the sun's movement, effectively erasing some three and one-half hours from their lives. The reason it was so hard to wake up at 7:00 A.M., Brown concluded, was because their bodies thought it was still only 3:30 A.M.

After shaving, bathing, and dressing—again into the same blue serge suit and blue RAF uniform, their only clothes—a sumptuous hotel restaurant breakfast was "eaten in an atmosphere of the deepest content" while reading newspaper accounts of their epic voyage. After breakfast and another brief Galway town reception, it was off to the railway station and the real circus.

All the way to Dublin on the Midland and Great Western Railroad, the Irish feted the two heroes, the long-bitter "troubles" between Home Rule and the British Empire momentarily set aside. Flowers, gifts, and brass bands appeared whenever the train slowed at each stop, with a host of military officers and local dignitaries offering honorifics. Inevitably, as Ted wrote, the "vanguard of the autograph hunters" came forward by the hundreds. At the time, neither man fully understood what all the fuss was about, though they always respectfully went along with it. Brown later speculated the people's joy was more prompted by the unprecedented exploit itself, the pure romance of men conquering the Atlantic by air, rather than for them personally—two fellows who were virtually unknown a few days earlier. After four years of the most terrible war in human history (sixteen million lives lost) and pestilence (the 1918 Flu Pandemic alone killed fifty million people worldwide), the great adventure was viewed as the beginning of a bright, new millennium.

In describing the epochal achievement, the world's newspapers pressed into service very nearly every known superlative in an attempt to outdo one another. The *Irish Times*, as reported by writer Brendan Lynch, captured the overall spirit of the moment with one memorable line: "The [US Navy's] NC-4 frustrated the obstinacy of the Atlantic with three sups; the Vickers *Vimy* has drained it at one gulp."

The victory tour was not without its comedic moments. The students at Dublin's venerable Trinity College were exuberantly celebrating Trinity Monday, that day each year when the school publicly recognized new Fellows and Scholars into their midst. A group of the students were among those welcoming Captain Alcock as he passed through Broadstreet Station—Brown had gone ahead to the next reception. The young men were suddenly seized by a serious case of pranksterism, managing to "kidnap" the pilot and whisk him away to the college. The provost soon rescued the victim and had the students reunite him with Brown at the Royal Irish Automobile Club—they playing host on behalf of the Royal Aero Club. The ultimate fate of the students is best left unrecorded, though one hopes none of them had earlier been singled out as prospective Fellows.

Already overwhelmed by Ireland's uninhibited fervor, Alcock and Brown could only wonder what lay in store for them once they reached England. On Tuesday, June 17, they sailed on the SS *Ulster* from Kingston to Holyhead, in northern Wales, a mere 125 miles west of Alcock and Brown's hometown of Manchester. In addition to the throngs of ordinary well-wishers meeting the daring duo were a host of *prominente*, including Reginald Pierson, the *Vimy*'s designer, and Claude Johnson, General Manager of Rolls-Royce. The celebration at quayside staggered the flyers; Alcock's earlier fears of Hawker and Grieve having exhausted public acclaim instantly vanished.

Arriving in Holyhead, Wales on the SS Ulster. Note the first Trans-Atlantic mailbag in the official's hand. (Alamy Stock Photo)

That was only the beginning. Dramatically accompanied along the way to London by swooping aeroplanes, the triumphant rail journey of England's newest heroes—perhaps the biggest outpouring the nation had seen since Armistice Day the previous November—drew tens of thousands as it came to each station. At one stop, Alcock caught a rose thrown by a group of giggling young ladies from a second story. When Jack fixed it in his buttonhole and blew a kiss at the girls, they squealed in ecstasy. The welcome at Rugby, after some 200 miles from Holyhead and eighty-five miles northwest of London, resembled a royal procession. "The crowd," *The Times* of London reported, "insisted on the airmen leaving the train during the halt. Suddenly an Australian soldier called to a porter, 'up with him!' and Lieutenant Brown was lifted shoulder-high so that all the people could see and cheer him. Another soldier with assistance hoisted up Captain Alcock."

For Brown, the stop at Rugby was particularly sweet. Major Kennedy had escorted his daughter to the city, from whence they surreptitiously slipped themselves into the flyer's salon car to surprise him. One can only imagine Ted and Micki's happy reunion. Jack Alcock, sensitive to the betrothed couple's desire to have a moment together, slipped out of the car to divert the crowd and reporters. When it came time for the train to depart, Alcock insisted the couple come outside and embrace their share of the cheering. As *The Times* reported, "Miss Kennedy [appeared] pretty, slim, tall, and daintily dressed."

After an already exhausting day, the two flyers at last arrived at Euston Station, London, where they were greeted by a tumultuous crowd of well-wishers numbering in the thousands. From there, they were whisked to the Royal Aero Club in an open Rolls-Royce motorcar, Union Jacks proudly flying on the two front wings. After RAC Vice-Chairman General Holden welcomed the two men home, Captain John Alcock ceremoniously handed over the St. John's, Newfoundland, mailbag, quipping, "I am the first trans-Atlantic postman!"

Alcock and Brown then traveled to the Brooklands Aerodrome to thank the men who had made it all possible. They received a euphoric reception, complete with flags, bunting, and a bold sign that read in capital letters, WELCOME! Eighty-year-old Albert Vickers, the son of the company's founder Edward Vickers (1804-1897), thanked the *Vimy*'s crew for carrying on the firm's longstanding tradition of excellence. Following the death of Albert, but a month later, Brown was moved to write, "[The occasion with Albert Vickers and his employees] was to be the welcome we appreciated most."

The flyers were greeted joyously all along their route. This photo most likely taken near Euston Station, London. (Alamy Stock Photo)

During the ceremonies, Brown found himself becoming mindful of his American compatriots—the US Navy NC trans-Atlantic team. He would later write, "That Lieut.-Commander Read, U.S.N., who commanded the American flying boat NC-4 in its flight from America to England, had left London before our arrival was a cause of real regret." Ted would later learn the instrument and weather issues the NC crews had faced were much more difficult than anyone had presumed at the time. In contrast to Harry Hawker's jaundiced views, Brown sincerely believed the events that spring and summer of 1919 had been a complementary Anglo-American accomplishment and that there was "the best possible feeling between [Read and his men] and all the British aviators." Indeed, after absorbing their initial disappointment, the English people gave the US Navy airmen an enthusiastic welcome. Commander Read had been moved to remark, "The British people are good winners; but they are wonderful losers!"

Thus began for Alcock and Brown a seemingly endless round of parades, receptions, and hearty greetings from everyday Englishmen, prominent citizens, government officials, and eventually royalty. It all culminated on Friday, June 20, 1919, at London's Savoy Hotel in a grand formal luncheon. Brown continued to wear his RAF uniform, as he had in all previous functions, but on this occasion, John Alcock shed his civilian suit and donned his RAF captain's uniform. The big moment came when Winston Churchill, Secretary of State for War and Air, who the ailing Lord Northcliffe had asked to substitute for him, presented Captain Alcock with the *Daily Mail's* £10,000 check. By that time, all of Britain had read accounts of their almost desperate journey and its close calls. Most were utterly amazed they had survived at all. As he handed it over, the inimitable Churchill remarked, "I really do not know what we should admire the most in our guests, their audacity or their good fortune."

And then came the icing on the cake. Moved by Lord Northcliffe's generosity, a Mr. Lawrence Phillips added £1,000 to the total, and the State Express Cigarette Company donated another 2,000 guineas (one guinea was worth one pound and one shilling). Altogether the two flyers found themselves harvesting a small fortune. Unexpectedly, Mr. Churchill staggered Alcock and Brown with yet one more surprise. To

Winston Churchill presents the Daily Mail's *£10,000 prize check to Captain Alcock. (Alamy Stock Photo)*

a mighty cheer, he said, "I am very happy to inform you I have received His Majesty's gracious consent to an immediate award of the Knight Commandership of the Order of the British Empire [KBE] to both Captain Alcock and Lieutenant Brown." They both were commanded to go to Windsor Castle the very next day for the investiture.

The Observer, London's oldest Sunday newspaper, reported the events that followed. "[Alcock and Brown] went down to Windsor by train and after a full civic reception at [Windsor Station] drove to the Castle in a Royal carriage, drawn by a pair of greys, and received a great ovation from the Eton boys, who surrounded the carriage and ran with it to the Castle, waving their top-hats and cheering."

After conferring their Knight Commanderships, King George V congratulated the two airmen on their great feat. The formal ceremonies over, the king and other royal family members spent some time chatting with the flyers. The fellows were pleased to learn their knighthood had been his idea. Brown was even more astonished to discover the king's comprehension of the complexities of marine/air navigation.

The garden party at Commander Trevor Dawson's home. Alcock is speaking to Mrs. Dawson, minutes after a formal portrait of the guests. Mrs. Douglas Vickers is speaking to Brown and Kay Kennedy, whose lovely face is unfortunately hidden by her wide-brimmed hat. (Alamy Stock Photo)

Later in the day, Commander Trevor Dawson, Vickers Director of Armaments, hosted a celebratory garden party at his home in Elstree, a quiet suburban village just northwest of central London. Mrs. Douglas Vickers, wife of the chairman accompanied Mrs. Dawson and represented her husband at the affair. In the photographs, John Alcock and Ted Brown beam exultantly, while the lovely Kay Kennedy stands primly by her man. Everyone was gloriously basking in the moment.

* * *

Alcock and Brown would never forget the critical contributions made by Monty Montgomery, Ernie Pitman, Bob Dicker, Rolls-Royce's Bob Lyons, and the seven mechanics, riggers, and carpenters. By mutual agreement, the two men allocated £2,000 of their prize money to be distributed among their treasured St. John's associates.

The trans-Atlantic flight likely rescued the Aviation Department of Vickers, Ltd. The foundry/engineering firm had been formed as a family business in 1828, specializing in iron castings, especially church bells. Through the remainder of the nineteenth century—becoming Vickers, Sons, & Company in 1867—the company continued to grow, branching out into the manufacture of marine shafts, ship propellers, and armor plate. Later came artillery production, and in 1897 Vickers acquired the Maxim ammunition and machine gun company.

In 1911, when the company expanded into flying machine manufacturing, the name was changed to Vickers, Ltd. After Alcock and Brown's flight, its Aviation Department would go on to produce the only partially successful *Vimy Commercial*, though the Royal Air Force purchased fifty-five military transport versions of the model, calling it the Vickers *Vernon*. The RAF would continue to operate large numbers of *Vimy* bombers and its variants until 1933 when they were finally retired, though the aeroplane would continue in training roles for a few more years. Its noble life finally ended, rather ignominiously, when in 1938, the remaining machines were used as target aircraft for antiaircraft searchlight crews. In 1927, the firm merged into Vickers-Armstrong, becoming a highly diversified company that made aircraft, armament, and ships. Eventually, market forces overwhelmed the company, and it went defunct in 1999, after 171 years of continuous operation.

The *Vimy*'s Atlantic success led to other record-breaking long-range successes for Vickers flying machines. In November 1919, Aussie World War One ace Ross Macpherson Smith, his brother Keith Smith, and two mechanics, flew a *Vimy* from London to Darwin, Australia. In perhaps a not so tongue-in-cheek plea for divine assistance, the flyers claimed their wing-painted registration letters G-EAOU stood for God 'Elp All Of Us. Logging only 135 actual flight hours, they made the harrowing trip in twenty-eight days, with just two days to spare to claim the £10,000 prize put forward by the Australian government. Inspired by the Smith exploit, Van Ryneveld and Brand departed London on February 4, 1920, bound for Cape Town, South Africa, in a *Vimy* they dubbed *Silver Queen*. It was an extraordinarily ambitious flight of some 8,000 miles over uninhabited desert and jungle; too ambitious it turned out. The aeroplane was battered from pillar to post by weather and malfunctions; over North Africa, the machine made a forced landing and was damaged beyond repair. The South African government provided a second *Vimy*, dubbed *Silver Queen II*, but it crashed in the Rhodesian bush, leaving the crew still 1,200 miles short of their destination. The indefatigable and somehow still uninjured flyers refused to accept defeat. The South African government came to the rescue once again, providing the men with a war-surplus AirCo/deHavilland DH-9 single-engine biplane bomber. On March 20, after forty-five days, Van Ryneveld and Brand became the first to reach Cape Town from London by air. In recognition of their extraordinary pluck, the South African government awarded them £5,000 each.

The 1920s would see an explosion of long-range over-ocean flights by British Commonwealth and American aircrews. In 1924, the US Army Air Service launched a 175-day around the globe flight in four single-engine Douglas World Cruisers, two of which completed the journey. May 1927 saw Charles Lindbergh's famous solo non-stop New York to Paris flight in the Ryan-built *Spirit of St. Louis*. One month later, US Army Lieutenants Maitland and Hegenberger flew the first non-stop flight from California to Hawaii in the *Bird of Paradise*, a tri-motored Atlantic-Fokker C-2 transport. In the summer of 1928, yet another Aussie, Charles Kingsford and his four-man crew, flew a three-stop 7,200-mile trip across the Pacific from Oakland, California, to Brisbane, Australia, in a tri-motored Fokker F.V11b/3m monoplane named *Southern Cross*. In 1929, a Ford Trimotor named after the late American pilot Floyd Bennett, piloted by the incomparable Norwegian-American Bernt Balchen, flew US Navy Commander Richard Byrd over Antarctica's South Pole. By the early 1930s, aeroplane and navigation technology had reached the point where nearly any point on the planet could be reached by air.

For the Rolls-Royce aircraft engine subsidiary, World War One had brought on a golden era. Throughout the 1920s and '30s, nearly every important United Kingdom military flying machine carried R-R engines. Established in 1904 by Charles Rolls and Henry Royce as a British luxury car manufacturer, World War One brought them into building aeroplane engines, quickly demonstrating their "best car in the world" reputation also applied to remarkably powerful and reliable flying machine power-plants. Their crowning achievement came in the mid-1930s and early '40s with the development of a series of liquid-cooled V-12 Merlin piston-driven gasoline engines. During World War Two, the latest versions of the Merlin were hung on over forty warbirds, including the Avro Lancaster, Handley Page Halifax, Bristol Beaufighter, de Havilland Mosquito, Hawker and Sea Hurricanes, Supermarine Spitfire, and the US North American P-51 Mustang. Later, the company's engine subsidiary followed the rest of the aviation industry by converting to jet engine manufacture. In the 1970s, Rolls-Royce was forced to liquidate its business, and a new government-owned company was formed, which soon sold it back into private hands. Later, in a too-big-to-fail step following fresh financial reverses, the UK government took back control and sold the business to the British public. Today, it is technically a subsidiary of Rolls-Royce Holdings, Plc.

After all the celebrating was over, Alcock and Brown discussed their aviation future together. Both were game for another big show, though what that might be, they had not a clue. Their immediate prospects, on the other hand, were more clear-cut. Alcock was still in his prime as a test pilot, and there were plentiful opportunities both for aero racing and exhibition flying, to say nothing of a guaranteed situation with Vickers. Additionally, John Alcock had long nursed a burning ambition to open and operate his own motorcar garage. With his share of the prize money, he could now pursue both passions. Brown's attention was focused on his upcoming July marriage to Kathleen Kennedy and building a home for himself, his new bride, and hopefully family to come. Percy Mueller had assured Ted he had a position as a Vickers aeroplane engineer for as long as he wished it.

As the summer of 1919 faded into early autumn, the future for Alcock and Brown could not have looked brighter—both individually and as a team. Neither could possibly have imagined they would never fly together again.

Alcock and Brown standing next to their restored Vickers Vimy, *August 1919.*
(Alamy Stock Photo)

EPILOGUE

Late Sunday Evening
October 3, 1948
Sir Arthur and Lady Whitten Brown's Home
Belgrave Court, Swansea

The doctor's expression was grave. "Lady Brown, I must be candid. Sir Arthur is in a bad way. The normal miseries we all endure with age have been greatly compounded by his increasingly troublesome war injuries. Not surprisingly, his depression has darkened correspondingly." The white-haired medico reached for his hat and coat. "Do what you can to cheer him up."

For weeks, a harried Kay's days and nights had been doing nothing less than precisely that, and her Irish flared. "My dear doctor, I do not need any such advice from you! You may be assured that since we lost our beloved son four years ago, I have done all in my power to comfort Ted." Close to tears, she turned away.

Realizing he'd handled the matter poorly, the doctor tried to make amends. "Of course you have, My Lady, of course you have." Seeing his words had little effect, he turned to go, murmuring, "Do not hesitate to call me anytime. I gave him a strong sedative to help sleep." He looked at her worriedly. "Please know it is essential he not have anything more along those lines for at least twenty-four hours." The doctor had become increasingly concerned his patient might wish to seek additional pain relief by self-medicating in some fashion.

"Yes, doctor," Kay said softly, more than a little embarrassed at having lost her temper. "We thank you very much. I'm well aware of this intrusion on your evening hours, and I shan't forget it."

The doctor managed a tight smile. "Good night, Lady Brown."

Kay made for what was now Ted's bedroom, having recently moved her toilette to the guest room. Caring round the clock for her husband, to say nothing of his constant restlessness and nightmares, had worn her absolutely ragged; it was Ted, wonderful dear that he was, who'd insisted upon the change. Despite his terrible afflictions, he had seen what his round-the-clock care was costing her.

As Kay had been careful to do since the crisis began, she peeked in to see if he was asleep; the last thing either of them wanted was to needlessly awaken him. Ted laid still in bed, eyes closed, his breathing even. Kay withdrew, gently closing the door behind her and immediately retiring to her own room. She was desperate for sleep and had long been relying on snatch naps whenever the opportunity presented itself.

* * *

Ted's eyes popped open the moment the latch clicked shut. He was grateful the doctor had left, grateful Kay had chosen not to come in, grateful most of all to be left alone. Despite the agonizing pain and his overall debilitation, he'd palmed the doctor's sedative. He wanted to keep a clear head . . . at least for a while longer. There was much to ponder.

How on earth could it have come to this? Three decades ago, when he and Kay first made a life together, the future could not have looked brighter. Oh, how glorious was that Tuesday, July 29, 1919! He could still picture it in his mind's eye as if it were yesterday. Arthur Whitten Brown and Marguerite Kathleen Kennedy taking their eternal vows at the Chapel Royal, Savoy, off London's Strand, he in a freshly tailored blue RAF uniform, she beautiful in a demure, classic white wedding dress. Alcock had come of course . . . oh my God, poor old Jackie. He'd attempted to blend into the background but, of course, was instantly recognized and hurrahed by all in attendance. Ted smiled inwardly from three decades away at his old friend's embarrassment. The glow from their crossing six weeks earlier had still not dimmed, and they both had remained subject to an increasingly annoying public acclaim. After the investiture and its aftermath, Ted was promoted to captain, RAF, on the disabled retired list. Jack hurriedly returned to Brooklands and test flying, staying continually on the lookout for flying exhibitions or perhaps another aero race. Both he and Brown were keen on rooting out another big challenge; perhaps something across the vast Pacific. Best of all, Alcock's old friend Bob Dicker had found backers for Jack's long dreamed of motorcar agency, to be located in the Burlington Arcade.

Ted reached out a hand for the water glass. He trembled so badly he had difficulty with grip, finally clutching it with both hands. It was infuriating that his mouth was always dry, and he had to sip liquids constantly; the doctor blamed it on the medications. He fell back heavily against the pillows, unaccountably winded from the effort and unable to recall what he had been thinking about. Oh, yes, Jackie was off flying new machines and happy as a clam, and indeed at the time, so was Ted. Percy Muller's word had been more than good; Ted settled in happily at Vickers behind an engineering draught table. In public utterances, both Alcock and Brown invariably minimized their own roles in conquering the Atlantic. Brown, in particular, both in his writing and conversation, always emphasized they had but stood on the shoulders of the many instrument inventors and flying pioneers who had gone before. Looking back, lying on his bed, it seemed to Ted that those months following the flight had slipped by in a flash.

Before the crossing and with his job prospects then at low ebb, Brown had toyed with the idea of he and Kathleen returning permanently to America. That fall of 1919, after much of the crossing hoopla had finally died down and with his desire to at least make an extended visit to the home country, Percy Mueller gave it his blessing. Ted and Kay sailed for New York. Their vessel was none other than the *Mauretania*, the same liner that had transported Alcock and him to their destiny in the New World a half-year earlier. Much to the passengers' delight, Sir Arthur Whitten Brown gave an in-depth lecture on how he'd navigated the *Vimy* across the North Atlantic. Following a celebrated arrival, Ted and Kay proceeded to have a wonderful time for the next two months—guided sightseeing, a flying boat tour of New York harbor, a lecture at Carnegie

Hall sponsored by the Aero Club of America, then off to the West Coast and San Francisco for more of the same.

San Francisco . . . Ted's eyes glistened as he mouthed the name, once more taking another large swallow from the large water glass Kay kept perpetually filled. The two of them had arrived in the Bay City in early December, thoroughly enjoying the deliciously pleasant weather and local scenery, especially the majestic Golden Gate, that providential narrows separating the huge, safe harbor from the near-boundless Pacific Ocean. Nothing, it seemed, could dampen the newlyweds' idyllic tour. The couple was further thrilled to read of events back in Britain on December 15. The Vickers *Vimy* had been restored to its original condition and presented to London's Science Museum. The papers reported that Sir John Alcock had been in attendance at the ceremonies and made most entertaining remarks after Mr. Douglas Vickers sardonically noted the curio hunters had got to the machine first and the Science Museum was not the only place where relics from the *Vimy* could be found. To which Captain Alcock had responded to much laughter: "I can vouch for that!"

The shattering telegram came on December 19. John Alcock had been killed the day before in France.

Even after all the many years, Ted still felt the acute pain of that moment. He never fully recovered from the blow, never mind the two had only known each other for less than a year. Their intense partnership, the deep bond the two had formed in that brief time, transcended any calendar reckoning. Brown was so profoundly affected that he never again flew as an aero crewman, drifting away from aviation friends and burying himself in his engineering work.

It needn't have happened. Alcock was to fly the prototype Vickers *Viking* Mark 1 flying boat to the much-ballyhooed Paris Air Salon—the first since the Great War ended—at Le Bourget aerodrome. The five-seat *Viking* featured new alternative fuselage and hull designs and a large, ground-breaking enclosed cabin. Jack had been determined to deliver the machine in time for the official opening. Fatefully, the weather intervened with low ceilings and rain. Succumbing to "get-there-itis" and ignoring the pleas of his fellow pilots to postpone, Alcock stubbornly took off anyway.

Brown had never stopped worrying about Alcock's unshaken belief in his ability to fly in cloud, despite their near-fatal stall-spin lesson over the North Atlantic. Ted was sure Jack became overconfident, having made the channel crossing to Paris any number of times. After all, what could the silly Channel do to him that the fearsome Atlantic couldn't? Ted had poured through his copy of the accident report until the pages were dog-eared. Alcock crossed over the Normandy coast and was almost certainly "scud running" up the Seine River toward Paris when what little ceiling he had closed to virtually nothing. The remarks of a farmer from Côte d'Evrard near Rouen were burned into Ted's soul. The fellow said he "saw a large plane speeding from the north. It became very unsteady in the wind. Then, it gave a great sway and fell to earth."

From the farmer's uninformed though unwittingly insightful descrip-tion, Brown understood precisely what had happened. Jackie had again lost his inner bearings—left, right, up, down became all a jumble—exactly in the same manner as had happened in their Atlantic stall-spin. The difference was that there had been the extra fifty feet of altitude that enabled a recovery over the ocean.

Amazingly, Alcock nearly pulled it off. The *Viking* clipped a treetop at a reasonably level attitude, which meant he was coming out of the spin. But his luck ran out there. The impact with the tree caused the machine to nose over and plow into the ground. Jack's head smashed against the windshield, fracturing his skull. Fatefully, rescuers were delayed getting to the wreck. He was at last rushed to No. 6 British General Hospital, Rouen, but it was too late. Captain John Alcock died a few hours later without regaining consciousness.

Ted groaned mournfully as the moment washed over him yet one more time. He rolled on his side, as if turning his back on the dreadful memory. Brown had been secretly grateful he was in America when it happened; too far away to attend what would have been the much too painful funeral service. It was all he could do to follow the proceedings via telegrams and then later read newspaper clippings friends sent from England.

Deep paroxysms of pain brought Brown abruptly back to the present, the agony having seemingly spread from the left leg to every part of his body. Time for the doctor's sedative. He fumbled for his water glass and downed the pill with a quick gulp, gratefully collapsing against the luxurious, overstuffed pillows his wife had specially made for him. *Oh, my sweet Micki. Always you think of me! What will the future hold for you?*

The strong medicine took hold within minutes, and Ted's labored breathing eased, though he was startled by how strongly he felt his heart beating. It was even more strange how his thoughts kept ebbing and flowing . . . memories darting in and out . . . images flashing. *Buster.*

Brown was suddenly weeping. Although the pill had somewhat eased his physical pain, it had reopened the door to Ted's greatest personal tragedy. The recent war, that damnable Second World War, had come in 1939. And it had stamped its ugly footprint on him and Kay in the most hideous of ways. In the evening and early morning hours of June 5 and 6, 1944, Flight Lieutenant Arthur "Buster" Whitten Brown, Jr., the boy who had determined to follow in his father's footsteps, was flying a 605 Squadron twin-engine de Havilland Mosquito over the Netherlands. On a patrol in support of the Allied Normandy Invasion, he and his navigator had been declared missing—apparently shot down by friendly fire over recognition signal confusion.

Then-RAF Lieutenant Colonel Sir Arthur Whitten Brown, who had been recalled to duty at the outbreak of war in 1939 to a posting near Swansea, Wales, had long since become disillusioned with his cherished post-Great War hope that global conflict was a thing of the past. Throughout the 1920s and early '30s, he'd publicly advocated for the peaceful use of the air while emphatically renouncing war, only to watch Hitlerism and his Luftwaffe put a lie to it all. Paradoxically, until the German airship *Hindenburg* destroyed itself over US Naval Air Station Lakehurst, New Jersey, in 1937, Brown insisted the future of transoceanic air travel rested with rigid, lighter-than-air dirigibles rather than heavier-than-air flying machines like the *Vimy*. The fatal blow to what little optimism he had left regarding the benefits of the flying machine to humankind came on June 12, 1944, when he and Kay officially received the crushing news their son's status had been changed from Missing to Killed in Action.

It had been a year earlier, in mid-1943, when Lieutenant Colonel Brown, who was teaching navigation and engineering to new aircrew, had finally to be invalided out of the Air Training Corps due to severe health problems. At the time, neither he nor Kay realized how much they'd pinned all future hopes on twenty-two-year-old Buster, their only child. A big part of the father and mother had died with the child. In the time left for Ted, with his health progressively worsening, he rarely strayed from home. Most of his days were spent reading and receiving old friends, with very occasional and physically demanding railway visits to London four hours to the east.

Most poignant of those trips were his flight anniversary visits to the Science Museum in South Kensington, London. Museum officials and attendants would long remember the gray, stooping figure limping through the Aeronautical Gallery to his usual bench and sitting quietly for an hour or more gazing at the *Vimy* and its adjoining displays.

During the summer of 1946, after seven long years of war confinement in Britain, Ted and Kay took "one last trip to America." They decided to go by air, in what became Brown's second and final aerial crossing of the Atlantic. He was not impressed; the comfortable and luxurious four-engined BOAC airliner flew so unadventurously above the sea and cloud they rarely ever saw the ocean. "They have taken all the fun out of flying," Brown told a New York reporter. He went on to say that although technically he was a British citizen, in his heart, he would always consider himself an American. It was an emotional moment, a belated valedictory to his origins and where life might otherwise have led him.

Brown glanced at his watch. It was time; he was at last ready. He fumbled open the nightstand drawer and withdrew a small bottle. After a moment's difficulty, he got the lid off—only vaguely noticing how badly his hands were shaking. He swallowed the contents and washed it all down with the remaining half tumbler of water. He closed his eyes and laid motionless for a time, not a little surprised at how relaxed he felt. His thoughts drifted back to that magical spring and summer of 1919.

Kay and the Major meeting him in the car at Rugby and being hoisted aloft by burly laborers—"Make way for Brown!"; the deeply touching welcome home given he and Alcock by everyone at Vickers-Brooklands; Churchill's perceptive inferences that chance played a larger role than

skill—an opinion completely shared by the two new Knight Command-
ers; the investiture and speaking privately with the king; the beautiful
July wedding . . . Oh, my lovely, lovely little Irish Mick. . . .

"Hi ho, Teddie!"

Brown blinked at the image forming just beyond the foot of his bed.
"Jack," he said wonderingly, "can that be you?"

"Who else," chimed the widely grinning man whose image suddenly
grew sharper.

It *was* Alcock! Why, he didn't look a day older than the day they
landed at Clifden! Amazingly, his old friend was dressed in the same blue
serge suit and flying coveralls used in the crossing, leather helmet still
unsnapped under his chin and goggles pulled up on his forehead.

Brown jumped out of bed and stepped toward Jack, abruptly stopping in his tracks. "My leg! It doesn't hurt! And I can walk easily without
my stick."

"Of course you can, old man. We're leaving all that rot behind."

Ted squinted his eyes at another figure forming behind and to one
side of Jack. Who's that, he wondered?

"Hello, Dad!" said the smiling, young RAF lieutenant, who oddly
enough was wearing a full-dress military uniform with all his awards and
decorations.

"Why, it's Buster!" Brown exclaimed. "But how can—" Ted stopped
himself in mid-sentence when suddenly all around him became a swirling, phantasmagorical stew. He felt like he was being picked up by a
great wave and gently lifted out to sea. While the sensations were not
unpleasant, there remained a certain hesitation.

"Steady, old man, there's nothing to fear," Alcock said to reassure
him. He was wearing that old Jackie smile. "Why, Buster and I have
been waiting for you. The three of us are going home together. Look over
there."

Jack was pointing at the *Vimy*, which had somehow been transported
from the Science Museum to Ted's bedroom. And what was that next to
it?

Alcock saw the question on his face. "Buster's Mosquito. He'll be
flying on our wing."

Ted looked down at himself. His pajamas were gone, replaced by his own 1919 RAF uniform and flying coveralls.

Alcock laughed at the look on his face. "I even had that bloody wireless repaired. You can listen in to your heart's content."

"What's our destination?" Brown asked dreamily, though he all at once knew the answer.

"Compass is 270 degrees, cruising speed and altitude infinity," Jack answered as Buster mounted his de Havilland and the two ancients climbed aboard their *Vimy*. "Teddie, my trusty and treasured friend, together the three of us have at last Gone West."

* * *

A Special Obituary Dispatch
Dated Saturday, October 16, 1948

It was announced only yesterday retired R.A.F. Lieutenant Colonel Sir Arthur Whitten Brown, K.B.E., died unexpectedly early Monday morning, October 4, 1948, at his home at Number 3, Belgrave Court, Swansea. He was 62 years old.

Sir Arthur was born in Glasgow on the 23rd of July, 1886, and educated in that city and Manchester. In 1902, at the age of 16, he became one of the earliest Westinghouse apprentices and he remained with that Company until 1914, when he joined the Universities and Public Schools Corps, later receiving a commission in the Manchester Regiment and serving in France. Subsequently, he was transferred to the Royal Flying Corps and was shot down, wounded, and taken prisoner by the Germans. He was later transferred to a Swiss internment camp and then, in a prisoner exchange, released late in 1917. For the balance of the war, he was employed by the Ministry of Munitions on the production of aeroplane engines and the testing of service machines.

In 1919, the possibility of flying the Atlantic was much debated among airmen. After Whitten Brown became acquainted with the racing pilot John Alcock, who had a brilliant war record in the air, they decided to make the attempt. Using a Vickers *Vimy* biplane they took off from Newfoundland on the afternoon of 14th of June, 1919, and sixteen hours later landed in a bog at Clifden, County Galway. Alcock and Brown won the *Daily Mail* prize offered for the first successful transatlantic flight in under 72 hours. Both were knighted. Sir John Alcock was tragically killed only six months later when his aeroplane crashed in France.

Following the great flight, Sir Arthur represented the Vickers Aviation Co. in the United States, China, and Japan. In 1922, he returned to his old firm, joining the Metropolitan-Vickers Export Co. in London, and since 1923, he had been manager of the Swansea office. During the last war he did very valuable work training navigators and engineers in the R.A.F. He married in 1919 Kathleen, daughter of Major D.H. Kennedy, who survives him. Their only son was killed on active service with the R.A.F.

An inquest was held, with a Swansea jury ruling that the cause of death was an accidental overdose of barbitone, a sleeping aid. The Colonel had been suffering from what was believed a nervous and physical breakdown. It has been reliably reported his grieving wife is convinced her own carelessness contributed to the accident, though she is somewhat comforted his agony is at last at an end. She remains under a doctor's care.

Sir Arthur Whitten Brown's ashes will be interred in St. Margaret Churchyard, Tylers Green, High Wycombe.

———

Selected Bibliography

Air Navigation: AF Manual 51-40, Volume 1. Washington, DC: U.S. Department of the Air Force. 1968.

Alcock, Sir John & Brown, Sir Arthur Whitten, with Introduction by Captain E.S.J. Alcock. *Our Transatlantic Flight.* London: William Kimber, 1969.

Barker, Ralph. *The Royal Flying Corps in France.* London, UK: Constable and Company, 1995.

Bowditch, Nathaniel. *American Practical Navigator.* Washington: U.S. Government Printing Office, 1939 Edition.

Brown, Sir Arthur Whitten. *Flying the Atlantic in Sixteen Hours.* London: Published in eleven installments in the Royal Air Force and Civil Aviation Record, 1920. (Public Domain Reprint.)

Card, Royal Navy Instructor Captain S.F. *Air Navigation: Notes and Examples.* London: Edward Arnold, 1919. (Forgotten Books Reproduction.)

Coombs, L.F.E. *Fighting Cockpits: 1914-2000.* Osceola, Wisconsin: MBI Publishing Company, 1999.

———. *Control in the Sky: The Evolution & History of the Aircraft Cockpit.* South Yorkshire, England: Pen & Sword Books Limited, 2005.

Conneau, Jean Louis Camille. *My Three Big Flights.* New York: McBride, Nast & Company, 1912. (Kessinger Legacy Reprints.)

Dixie, Royal Navy Lieut.-Commander A.E. *Air Navigation for Flight Officers.* New York: D. Appleton & Company, 1917. (Nabu Public Domain Reprints.)

Harbold, Retired U.S. Air Force Maj. Gen. Norris B. *The Log of Air Navigation.* Manhattan, KS: MA/AH Publishing/Naylor Company, 1970.

Hawker, H.G and Grieve, K. MacKenzie. *Our Atlantic Attempt.* London: Methuen & Co. LTD, 1919. (Forgotten Books Reproduction.)

Heather, Alannah. *Errislannan: Scenes from a Painter's Life.* Dublin, Ireland: The Lilliput Press LTD, 1993.

Johnston, Andrew K., et. al. *Time and Navigation: The Untold Story of Getting from Here to There*. Washington, DC: Smithsonian Books, 2015.

Lynch, Brendan. *Yesterday We Were in America*. Somerset, UK: Haynes Publishing, 2012.

Morgan, George M. *Alcock and Brown and The Boy in The Middle*. St. John's, Newfoundland: Tuckamore Books, 1994.

Nevin, David and the Editors of Time-Life Books. *The Pathfinders*. Alexandria, Virginia: Time-Life Books, Inc. 1980.

Pike, Dag. *The History of Navigation*. South Yorkshire, England: Pen & Sword Books Limited, 2018.

Potter, Capt. Leslie S. *The Navigation of the Air and Meteorology*. New York and London: Harper & Brothers Publishers, 1931.

Rosen, Mike. *The First Transatlantic Flight*. New York: The Bookwright Press, 1989.

Sloan, Carolyn. *An Incredible Journey: The Story of Alcock and Brown*. Parsippany, New Jersey: Silver Burdett Press, 1998.

Smith, Richard K. *First Across! The U.S. Navy's Transatlantic Flight of 1919*. Annapolis, MD: Naval Institute Press, 1973.

Sobel, Dava. *Longitude*. New York: Walker and Company, 1995.

Sumner, U.S. Navy Captain Thomas H. *Finding A Ship's Position at Sea*. Boston: Thomas Groom, 1845. (Nabu Public Domain reprints.)

Turner, P. St. John. *The Vickers Vimy*. London: Patrick Stevens Limited, 1969.

Wallace, Graham. *The Flight of Alcock & Brown: 14-15 June 1919*. London: Putnam, 1955.

Weems, Retired US Navy Lieutenant Commander P.V.H. *Air Navigation*. New York and London: McGraw-Hill Book Company, Inc., 1943.

Wimperis, H.E. *A Primer of Air Navigation*. New York: D. Van Nostrand Company, 1920.

About the Author

Robert O. Harder has much in common with his subjects. Like Captain John Alcock he was a multi-engine (piston/propeller) pilot—as well as an instrument-rated commercial pilot. As with Lieutenant Ted Brown, he was an Air Force navigator. Like both men, he has flown heavy bomber combat missions over the ocean using dead reckoning and celestial navigation (sextant).

Harder was an Air Force ROTC Distinguished Military Graduate, commissioned in 1966 at the University of Minnesota, Duluth as a Regular Air Force Second Lieutenant. A set of slightly myopic eyes set him on a course to Mather AFB, California, where he won his Navigator wings.

He was assigned to Navigator-Bombardier (Radar) Training, which included a four-week Special Weapons (Hydrogen Bombs) School. During the Cold War, he served in the 306th Bomb Wing of the Strategic Air Command flying nuclear training sorties and standing Pad Alert. Harder flew 145 combat missions as a B-52D Stratofortress Navigator-Bombardier during the Vietnam/Southeast Asian War. Decorations include the Air Medal with 6 Oak Leaf Clusters and the Air Force Outstanding Unit Award with V (Valor).

A retired retail executive and real estate investor, Harder is a freelance writer. He has authored a four-volume regional history of northern Minnesota, over a half-dozen aviation/military history articles, and five short stories—several of which won awards. This is his third published book about aviation history. He and his wife, Dee Dee, live in Chicago and at their summer cabin on Big Sandy Lake, Minnesota.

CPSIA information can be obtained
at www.ICGtesting.com
Printed in the USA
JSHW020748290722
28478JS00002B/110